Sacred Scroll of Seven Seals

-The Lost Knowledge *of* Good and Evil-

Judah

Truth Flasher Books

Copyright © 2016 All rights reserved.

This book or any portion thereof may not be reproduced or used in any manner whatsoever without the express written permission.

Printed in the United States of America
First Printing, 2016

23573 S. Malnetta Road, Crown King, Arizona, 86343
You may correspond with the Author of this work at the following url (below):
TheWindows*Of*Reality.com

Table of Contents

Title Page
Copyright Page
Table of Contents
Preface
- 1—There's Something Rotten in Denmark
- 2—The Little Book
- 3—The Order of Skull and Bones
- 4—The Tower of Babel
- 5—East India Company
- 6—The Four Horsemen of the Apocalypse
- 7—The National Order of the Knights of the Golden Horseshoe
- 8—The Order Terrorizes North America
- 9—The Improved Order of Red Men
- 10—Fifteen Known Men
- 11—Thor's Hammer
- 12—Illuminati & The Age of Enlightenment
- 13—The Nine Unknown Men
- 14—What is 'The Order?'
- 15—The Jesuit Order
- 16—Unholy Whispers
- 17—The Phony Express
- 18—Slave Ship Flag
- 19—Salty Tea Time
- 20—Russell Military Academy
- 21—The Order Founded the KKK

22—Opposing Horses
23—Civil Terrorism
24—The Lincoln Rope-a-Dope
25—The Prescription is War
26—Dirty Showers
27—World War Too
28—Muggy Whisperings
29—Famous Supporters of Eugenics
30—Grandpa Bush's Human Zoo
31—Segregation of Judah
32—Stoned with Horror
33—The Flight of Lilith
34—Acting Foolish Around San Francisco
35—Bull-B-Q
36—Whoring Around
37—Blasphemous Names of Revelation
38—Conquering the Papacy
39—Bohemian Trap City
40—The Du Rozel Code
41—British 'Israelism'
42—The Order's Siege Upon Jerusalem
43—The Un-holy Grail
44—Supposed Disbanding of the Knight's Templar
45—Breaking the Seals
46—The Nazi Rites
47—The Indian Head Scalping Lie
48—American Education
49—The Ordure of Yale University
50—Yale's Bible Reveals the Antichrist

51—Why The Order Hates The Bible
52—All Fired up
53—The Greatest Lie Ever Told
54—Sex-Ed
55—The Yale Spooks (CIA)
56—How The Order Killed Christ
57—King Solomon's Temples
58—Flat Crazy
59—The Idol and the Ephod
60—Dirty Dan
61—The Reptilian Drain
62—Ancient Satanists
63—Russell Family Viking Kings
64—Rollo Russell's Magic Plate
65—Early Viking Presence in America
66—The Greatest Sailor Who Ever Lived
67—Kennedy's Fatal Mistake
68—The Nimrod Code
69—Three Geronimos and a Nimrod
70—I Will See You Again
Poem—The Way
The Real 'Rules'
Suggested Reading List

In Evil We Trust

Preface

Originally this work set out to be a wake up call for government officials and medical professionals, and to potentially serve as a guide with which we American citizens could solve the ghastly opiate problem. Then it became something of a battle cry, almost like Thomas Paine's, *Common Sense,* the sequel.

But, as I researched, I discovered that *Common Sense too* was contrived fecal matter, and a dark shadow grew into a size and form which cast that darkness upon our entire medical system, government, churches, educational system, banking systems, and corporations. You will see for yourself that they all appear to blend into one indistinguishable amalgam.

As you read, keep in mind that I *wasn't* religious; I *didn't* have an agenda, political, racial, historical, monetary, or otherwise. This *wasn't* a persuasive paper—if things don't change, it *may* just be a pathetic, voyeuristic last look at a beautiful, intelligent life-form riding piggy-back on a bountiful blue planet which is doomed.

While we explore this work, a long golden thread of coincidence will unfurl, revealing to you our planet's authentic, unmolested history. We will track a dark shadow who seems to rush through time on the backs of generations of greedy men, without conscience—an evil epic of conquest, cannibalism, magic, money, drugs, corruption, sex, oppression, slavery, pestilence, war, and death. Is it all true? Yes, but, on matters such as these...you, the reader, had better verify and decide for yourself. There is so much readily available information on this topic that it's hardly worth citation.

John likely would have preferred to scribe what he knew was taking place during his Biblical times rather than the coded epic which ends the book collection of God's Word. Upon his writing of the account of Revelation, John would have been struck dead for uncovering the ugliness which you yourself are now preparing to behold moving forward in the text. Looking back, I would have to assume this to be true since most of the things which John so colorfully described as evil are still going on today in the same fashion in which they were then. This is not to discount the amazing accuracy in which John's prophecies have unfolded to this point in history.

But, what has changed? With the age of information also came the opportunity for one man *or woman* to circumvent our modern censures, and to broadcast these accounts in realtime—everywhere. The Order also failed to realize that the key to their 'magic,' which is written of extensively in the Holy Bible, *was* the technology of confusion by having many different people, speaking multiple languages, over many different lands, of whom to take advantage. In today's world we again all speak the same language, thanks to The Order's subsequent technology of instantaneous global communication, which, with God's will, was their fatal oversight.

To know of a terrible injustice is a tragedy, but to know of a tragedy and not speak of the horrific injustice is, in itself, *a crime against humanity.*

s.S.O.S.s.

1. There's Something Rotten in Denmark

As I began to discover that America *is* 'number one,' but mostly in things which are negative, I began to seek answers. Eventually, I found myself questioning irresponsible policies in America which have made us *number one,* around the world, in things like….

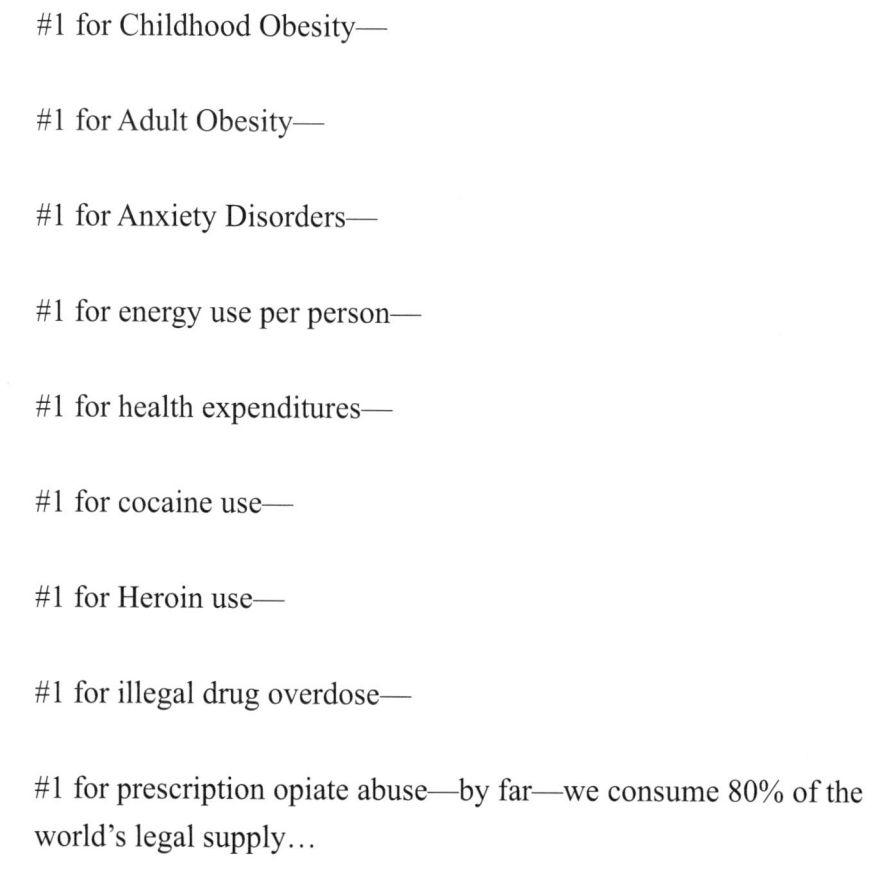

#1 for Childhood Obesity—

#1 for Adult Obesity—

#1 for Anxiety Disorders—

#1 for energy use per person—

#1 for health expenditures—

#1 for cocaine use—

#1 for Heroin use—

#1 for illegal drug overdose—

#1 for prescription opiate abuse—by far—we consume 80% of the world's legal supply…

s.s.O.s.s.

Top three countries who now lead the world in opiate abuse:

3. China—1,367,485,388 total population

2. India—1,251,695,584 total population

#1—United States—321,368,864—though we have a relatively small population, we use nearly as many prescription opiates as the remainder of the world—COMBINED…

World Population—7,256,490,011

#1 for prescription drug overdose—

#1 for imprisoning our citizens, and converting them into slave laborers for large corporations.

After citizens lose their rights due to incarceration they are no longer protected by the minimum wage. And, therefore, are available to work for only pennies per hour. **2,220,300 adults were incarcerated in the US as of 2013.**

Geo Group is the corporation which is buying up prisons in the united states, and around the world, as fast as they can get their grubby hands on them. The publicly traded company is a branch of the clandestine mercenary for hire group, Wackenhut. You would call Wackenhut for services ranging from, escorting your high profile child to school, to waging a private war against a third world country.

s.s.O.s.s.

Many sources have identified Wackenhut to be the security group which protects the interests of the stealthy Russell Trust Association, *which in turn manages the assets of the Secret Society of Skull and Bones*—a group which is *so secret* that they are the only 501c3 (nonprofit) group whose books are off-limits, *even to the IRS*. If Skull and Bones is indeed just a crazy group of frat boys, as they proclaim to be, it is hard to understand why *their* silly little group is not subject to the same financial scrutiny which *haunts* the rest of us.

Not only is Wackenhut now a publicly traded prison-owning conglomerate, but they have recently diversified their attention to contractual border patrol services. Wackenhut's, *Geo Group,* has announced that they will be creeping into the detainee and deportation game, which coincides perfectly with the racial roundups which seem inevitable for our country's coming years. I don't know about you, but there is something *very* disturbing about a group of executives sitting in a hotel meeting room, while their hopeful incarceration and deportation projections for the upcoming year are flashed upon the wall, like a company rally for a real estate conglomerate. Chanting and spiff programs for human bondage just doesn't settle right with me. Just take a look at their boisterous timeline **on Geogroup.com**.

And though being a contractor for many of America's super secret US government agencies, Wackenhut recently sold out to a couple of *unAmerican* organizations. First, in 2002, the company was acquired for $570 million by a Danish Group, known as 4 Falck, which then merged to form British company G4S in 2004.

These stats told me only one thing…with the amazing resources America has, these things have to be intentional.

S.S.O.S.S.

Upon discovery of these nearly abysmal facts, I began a quest which did not stop until *truth* was found. The truth may hurt you as it initially did me, but you will find for yourself that this story has a happy ending, if you too are willing to recognize *truth* when you see it.

The research which started me down this trail led me to a long list of what I like to call the '*Great American Opiate Dynasties*'—disastrous opiate epidemics, for which The Order only offered a stronger, more synthetic, opiate as the cure for the last contrived epidemic. We are still doing this today—the original essay is on the website: TheWindows*Of*Reality.com. Below are a list of the Great American Opium Dynasties:

Great American Opium Dynasties
I. Opium—*problem*
II. Morphine/Syringe—solution for Opium epidemic—*turned problem*
III. Heroin—solution to Morphine epidemic—*turned problem*
IV. Oxycodone—solution to Methadone epidemic—*turned problem*
V. Suboxone—*new miracle opiate cure, and America's next opiate epidemic (along with Heroin) Suboxone is the strongest opiate ever designed in a lab.*

Starting with Opium Dynasty II each subsequent opiate (which was even more-potent than the last) was billed by The Order as the cure for the prior. And, toward the end of each cure's cycle, all out pandemonium struck, as is happening now. At the end of this trail of Opiate Dynasties, I found that President

s.S.O.S.s.

Franklin Delanor Roosevelt's grandfather (Warren Delano) was a leader of the greatest drug cartel ever formed.

While visiting Geo Group's timeline (mentioned prior), I would like for you to also take notice that, Geo Group has become heavily invested in drug rehabilitation programs as well. This move also coincides with Obama's recent Suboxone *'shift'* speech, and crackdown on heroin (again, TheWindows*Of*Reality.com website will make the dirty details of this opiate 'epidemic' *'perfectly clear')*.

I kept digging, and when I reached the Russell family (who also formed the *Order of Skull and Bones on Yale University*), I knew that I was on to something BIG—I just didn't know, at the time, how *BIG*. Then, through a random Google search I discovered a tiny little book which would make all of the puzzle pieces fit, in a way which rocked every belief I had ever been handed. This book is called *Memoirs of the House of Russell*. My life hasn't been the same since. And, neither will yours....

Quote:

"It is said that no one truly knows a nation until one has been inside its jails. A nation should not be judged by how it treats its highest citizens, but its lowest ones."

—Nelson Mandela—

Fun fact: One thing for which America does *NOT* rank # 1 in is education....**Sadly, the US currently ranks #17 in the world for education.**

2. The Little Book

The *little book, *which I discovered,* revealed a bloodline of savages who seem to have been responsible for every single conflict and human calamity, throughout time.

*Memoirs of the House of Russell: From the Time of the Norman **Conquest**,* is the full title of the work, and it was written by, poet, *Jeremiah Holmes Wiffen*—it was published in 1833. The publication was never meant to be studied by the common man. The work chronicles the Russell family's sinister conquests, back to the very start of recorded human history. It places them in the wrong places, at the wrong times, for the destruction of countless peoples, of many races, of which there doesn't seem to be any level of discrimination. People with land and resources were conquered, indiscriminately, regardless of their *color.*

As stated, the book was only for the Russell family—only 250 original copies were produced (to ensure that), so that subsequent family members could revere the incorrigible men who were responsible for their privileged upbringings. Conceit itself was their fatal mistake. But I would also assume that they couldn't have imagined that the whole world would one day be connected, in a way which one man sitting on a postage stamp sized piece of land could access a world of information, using only God's guidance and the fingertips, with which his God had blessed him.

As it turns out, *Wiffen,* the Poet who wrote the **Russel Memoirs, even hid some secret messages from the past in the nuances of his text—he too must have been disturbed by the ugly deeds which were sown by this family. After years of secrecy, this incredible piece of history, in the form of a secret *little book,* must have mindlessly been scanned and uploaded into the public archive, by someone who had no idea of its implications.

This 'Little Book' really wasn't so 'Little.' Its discovery was made while searching for another Russell Memoirs book which *was* small—*William Russell and his Descendants.*

And though I rarely refer to the original 'Little Book' in this piece, it still holds great historical significance (there was only so much I could fit between this book's covers as it were).

And since both said, 'Russell Memoirs' works are digital, leaving me unable to visualize their girth, I have since always referred to the primary book of reference (Memoirs of the House of Russell) as the 'Little Book.' But, *William Russell and his Descendants,* was the original 'Little Book' in which this clan's horrific deeds were initially unveiled to me.

Note**: Throughout this work, I may refer to this book by its proper name, *Memoirs of the House of Russell,* simply as, *'Russell Memoirs,'* or just, *'The Little Book.'*

I used another leak from *The Order of Skull and Bones* in conjunction with the *Memoirs of the House of Russell* book, to decipher the evil emanating from this dark fraternity. An outtake from Antony C. Sutton's publication, *America's Secret Establishment,* best illustrates the public offering of:

The "Address" Books...

S.S.O.S.s.

As The Order is a secret society it does not publish minutes or journals. As Rosenbaum suggests, "they don't like people tampering and prying."

This author does, however, possess copies of the "Addresses" books, which used to be called "Catalogues." These are the membership lists all the way back to 1832, the founding date in the United States. How did this material make its way into outside hands? It is possible that one or more members, although bound by oath, would not be dismayed if the story became public knowledge. That's all we will say.

Other material exists, Skull & Bones is always a lively topic for Yale conversation. Some time back a few practical minded students made their own investigation; they did a break-in job, a "Yalegate." A small hoard of Bones momentos, a layout diagram and considerable embarrassment resulted.

The core of the research for this book is the "Addresses" books. With these we can reconstruct a picture of motives, objectives and operations. The actions of individual members are already recorded in open history and archives.

By determining when members enter a scene, what they did, what they argued, who they appointed and

s.s.O.s.s.

when they faded out, we can assemble patterns and deduce objectives.

Cross-referencing these two works along with the Holy Bible, and *many* other historic accounts, allowed me to identify the evil-doers, and to unmask them before you! And now, the moment for which you've been waiting your whole life—the glorious dawn of the *true* Story of Man.

Prepare to read, for yourself, the book for which *Chariots of the Gods*, and *The Da Vinci Code*, were written in order to prevent…*Sacred Scroll of Seven Seals*….

3. *The Order* of *Skull and Bones*

The American Chapter of the German Order of Skull & Bones was supposedly established on the campus of Yale University in 1833 (though the prior S&B 'minute' stated its founding as '1832'). S&B founder, William Huntington Russell (1809-1885), comes from a bloodline of the most privileged, savage warlord families in history. He was a descendant of several old New England families, including those of Pierpont, Hooker, Willett, and Bingham, among countless others.

Alphonso Taft **(Skull & Bones 1833)**, father to President, William H. Taft **(S & B 1878)**, co-founded the dreaded institution with Russell. Russell was the financiér of the endeavor, and, both gentleman were quite privileged Yale attendees.

There were 13 other 'Bonesmen' chosen that charter year, whom were all among America's financially elite families. There have been 15 students chosen as Bonesmen every year at Yale since. The Bones Chapter, which supposedly approved Yale Chapter 322 of *The Order of Skull & Bones,* was in Berlin, where young William Russell was sent off to study as a lad in 1831.

Germany was at the center of "new ideas," and scientific revolutions in psychology, philosophy, and educational reform, which were evolving quite rapidly in those times. In 19th-century Germany, education according to the "scientific method" was being taught. *Scientific Method teaches individuals what to think, and how to think it, as well as total obedience to the state.* Russell was particularly impressed with the concept of "thesis versus antithesis" and Hegel's historical dialectic: *the state is absolute, indi-*

viduals are granted their freedoms based on one's obedience to the state, and, the art of **controlled conflict by an intellectual elite which can produce a pre-determined outcome.**

Supposedly William Huntington Russell learned *The Scientific Method* and the ideas and philosophy of Georg Wilhelm Friedrich Hegel first hand, since Hegel himself held the Chair in Philosophy at the University of Berlin from 1817 until his death in 1831. It is said that William Russell identified with the death head creed, which would later breed Adolf Hitler's brand of Hegelian beliefs, so well, that Russell brought the evil home with him and planted it in the USA, just in time for the American Civil War. But as we proceed, you too may feel differently. (After less than a generation, Hegel's philosophy was banned by the Prussian right-wing, and was shamed by the left-wing in multiple official writings.)

The royal family of Taft's frat-Bro, William Russell, *owned East India Company (discussed in the following chapter)*, who also owned American commerce and held all of her power in early America.

Russell's *frat-Bro* business partner, Taft, went on to act as Secretary of War and Attorney General (the only man ever to have held both offices), under Ulysses S. Grant—Taft's running mate, Grant is a guy who managed the demise of 600,000 Americans, upon the ground on which you are currently sitting, during what is known as the American Civil War.

Here is what First Lady, *Mary Todd Lincoln,* had to say about Grant:

s.S.O.S.s.

"He is a butcher and is not fit to be at the head of an army. Yes, he generally manages to claim a victory, but such a victory! He loses two men to the enemy's one. He has no management, no regard for life." [Conversation with Abraham Lincoln regarding General Ulysses S. Grant. SOURCE: *Behind the Scenes, Or, Thirty Years a Slave, and Four Years in the White House* by Elizabeth Keckley (New York, Penguin Books, 2005), p. 59.]

    Skull and bones, or *The Order* as *Bonesmen* call it, has been written about extensively and so have their atrocities, so I will not make a futile attempt at explaining them all. You and I wouldn't have time in our entire lives to sift through the human misery, deceit, and historical facts which have been lain waste by Skull and Bones anyway.

    Skull and Bones did do damage enough to our planet earth and its unfortunate inhabitants that, we will easily follow one of the many long droppings of factual breadcrumbs, which now apply to you and I. As we continue, we will begin to understand the true American & World Histories, and how those consequential events apply to *our* times.

    Despite what you learned in school, we didn't "feast" with the Native Americans and they didn't willingly teach us how to farm either. These bloodthirsty warriors feasted on Native American resources and made, *Skull & Bones,* of their peoples; including Geronimo, one of their great leaders.

    Today, Geronimo's skull makes its home in *The Tomb* on High Street, located *ON* the Yale campus.

    "The Tomb" serves as a meeting place where William Huntington Russell's creation, *The Order of Skull & Bones,* acts

s.s.O.s.s.

out their macabre rituals and hold their satanic meetings. *Some silly pranksters at The Order thought it would be cute to dig up the Native American relic (Geronimo's skull), and house it in their creepy little haunted house on Yale's Campus.*

The Order of Skull & Bones is said to have "crooked," many skulls—Pancho Villa's, and US President Martin Van Buren, are among their unusual collection. In a publication printed by The Order, *The Continuation of the History of Our Order,* for the Century Celebration, 17 June 1933, written by one of the organization members, one of the six grave robbers recalled the night of the tragic grave robbery of Geronimo's head:

> "The ring of pick on stone and thud of earth on earth alone disturbs the peace of the prairie. An axe pried up the iron door of the tomb, and Pat[riarch]. Bush entered and started to dig. We dug in turn, each on relief taking a turn on the road as guards... Finally Pat. Ellery James turned up a bridle, soon a saddle horn and rotten leathers followed, then wood and then, at the exact bottom of the small round hole, Pat. James dug deep and pried out the trophy itself... We quickly closed the grave, shut the door and sped home to Pat. Mallon's room, where we cleaned the Bones. Pat. Mallon sat on the floor liberally applying carbolic acid. The Skull was fairly clean, having only some flesh inside and a little hair. I showered and hit the hay... a happy man..."

s.s.O.s.s.

The man this fellow is calling "Pat [riarch]," is the *Patriarch* of the vile bloodline which produced, *George Herbert Walker Bush **(S&B 1948)**, and George W. Bush **(S&B 1968)***. You really should google image the photo: 'Prescott Bush posing with Geronimo's skull.'

Fun fact: The word 'crook' (which The Order of Skull & Bones uses to describe their ritualistic crookings) is Norse in origin.

4. The Tower of Babel

In order to understand the following story (of a pirate who took over the world), you must first understand the Bible Stories which *The Order* themselves so revere. As you will see throughout this story, most everything The Order loves about The Bible was not from the deeds of the good guys but, from those of the dark side:

Genesis 11:1-9 New King James Version
The Tower of Babel
11 Now the whole earth had one language and one speech. **2** And it came to pass, as they journeyed from the east, that they found a plain in the land of Shinar, and they dwelt there. **3** Then they said to one another, **"Come, let us make bricks and bake them thoroughly." They had brick for stone, and they had asphalt for mortar.* **4** And they said, "Come, let us build ourselves a city, and a tower whose top *is* in the heavens; let us make a name for ourselves, **lest we be scattered abroad over the face of the whole earth.**"
5 But the Lord came down to see the city and the tower which the sons of men had built. **6** And the Lord said, **"Indeed the people *are* one and they all have one language, and this is what they begin to do; now nothing that they propose to do will be withheld from them. 7 Come, let Us go down and**

S.S.O.S.S.

there confuse their language, that they may not understand one another's speech." 8 So the Lord scattered them abroad from there over the face of all the earth, and they ceased building the city.
9 Therefore its name is called Babel, because there the Lord confused the language of all the earth; and from there the Lord scattered them abroad over the face of all the earth.

Note*: The people who built the tower of Babel were mocking God. Since God had previously destroyed the world by flood (only three generations prior), the evildoers were saying, "Bring it on…Our tower stands so high, that you cannot flood us out. We will just climb to the top and escape your deluge." There are now countless *Towers of Babel*, or "stepped pyramids," in abundance on planet earth—too many to count—and we are discovering more giant pyramids all the time. And the heart of every city is filled with modern versions of the pyramid—*the skyscraper.*

    The story of the Tower of Babel is where the enigmatic *Order of the Freemasons,* originally derived their name—listen again:

****'Come, let us make bricks and bake them thoroughly.' They had brick for stone, and they had asphalt for mortar."***

s.S.O.S.s.
And, the Masons were born.

"The Order" (a name I apply to any one of the secret organizations *outlined in this paper*) who you will soon learn about, were responsible for physically scattering our 12 tribes, for their own purposes of taking advantage of God's children, in ways which you will now have the privelage of reading about; ways which are responsible for the crumbled ruins which now litter our tired planet.

Most of those societies have taken a shine to building pyramid-shaped structures, and most, if not all of them, sacrificed humans; many times children.

The internet gives a reader the ability to fact check the events, and to even contribute to the work for one's self. As previously suggested, I will simply give the very end of the thread of Gospel truth a tug, and allow the reader to finish the unfurling as they see fit. That is if they have the stomach for the task. This work will serve as a sort-of Rosetta Stone with which to understand the book of Revelation, as well as serving as a guide, or a key code, with which to understand the rest of the Biblical books with divine clarity—now all one truly has to do is open one's eyes and, behold, for the Lion of Judah cometh!

Revelation 3:20-22 King James Version
20 Behold, I stand at the door, and knock: if any man hear my voice, and open the door, I will come in to him, and will sup with him, and he with me.

s.s.O.s.s.

21 To him that overcometh will I grant to sit with me in my throne, even as I also overcame, and am set down with my Father in his throne.

God's Holy Word is said to be a Book of Truths, *The Gospel,* and its might known to cut through men, cities, and countries, like a double-edged sword—The Bible has been ridiculed, and become an object which God's people hide, and for which they've made excuses, exceptions, and for which they've had to *evolve* for the sake of *science.* For those of you who proclaim to be 'illuminated,' 'enlightened,' 'lover's of truth,' 'perfection,' or of *'the light'—touché.*

Strange times are these in which we live when old and young are taught in falsehood's school. And the person that dares to tell the truth is called at once a *lunatic* and *fool.*
Plato (427 - 347 AD)

Enjoy the warm Sunshine!

Fun fact:

5. East India Company

The new American Colonies were all individually founded by publicly traded British companies—the most deadly of them all being *East India Company.* EIC was also known as: "The Deadliest Company in History." Elite financial backers in Britain pooled funds to bet on these warlords who, as you will soon learn, then went on to conquer most of the globe quite-handily, including the "Americas."

Previously discussed Skull & Bones Founder, *William Huntington Russell,* was quite learned in the art of death, oppression, and destruction for hire; below are only a handful of the great accomplishments of his forefathers' company, East India Company, before they dissected and incorporated America:

—**Widespread Famine**—Prior to founding EIC's new company, "America" (under 12 separate, British Crown approved corporate charters), EIC Starved over eighty-five million people in India, to death, during over two-hundred years of tyranny, as a result of exportation of *all* of India's resources! East India Company forced the Indian citizens to grow opium in place of life-sustaining grains and crops, which devastated the food stores for the country. Some estimate the genocidal number to be in the hundreds of MILLIONS!

There was no need for a concentration camp, back then, since these seed Nazis effectively turned the whole country of India into a Gulag.

s.S.O.S.s.

—**Widespread Slavery**—East India Company sold untold rabbles of Africans into slavery in North America, and around the world. Estimates as high as 75% of slaves traded came to the New World courtesy of EIC's shipping merchant operation. Some report the number of humans traded by East India Company to be well over ten million.

—**Widespread Dope-dealing**—EIC Spread the potent Opium, grown by Eastern Indian slaves, around the globe. EIC's international dope ring economically oppressed, and chemically & physically enslaved the people whom they sold the dope to—even in their new business, America, but we will get to that.

—**World Domination**—EIC maintained full control of the government, industry, commerce, and trading around the globe. When I say trading, I mean piracy! *The History Channel* and Miss Honey at school only call it "piracy" when fellow *pirates* robbed EIC's massive fleet of *pirate ships*. These rogue *"pirates,"* were originally learned in the art of *"piracy"* under the tutelage of their ex-employer, East India Company.

—**EIC Conquered and Owned the Entire Country of India**—The country of India was won as plunder as a result of the *Opium Wars*.

You heard right, the **East India Company OWNED INDIA** before its plutocratic British owners founded America! Skull **& Bones Founding Member's relative, Sir William Russell, was CEO** of a *publicly* traded (he and his buddies) company which enslaved India's people and monopolized every single trade and industry, in nearly the whole country. The tyranny continued for around two-hundred-seventy years of reign. At minimum, a hundred million people are reported to have fallen to the Skull & Bonesman's family business in India during EIC's reign—some reports dwarf this estimate. The following are the death tolls during East India Company's Opium '*Wars.*'

Opium "*War*" I—Also called the First Anglo-Chinese War
Reported East India Company Casualties—69 Troops
Reported Chinese Casualties—18,000 Troops
Results: East India Company gets trade rights, access to five treaty ports, and Hong Kong

Opium "*War*" II—Also known as the Arrow War or the Second Anglo-Chinese War, although France joined in.
Reported Eastern India Casualties—approximately 2,900 killed or wounded
Reported Chinese Casualties—up to 30,000 killed or wounded

> Note: These documented casualties, I am sure, are quite light....But, the low number of casualties for such a large conquest (the entire countries of both India AND China) too show a heavy existence of The Order's signature infiltration, long before these '*Opium Wars.*'

Our history books claim that those EIC deaths were British Casualties which isn't true, those were all part of a private company's war machine, sponsored by East India Company. One could argue that East India Company had one of the greatest, most calculated and brutal military forces on the planet—they'd be right.

East India Company was originally founded in 1600 by John Watts (another fellow Russell). William was sworn a free brother of the East India Company on 20 October 1609, having formerly bought Sir Francis Cherry's *adventure*, and became a director on 5 July 1615. In May 1618 Sir William Russell bought the treasurership of the navy from Sir Robert Mansell—leaving the sinister group in possession of the entire British Navy, not long after he took control of EIC. East India Company reported as many as 2,800 vessels to have been in EIC's fleet at the time. At its peak, East India Company had the largest Navy on the planet, and they dominated the Globe in trade and industry.

Britain awarded East India Company a monopoly on pillage, and tyrannical reign over any peoples EIC could reach with their pirate ships.

The ruthless dominion, oppression, and incorporation, of the entire country of India was just one of the many dirty deals this early Nazi seed company was involved in. East India Co. also oppressed, enslaved, conquered, raped, and financially manipulated every small settlement, country, and tribe along its trade routes, which were vast.

Think about it, the entire country of India, including the incredibly powerful army who won India as a war trophy, was controlled by the family of Founder of Skull & Bones, William Russell. When I say elite, Russell was a king. No, kings have some sort of duties in the way of pageantry and *or* morality, but, not the *king* of a publicly traded company.

S.S.O.S.S.

The Opium Wars, weren't simply another form of trade for East India Company, they became another form of bondage, chemical bondage. Whence EIC had control of the strongest Opium poppies in the world, they spread one of the most evil and oppressive forms of control and misery that a human being can endure, which is why many *don't* endure it. I won't elaborate on this since the book, *The Windows Of Reality,* covers the evil bondage qualities of the chemical hell quite well, if you're interested (available at amazon.com).

Below is a shortlist of the *Opium 'Wars'* in which the East India Company was involved, though, ***most*** were left out of the books. I will list the battles which the company had no choice but to record, alphabetically, for convenience sake:

A
- Siege of Ahmednagar
- Battle of Aliwal
- Battle of Argaon
- Battle of Arnee
- Battle of Assaye

B
- Battle of Quilon
- Siege of Bharatpur (1805)
- Battle of Buxar

C
- Battle of Calicut
- Battle of Chillianwala
- Battle of Chingleput
- Battle of Chinsurah

s.s.O.s.s.

- Cotiote War

D

- Battle of Deeg
- Battle of Delhi (1803)

F

- Battle of Farrukhabad
- Battle of Ferozeshah

G

- Battle of Golden Rock

H

- Capture of Hooly Honore

J

- Battle of Jaithak

K

- Battle of Khadki
- Battle of Koregaon

L

- Battle of Laswari

M

- Battle of Mukandwara Pass

N

- Battle of Nalapani

O

- Capture of Ormuz (1622)

P

- Battle of Plassey
- Battle of Pollilur (1781)
- Battle of Porto Novo
- Battle of Pune

s.s.O.s.s.

R
- Battle of Ramnagar

S
- Battle of Seringham
- Battle of Sholinghur
- Siege of Bharatpur

W
- Battle of Wandiwash

East India Co. eventually ran the country of India into the ground; the country was devastated in every way. East India Company written history books lead one to believe that in 1876 financial interest in India had waned enough that the native people were able to overtake what was left of East India Company's military assets, and to re-establish rule of their homeland. But, Actually, India was handed back over to Britain to clean up the mess that East India Co. had made over almost three centuries of tyranny. This allowed the common man, or slave, in Britain to foot the bill for the India disaster, leaving East India Company's imperial bloodline owners financially divorced from the wreck.

East India Company was the first business to ever be traded publicly, and would be the model by which all business in America, and around the world, would follow.

Below is a series of quotes about East India Company, which will give you the reader a better idea of the working dynamics which made this company successful:

—Quoted by Michael Tsarion

s.s.O.s.s.

"The sinister element that sets the British oligarchy apart from the popular image of the mafia family is its unshakable belief that it alone is fit to rule the world...The inheritors of the British East India Company, the same British monarchy and some of the same banking houses, have launched the new Opium War just as they did the first: to loot nations, destroy them, and exalt the power of the Empire...to become the 'The Third and Final Rome'"
Lyndon Larouche—

—Quoted by Michael Tsarion
"On May 10, 1982, addressing a celebration at the Royal Institute for International Affairs at Chatham House in London, Kissinger boasted that throughout his career...he had always been closer to the British Foreign Office than to his American colleagues, and had taken all his major policy leads from London...Chatham House is a successor to the old British East India Company, and serves as the think-tank and foreign intelligence arm of the British Crown"
Lyndon Larouche—

—The Committee of 300
"BEIC profits, even in those years, far exceeded the combined profits made in a single year by General Motors, Ford and Chrysler in their opium-profit years."
Dr. John Coleman

—The Committee of 300
"Remember the British East India Company? Officially, its business was trading in tea! *But Lord Palmerston crafted an official opium policy for the company and the British Government en-*

forced it. [...]Later, the British Crown, or Royal Family, joined the East India Company by granting it a charter that enabled the company to fight wars and conduct foreign policy."
Dr. John Coleman—

—The Committee of 300
"The truth is that the supply of Indian opium to China was a British monopoly, an official monopoly of the East India Company and official British policy."
Dr. John Coleman—

—The Committee of 300
"In 1702, the East India Company was revamped and became known as the *United* East India Company and then the British East India Company. The system of operations and banking learned in India was adopted almost *in toto* by the Bank of England under Norman Montague and the Federal Reserve Bank instituted by Woodrow Wilson."
Dr. John Coleman—

—The Committee of 300
"By 1830 all of India was under the control of the East India Company, a truly breathtaking achievement."

Dr. John Coleman—
"In 1661, King Charles II (Stuart) granted the East India Company the power to add to its charter the right to make peace or war with sovereign nations, an extraordinary event without parallel. Here

S.S.O.S.S.

was a private company given powers to make war with sovereign nations!"

Dr. John Coleman—

Fun fact: The East Indian word, *loot*, entered the English language thanks to the East India Company. The word *loot* was rarely heard outside the plains of north India until the late 1700s, which was when it became popular across Britain, as a result of being brought home by East India company employees, along with the actual treasures which were, 'looted,' from the country of, what is now called, *'India.'*

6. The Four Horsemen of the Apocalypse

'The Four Horsemen' get tossed around in movies, song, and other areas of pop culture, but who are they?

Revelation 6:1-7 New King James Version

First Seal: *The Conqueror—Pestilence*
6 Now I saw when the Lamb opened one of the seals; and I heard one of the four living creatures saying with a voice like thunder, "Come and see." **2** And I looked, and behold, a white horse. He who sat on it had a bow; and a crown was given to him, and he went out conquering and to conquer.

Second Seal: Conflict on Earth—*War*
3 When He opened the second seal, I heard the second living creature saying, "Come and see." **4** Another horse, fiery red, went out. And it was granted to the one who sat on it to take peace from the earth, and that *people* should kill one another; and there was given to him a great sword.

Third Seal: Scarcity on Earth—*Famine*
5 When He opened the third seal, I heard the third living creature say, "Come and see." So I looked, and behold, a black horse, and he who sat on it had a pair of scales in his hand. **6** And I heard a voice in

s.S.O.S.s.

the midst of the four living creatures saying, "A quart of wheat for a denarius, and three quarts of barley for a denarius; and do not harm the oil and the wine."

Fourth Seal: Widespread Death on Earth— *Death*

7 And when he had opened the fourth seal, I heard the voice of the fourth beast say, Come and see.
8 And I looked, and behold a pale horse: and his name that sat on him was Death, and Hell followed with him. And power was given unto them over the fourth part of the earth, to kill with sword, and with hunger, and with death, and with the beasts of the earth.

Since the true famine numbers are always in question by The Order's so-called 'experts,' here are The Order's 10 greatest, well-documented, contemporary *famines *that you've never even heard of:*

10—Great Famine of Ireland 1845-1853—1.5 million dead

9—Vietnamese Famine of 1945—2 million dead

8—North Korean Famine 1994-1998—3 million dead

7—Russian Famine of 1921—5 million dead

S.S.O.S.S.

6—Bengal Famine of 1943—7 million dead

5—Bengal Famine of 1770—10 million dead

4— Soviet Famine of 1932-1933—10 million dead

3—Chalisa (India) famine 1783—11 million dead

2—Chinese Famine of 1907—25 million dead

1—Great Chinese Famine 1959-1962—43 million dead

Many contemporary famines, including the *many* in Africa, aren't even listed here.

7. The National Order of the Knights of the Golden Horseshoe

A more modern version of William the *"Conquerer,"* William James Russell (Sr.) of Virginia (1678-1757), aka William ***"the Ranger"*** Russell, was responsible for the forming of *The Order of the Knights of the Golden Horseshoe expedition*—the branch of The Order which laid claim to the Louisiana Territory. Only the following are known by name to have taken part in the charter of The Order of the Knights of the Golden Horseshoe expedition:

—*Lt. Governor Spotswood

—John Fontaine, Robert Beverley, Jr.

—William Robertson

—Dr. Robinson

—Mr. Todd (possible secret Mary Todd Lincoln connection—Mary
Todd was from Lexington, KY)

—William Clopton, Jr., (second son of William Clopton and Ann
Booth Clopton; a John Wilkes Booth relative)

s.s.O.s.s.

—James Taylor (great-Grandfather of US Presidents James Madison and Zachary Taylor)

—Robert Brooke (grandfather of VA Governor Robert Brooke)

—George Mason III

—Capt. Smith

—Jeremiah Clouder

—"Old Edward Sanders" was identified as a Knight of the Order of the Knights of the Golden Horseshoe, upon a family will reading.

—William Russell (General, Russell CO, Virginia, Fort Russell)

Note*: "Governor Spotswood," was another descendent of the Russells'—*he* was the Lieutenant Governor of "Old Dominion"—A name given to the Virginia Company, since she was **the seat of government for The Colonies.**

North America's abundant resources, and the rate at which the early colonies were being settled, motivated The Order of the Knights of the Golden Horseshoe to scout, and "claim," what was

s.s.O.s.s.

to the west of the Blue Ridge Mountains. (Though as the story progresses, you too will realize that these adventurers were simply carving off another slice of land which their Order had been aware of for a *LONG* time.)

In 1716, the ragtag group of killers easily made it to the top of the mountains, which over-stood a great river they dubbed, the *"Euphrates."* The name never stuck, and instead remained the Shenandoah, which was the Native American name for the river. Interesting Biblical Prophecy connection in Revelation:

> **Revelation 9:13-15 King James Version**
> **13** And the sixth angel sounded, and I heard a voice from the four horns of the golden altar which is before God,
> **14** Saying to the sixth angel which had the trumpet, **Loose the four angels which are bound in the great River Euphrates.**
> **15** And the four angels were loosed, which were prepared for an hour, and a day, and a month, and a year, **for to slay the third part of men.**

Note: The Order named a couple of mountain peaks, "Mount George," in honor of the king, and, "Mount Alexander," after the Governor of Virginia.

The group then hiked down the West side of the Blue Ridge Mountains and buried a note in a bottle which read the following:

s.s.O.s.s.

"This whole valley belongs to George I, King by the Grace of God *of* **Great Britain, France, Ireland** and **Virginia**."

This swath of America now feeds most of the world. The stone monument which still stands at the spot where the clandestine land-grab was made, is of fieldstone, and is fittingly designed in a pyramid shape.

The Order of the Knights of the Golden Horseshoe later evolved into several other "Orders"—among them:

—**The Secret Society of *the Sons of Liberty,*** which covertly organized the Revolutionary War, was a spinoff of The Order of the Knights of the Golden Horseshoe.

—***The Knights of the Golden Circle*** was The Order's ***Northern-*** **created** and sponsored secret society, which was a spinoff of The Order of the Knights of the Golden Horseshoe.

This faction, of The Order of slave-drivers, was responsible for attempting to expand slavery into 25 new slave states which would be formed from Mexico. The Order *planned on* expanding the States, of what would become America, by commandeering the entire country of Mexico. Polk's "Manifest Destiny" mission stopped far short of that when we took the American west from Mexico, but, he had considered drawing the international border as far south as Mexico City.

Cuba was also part of the mission, but that was never realized (which explains why Castro wanted nothing to do with us, or,

S.S.O.S.S.

the rest of the world, for that matter). The Knights of the Golden Circle theorized that the introduction of slave states, clear into South America, would allow their trade of slavery a stronghold which could "never be dislodged."

But when their plans of spreading Slavery across the Western world failed, they switched gears, and acted as *their own army* which pursued the financial interests (aka death squads) of *The Order,* during the American Civil War.

Many have fantasized The Order of the Golden Horseshoe as a myth, but the 200 year old 'little book' which I found online confirms these accounts.

Here is what the Russell's 'Little Book' has to say about the Knights of the Golden Horseshoe:

> Tradition also tells us that he (William Russell) was one of the party of cavaliers who accompanied Gov. Spotswood in his expedition across the Appalachian Mountains, and that, consequently, he was one of the famous "Knights of the Golden Horseshoe." The very meagre records of that period afford us but little of a definite character. The old account says further, that he had obtained large grants of land from the British government. The records of the Virginia Land Office show where many of those grants were located. In 1712 he purchased from Lord Fairfax several thousand acres, which were located in part not far from Germanna, the settlement made by Gov. Spotswood in what was afterwards Spotsylvania County. Many entries of land

S.S.O.S.S.

are found, aggregating over forty-thousand acres. In 1730 he purchased two tracts of land, containing respectively ten-thousand, and six-thousand acres, also in Spotsylvania. [William Russell and His Descendants, Pg 3.]

After the above account, along with the publishing of the diary of Governor Fontaine's *(Grandson of Governor Spotswood)* account of the expedition and formation of the so-called "The Knights of the Golden Horseshoe," there is no more denying the land-grab escapade. Spotswood's diary, which features a star-studded political cast who all got their hands in the dirty deal, is readily available online. Most, *if not all* of the cast of greedy characters included kindred to future US presidents and politicians.

Below is an outtake from a book of short stories—the story is titled, *Knights of the Golden Horseshoe,* By, Etta Belle **Walker**:

The Governor was a romantic person, as well as practical, so he wanted to have something tangible by which all of his party might remember their thrilling trip. He asked some of his men what they thought of the idea and someone suggested, no doubt in fun, that they call themselves the "Knights of the Golden Horseshoe". Anyway, historians relate that when he returned to Williamsburg, he promptly wrote a letter to His Majesty and told him of the wonderful country "beyond the mountains".

s.S.O.S.s.

He also asked for a grant for the Order of the Knights of the Golden Horseshoe. In due time a proclamation arrived from England creating The Order of the Golden Horseshoe and also ***fifty tiny golden horseshoes** inscribed in Latin "*Sic jurat transcerde mantes*" (meaning, "thus he swears to cross the mountains"). There was a seal and a signature and the title of Knight was conferred upon the Governor. The King also had his own sense of humor and included with all the rest, the bill for the golden horseshoes! And we are told the sporting Governor paid for them out of his own pocket without any regrets.

Note*: What is wrong with this picture? Listen again:

*"In due time a proclamation arrived from England creating The Order of the Golden Horseshoe and also ***fifty tiny golden horseshoes** inscribed in Latin..."*

The problem herein, is the fact that, *only 13 men took part in this expedition,* and the King expedited to the group *"fifty tiny golden horseshoes."* This, no doubt, shows the group's far more sinister motives to expand their swath of conquest and influence. It also gives us another small glimpse into the working dynamics of The Order's uncanny ability

38

s.s.O.s.s.

to form, on a moment's notice, the tight knit groups of men which it would take to conquer an entire planet.

The cute brooch idea was certainly *Knight* William Russell's idea, since The Order of Skull & Bones, *and all of the other secret clubs created by the Russells* (aforementioned), share the very same brooch tradition. Yale's, *The Order of Skull & Bones,* pin was made by Tiffany & Company—you should google image it —it really is quite pretty.

8. The Order Terrorizes North America

For this section we will simply review, and comment on, an article which describes a great, native American biological Genocide. The article describes *the truth* about the ugly mechanism which cleared the Native Americans from their continent, to make way for the British Imperialists who settled here:

Native History: Inventor of Biological Warfare Against Indians Dies
ICTMN Staff
8/3/13

This Date in Native History: On August 3, 1797, Lord Jeffrey Amherst, the first military strategist to knowingly engage in biological warfare by giving smallpox-infected blankets to Native Americans, died.

The spring of 1763 began Pontiac's Rebellion, a series of relatively successful frontier attacks. This was when the use of the blankets to slow the Indians down was first suggested by Colonel Henry Bouquet and Amherst.

Carl Waldman's *Atlas of the North American Indian* has an account of the use of the infected blankets: "...Captain Simeon Ecuyer had bought time by

s.s.O.s.s.

sending smallpox-infected blankets and handkerchiefs to the Indians surrounding the fort—an early example of biological warfare—which started an epidemic among them. Amherst himself had encouraged this tactic in a letter to Ecuyer."

It's estimated that three-quarters of the Native American population died in smallpox outbreaks.

Amherst was a big shot among his British brethren. He was a commanding general of British forces during the final battles of the so-called French & Indian War (1754-1763) and he won victories against the French to acquire Canada for England, making England the world's top colonizer at the end of the Seven Years War (1756-1763).

The towns of Amherst, Massachusetts and Amherst, New York as well as Amherst College are named after him. Though, it's said that those living in the town in Massachusetts wanted to name it after the Indians whose land they took—calling it Norwottuck, but they were overruled by the colonial governor. Amherst returned to Britain in November 1763 and never returned to take the governorship of Virginia he was rewarded for his military success.

s.S.O.S.s.

The governorship of Virginia went to second-fiddle player, George Hamilton, 1st Earl of Orkney, who in 1710, appointed Alexander Spotswood as Lieutenant Governor of Virginia.

The Virginia company, however, was virtually ran and owned, by, William *The Ranger* Russell, *from behind the scenes.* The Giddy Spotswood seemed tickled just to be part of the fateful ride, with almost a Sancho Panza type of enthusiasm.

As mentioned in the above article, Jeffrey Amherst (also known as 1st Baron Amherst) cleared the whole continent of North America, by handing live smallpox infected blankets over to the true owners' of America. What the article doesn't say, however, is that the wielder of smallpox blankets was rewarded for his bravery, by taking governorship of the very first British territories in Canada—the top sliver of the Louisiana Territory, which the Baron had saved for himself. Maybe after all of that underhanded genocide the Baron just wanted to enjoy a more basic life than The Order's plans for America had projected.

As mentioned in the article above, there are many places named in the honor of the king of biological warfare against the Native Americans: Amherst Massachusetts; Amherst New York; Amherst College—just to name a few. There are many more in Canada, as you can only imagine.

Joe Sark (a spiritual leader) called the name of Fort Amherst Park of Prince Edward Island a 'terrible blotch on Canada,' he remarked....'To have a place named after General Amherst would be like having a city in Jerusalem named after Adolf Hitler...it's disgusting.'

s.S.O.S.s.

Did you ever stop and wonder, *how did a group of pirates hand out smallpox-laden blankets to 'Indians' without dying of the terrible disease themselves?...With no hazmat suits on?*

Well, more than two decades before Edward Jenner supposedly 'invented the smallpox vaccination,' five investigators in England and Germany *successfully tested a cowpox vaccine against smallpox.* Also, in 1774, Dorset England farmer, *Benjamin Jesty,* successfully vaccinated his wife and two children during an epidemic.

Though Edward Jenner was credited with the discovery, and is even being called *The Father of Immunology,* this story also bares a strong stench of The Order.

In the late 1910s, the Spanish Influenza, or, 'Spanish flu,' is said to have killed upwards of fifty-million people (more casualties than the entire first World War). An estimated half-billion people were infected with the virus, which was a third of the world population, at the time. The flu pandemic broke out in 1918, which also just happened to be the end date of the War.

Spanish Flu is a mystery, with its suspected origins ranging from Spain to China. One thing that is not a mystery, however, is the fact that, the War *is* what spread this virus allover the planet— so, whether intentional or not, that too, was brought to you by *The Order.*

Fun fact: America was given her name in honor of Amerigo Vespucci, who supposedly made two trips to the 'new world' as a navigator in the 1500s. Amerigo, was one of the very many who claimed to have discovered the continent of North America. We now know this as complete dung.

s.s.O.s.s.

The name Amerigo, is Germanic in origin, which literally translates to **work ruler.**

9. The *Improved* Order of Red Men

After the North American continent had been cleared of undesirables, an Order of Native Americans called the "*Improved* Order of Red Men" was established in, get this, 1776. The new Order was chartered by an Act of Congress.

At the time of its official charter in 1776, The Improved Order of Red Men was said to already have been in operation for several hundred years, placing its origin right about the time of the shameful smallpox blanket give-away program. This is a rare glimpse at the working dynamics of these groups, who use infiltration of their so-called enemies' tribes, to do the dirty work, when bludgeoning their opponent into submission.

Many high-ranking members of the militia groups and armies, which cleared the Native Americans from their home, were said to have been given higher-ranking positions among the new Order of 'Red Men,' after marrying into their tribes. These new Anglo-Native-American-hybrid humans completely blent-in with the subjugated races to ensure their DNA lines, and to take their promised thrones among the native peoples. Their evil intentions become deeply rooted into the heart of a culture—ruthlessly ensuring that their impious ways live on to rule the new Order.

A new organization of men, who can be called-on for favors *(or even wars),* had been formed among the Red Men. Throughout time these esoteric devils have bred their way into the elite of all races, even on the fringes of the four corners of our world.

s.S.O.S.s.

Many times (as in the case of the creation of Nazi Germany), the group will call on an Order, in order to harvest the controlled conflict which they had been nurturing for decades, and sometimes centuries—both sides will then invest strategically, engage, and then profit handsomely from the evil purge of their own people. Promises of a protected bloodline, and financial backers who have the power and wealth to change mens' minds, are among The Order's irresistible bag of tricks.

Again, many think William Huntington Russell (creator of the Skull & Bones Chapter 322) learned his beliefs from the Germans in Berlin "while away at school." But, I think, more than likely, Russell was simply calling upon a historic event which they had been propagating for decades, if not centuries. These devils farm civilizations and wars over generations, and even lifetimes. If you will look at the timeline, Russell was in Germany in 1831-1832, and in just outside of a century the entire world was at war, and Germany was at the epicenter of the conflict.

My state of origin, "Indiana," was initially incorporated as a company owned settlement. Indiana was allotted to the "Indian leaders" and the families who The Order infiltrated and coaxed to turn on their own people. The new "Order" was established amongst those Native Americans made 'settlers,' and is now controlled by the established hierarchy of The Order—the same Order which had been imposed on the rest of us new Americans, and the known world.

Britain's conquest of North America was a great model for studying the inward mechanical operation of The Order. A close-up of The Order's submission hold which infiltrated that group of native men can easily be observed from this vantage point. Insight into the corruption, of the corruptible among the group's leaders, can be gained from this observation. The Order now controlled the 'Red Man' from within, in perpetuity.

This was surely the case with Geronimo *'the Terrible'*—a timeworn epithet, often issued for the perceived enemies of The Order. Remember? Ivan "the Terrible" was busy terrorizing Russia, for The Order, only a few hundred years prior.

The epithet, **The Terrible**, or ***el Terrible***, has been applied to:

—Afonso de Albuquerque (c. 1453–1515), Portuguese empire builder

—Charles the Bold (1433–1477), last Valois Duke of Burgundy

—John III the Terrible (1521-1574), Voivode of Moldavia

—Ivan the Terrible (1530–1584), Tsar of Russia

—Shingas (fl. 1740–1763), another Native American warrior and leader during the French and Indian Wars

—Roger and Tommy Touhy (1898-1959), American gangsters in Chicago

—Abdul the Terrible, was a Turkish sniper assigned to kill Chinese-Australian sniper Billy Sing during World War I

—And countless others…

s.S.O.S.s.

One day Geronimo returned to camp, and found his people slaughtered (among them, laid Geronimo's own mother, wife, and three children). Geronimo's family were killed by the Mexicans. The raid kicked-off a legendary killing spree, deep into Mexico, which won him his Mexican name, Geronimo—"One Who Yawns." Geronimo's quest for revenge left him viewed as a great war leader, even credited with having *mystical powers*, but he was never truly a Chief among his people.

An indian agent captured Geronimo in 1877, but strangely, Geronimo "The Terrible," was released after being transferred in shackles, to Arizona, just in time to rejoin the war in 1879.

After a raid on San Carlos, in which Geronimo liberated the dead Victorio's people (now led by Chief Loco), Chief Loco made a startling claim…Loco and others said that they had been kidnapped (not rescued), and they blamed Geronimo for his tribe's misery, following the shady event. Geronimo then fled back to the safety, which he had strangely previously enjoyed, on the northern side of the border.

This time was different, though…After realizing that he had no sanctuary in Arizona, Geronimo agreed to surrender, but got drunk and fled the scene in the final hour—why was Geronimo "The Terrible," not in shackles?

5,000 American troops (a quarter of the US Army) were tracking Geronimo by the summer of 1886. (Remember, Russell's British company [East India Company] had 2,800 ships in its Navy, which were all load to the gills with savage, bloodthirsty killers [two-hundred years prior] And, 'America,' *in 1877*, only

s.S.O.S.s.

had 20,000 soldiers, TOTAL?) Geronimo finally surrendered in 87, to end the charade. Geronimo was still not a prisoner!

Geronimo became a celebrity, over time, as memories of his terroristic activities faded. Geronimo was a favored attraction at the 1898 Omaha exhibition, and at the 1901 Pan-American Exposition in Buffalo, New York. Ironically, Geronimo was even on display for the 1904 St. Louis Louisiana Purchase Expo (a celebration of the genocide of America's native peoples). Geronimo even had his own booth, where he sold his autograph for 10 cents and photographs for $2. Exhibit organizer SM McCowan had this to say about Geronimo: "The old gentleman is pretty high priced, but then he is the only Geronimo."

A more-detailed study of this topic will reveal that Geronimo *the Great* was the leader of a terrorist organization which was formed by The Order—Geronimo was a *traitor*.

Geronimo *the Great* was hated on both sides of the border, and was finally hunted down by his own people for the atrocities which he committed—but was released and made a high-demand celebrity instead of being lynched. Now long-forgotten, however, are the calloused killings and deportations of his own men, women, and children. Geronimo's, is an amazing tale of the near-miraculous shifting public view of a man who was hated by all, to becoming something of an American icon, and even a hero. Both sides of the conflict now celebrate Geronimo's bravery, which is an enigma comparable with Osama Bin Laden being revered by Americans now.

Perhaps, Geronimo's crowning achievement was when he marched in President Theodore Roosevelt's March 1905 inaugural parade. Near the end of his life he was asked if he had any regrets.

s.S.O.S.s.

"I'm sorry I did not kill more Mexicans," was Geronimo's simple reply.

President William McKinley was the president during said times. McKinley was known as the 'hard money' man, since he had been a fierce advocate of a gold standard. Mckinley's opponent, William Jennings Bryan, advocated the 'easy money' *with no backing* philosophy (money printed by privately owned "banks" *at interest* to its borrowers—*American Citizens—like we do now*). Gold-backed American currency was the very foundation of McKinley's 1896 & 1900 successful campaign against William Jennings Bryan who advocated for "*free* and *unlimited* coinage of silver."

McKinley's staunch opposition to "easy money" (fiat paper currency) sealed his death warrant. While Geronimo was posing for fan photos at the 1901 Pan-American Exposition in Buffalo, New York, President Mckinley was shot down (across the grounds) at the same event, for protecting Americans from the inevitable complete financial collapse of the US dollar.

Fun fact: The American dollar has crashed before—hard!

The American Colonies began printing paper money as early as 1751. In addition, the Continental Congress began to issue even-more *Continental currency,* to fund the war effort. Our new worthless form of currency depreciated to nearly nothing by the end of the war due to over-printing. Today, with the advent of the computer, printing money isn't even necessary for further debasing our currency, since data entry is instantaneous.

On the day this passage was written, the national debt was up to $66,319,912,000,000 (an *estimate* since the "debt clock" was

s.S.O.S.

moving so rapidly). A common response to this mounting debt is "don't worry, they'll just *print* more"—here is the math behind that falsehood: All of the US mints combined can produce roughly $541 million per day, 95% of which is printed just to maintain the replacement of tattered or ripped bills, leaving a daily surplus of $27 million in *new* notes.

Based on our current money-printing capacity, it would take 2,451,752 days to "print" 66 trillion dollars—**6,717 years.** If we used the entire printing capacity of the US government to make the bills (not accounting for the normal maintenance of our tattered currency), it would still take us 122,587 days to do so. This means that if we used every penny of our freshly minted money to repay our national debt, *it would still take 335 years to repay.*

S.S.O.S.s.

10. Fifteen *Known* Men

—Decoding Skull and Bones—

The meaning behind the infamous *"Chapter 3:22'* on the Bones insignia:

Holy Bible—Genesis *Chapter 3:22*

22 And the Lord God said, "The man has now become like one of us, **knowing good and evil.** He must not be allowed to reach out his hand and take also from the tree of life and eat, and live forever."

The Order of Skull & Bones, on Yale University, was founded in 1833, by William Huntington Russell (as aforementioned). Below is a list of satanic, Biblical, and ritualistic creepiness, which occurs at the trust of the most vile, and clandestine society ever dreamt-up by the evilest of evildoers who have ever strayed planet earth—

s.S.O.S.s.

—New recruits are simply "tapped" on the shoulder while going on about their day on campus, to acknowledge the potential pledge's position of eligibility within The Order.

—The society anoints the initiate with a new name, symbolizing his rebirth and rechristening as **Knight X**, a member of the Order. The rookie "knights" are then introduced to the many creepy artifacts in the tomb. A set of Hitler's silverware (among other Hitler tchotchkes); crowds of skulls and full skeletons, human organs, other halloween-worthy relics, and who knows what else is in their dark collection? "The Bones whore," is the tomb's full-time resident, who supposedly caters to any sexual needs of the spooks.

Mentally assuming an all-new evil persona is the first step toward creating a psychopath; they are not "born that way" as The Order's lying educational system leads you to believe, at The Order's so-called *Universities*, or on The Order's so-called *"Discovery"* Channel programming. *We shall delve into this fecal matter later.* In the good guys' version of The Bible God changed peoples' names, to change humans into new creatures of good—God changed Abram's "high father" name to "Abraham," "father of a multitude" (Genesis 17:5), and his wife's name from "Sarai," "my princess," to "Sarah," "mother of nations." I would have to assume that in the same way these fellows believe to be inviting demons to take over their bodies.

By the way…it doesn't matter if you believe any of this Bible stuff, *or not*; you will soon believe that *these evil bastards do…*

s.s.O.s.s.

An article titled *Last Secrets of Skull and Bones,* by Ron Rosenbaum *(Esquire, September 1977)*, gives us a rare peek at The Order's name-changing ritual:

> **"Tonight he will die to the world and be born again into The Order** as he will thenceforth refer to it. The Order is a world unto itself in which he will have a new name and fourteen new blood brothers, also with new names."

Rosenbaum (the Author of these passages) was a Yale graduate attracted by the 'fictional' possibilities of a secret society who were 'out to control the world.' When Rosenbaum inquired about The Order, he was told:

> "They don't like people tampering and prying. The power of Bones is incredible. They've got their hands on every lever of power in the country. You'll see—it's like trying to look into the Mafia. Remember they're a secret society too."

—List of known Skull & Bones nicknames by which the shameless recruits will be 'known for life' within the society...

Long Devil—is assigned to the tallest member.

Boaz—goes to any member who is a varsity football captain. The name Boaz means strength. One of two symbolic columns sup-

s.S.O.S.s.

porting the porch of Solomon's Temple was named after the devil Boaz.

Look:

The monolith, or circular pillar, standing alone, was, to the ancient MMD (Master Mason's Deacon), a representation of the Phallus, the symbol of the creative and generative energy of Deity, and it is in these Phallic pillars that we are to find the true origin of pillar worship, which was only one form of Phallic worship, the most predominant of all the cults to which the ancients were addicted. PILLARS, PILLARS, Pillars of Cloud and Fire.

The pillar of cloud that went before the Israelites by day, and the pillar of fire that preceded them by night, in their journey through the wilderness, are supposed to represent the pillars of Jachin and Boaz at the porch of Solomon's Temple. We find this symbolism at a very early period in the last century, having been incorporated into the lecture of the Second Degree, where it still remains.

The passage (above), from the Freemason's own encyclopedia, finishes with an explanation of the cloud and fire pillars being a 'representation of deity.' These two 'Deity' Pillars are very important to the Freemasons, and the symbolic pillars are duplicated and placed in every masonic lodge around the country—there is probably at least a pair in your town.

s.S.O.S.s.

To me this means that the Freemasons view themselves as the god of the common man (us)—their actions, when studied at any length, prove the same. By placing the cloud and fire before the congregation, which is how God led the Israelites, the Freemasons are symbolically acting as *our god*. The fire and cloud guided the Israelites by night and day—the Freemasons are quite obviously guiding us in the same way.

The Pillars of Solomon's Temple **(google image 'Freemason Pillars')** could easily represent the rebuilding of the *Temple of Solomon*. (One of the few remaining unfilled prophecies, which need to be fulfilled before the second coming of the Messiah, as described in The Bible.) By referring to a member as 'Boaz' the Society of Skull and Bones are showing us that they have an affiliation with the *Freemasons*.

Sancho Panza—was a fictional character in literature, and is a neighbor to Don Quixote. He is an illiterate laborer who joins Don Quixote's squire, in hopes to become governor of an island as a reward for some adventure *(this sounds familiar)*.

Sancho starts the adventure as an introvert fellow. But, gradually, Sancho becomes more loquacious. He recites proverbs, and becomes an accomplice to Don Quixote's madness. He also functions as the jester, or the gracioso—the buffoon of Spanish comedy archetype. This name is also said to be assigned to one of the 15 initiates.

McGeorge Bundy **(S&B 1940)**, Special Assistant for National Security Affairs National Security Advisor, was **Odin**, of Norse mythology.

s.S.O.S.s.

Odin is associated with healing, death, royalty, the gallows, knowledge, battle (war), sorcery, poetry, frenzy, and the Runic alphabet (a juxtaposed grouping of gifts)—Odin was a trickster. Odin was a Norse deity who was passed on through necromancy—visitation with the dead via their remains—and was a war-making deity with little care for fairness (or justice).

A human life was the most valuable sacrifice that the Vikings could make to the god (shocker right?). Odin is known as the king of the gods.

But one thing which they don't tell you when studying 'mythology' (Greek, Norse, or otherwise), is the fact that, many *if not all* of these so-called 'mythological' *god's were* living men in Biblical times, and they were held in such reverence by their admirers that they had become objects of worship—*idols*. (Hence the ritualistic collection and worship of the bones of these men.)

It was important that these heathens discount the existence of the 'Greek' (and otherwise) versions of their Biblical heroes—the *bad guys*. Through the confusion of changing the names of the Biblical bad guys, whom they worship, the existence of the Biblical *good guys,* and **God,** can continue to be haled as myth as well. And since the very foundation of the threshold to satanism revolves around the notion that God *nor the devil* ever actually existed, they continue teaching your child *(at public school)* about the Greek 'gods' who they themselves worship, and The Bible becomes more and more an object of ridicule, and *myth*, as time passes.

So now let us look at whom Odin really was in The Bible... Odin is a cryptic name for King Nimrod, who definitely existed.

S.S.O.S.s.

As a matter of fact, Nimrod may be one of the most documented people of ancient times, in The Bible, *and* by scholars of the times.

Nimrod, or ***Odin,*** was the King of Babylon, which was one of an entire kingdom of cities over which King Nimrod ruled. Nimrod was known to be a powerful man—a great trapper of animals *and men.* Nimrod was a nasty man. Nimrod actually claimed that he had had a battle with God in the mountains, but that he had defeated and beheaded God, so his people would depend on, and worship, Nimrod, instead. Many, both satanists and believers, believe that Nimrod actually *was* satan, which explains why Bonesmen and Freemasons alike worship the guy.

Nimrod was the Babylonian King who would have presided over the building of the Tower of Babel—The Bible story which kicked-off the beginning of our adventure. Remember, the Ancient Babylonian City who continued building 'ever higher' in protest to God's great flood? They thought that their stepped pyramid technology could save them from the drowning waters—if the floods came they would all simply run to the top and save themselves.

Well, interestingly, Noah (who saved the world aboard his ark) was Nimrod's great, great, grandfather. Noah is mentioned dozens-and-dozens of times in the 1916 version of the Encyclopedia of Freemasonry—they literally worship the great Sailor.

Averell Harriman **(S&B 1913),** was **Thor**—One Skull & Bones member whom shared the nickname 'Thor' had *his* dead head turned into a ballot box for any voting done by Bones members **(an image can be easily searched online).** (Note: One of the femurs of the ballot box has his moniker, Thor, carved into it.)

s.S.O.S.s.

The Thor suggestion box turned up in an estate, and was up for auction at one of the haughty auction houses in New York. An 'unnamed claimant,' who had 'lost' the unidentified human head, phoned *Christie's,* before the auction was set to begin, and the relic was returned to his 'rightful owners,' I will give you two guesses who these fellas were, and your first guess *'don't count.'* And yes, **Thor too demanded human sacrifice,** *or else* he would become very cranky. (*Thor* is the *son* of Odin—this means that, "Thor," is *Nimrod's son.*)

Henry Luce (**S&B 1910**), **co-founder of Time-Life Enterprises, was Baal. The worship of Baal extended to the early Jews, and Canaanites, of The Bible. Baal is synonymous with *Lilith*. The demon Lilith, who many times came in the form of an owl, was an alternate form of the same god,** *Baal.* **The last name, 'Luce,' actually translates to, 'Lily,' or, 'brightness'** (*Lucifer*) **and its origin can be traced back to The Bible, and to the name,** *Lilith*, **itself.**

Baal is also the same satan god known as Molech in The Bible—the golden calf god from the Moses and the Ten Commandments story—the Ancient Greeks knew the fellow as Zeus. Baal was also known as Jupiter and, Amon, to Ancient Egyptians. Worshippers of Nimrod in the form of 'Dagon' wore fish head costumes, and still do. The Pope typically wears a 'Dagon' miter—the Pope's Dagon fish head even has x's for dead eyes.

> Note: The Order has made the task of keeping up with all of their Gods extremely complicated for good reason—the horrible ritual of human sacrifice

s.s.O.s.s.

to these deities eventually signaled the end of all of these civilizations. What *is* important is that, you remember that they all just represent the same evil Biblical King—*King Nimrod.*

Dagon is another rebellious form of Nimrod. Dagon myth claims that he survived God's dreaded flood, so the fish getup is another slap in God's face, since Dagon depicts King Nimrod as a fish who would survive earth's destruction by water. Poseidon and Neptune are both evolved versions of Dagon (Nimrod), and both hold tridents—*the devil's pitchfork.*

As you can see, by studying the face of all of these demons, they are all exactly the same no matter what time period in which he was worshipped—*they are all just King Nimrod!*

Jeremiah 19:4-6 King James Version
4 Because they have forsaken me, and have estranged this place, and have burned incense in it unto other gods, whom neither they nor their fathers have known, nor the kings of Judah, and have filled this place with the blood of innocents;
5 They have built also the high places of Baal, to burn their sons with fire for burnt offerings unto Baal, which I commanded not, nor spake it, neither came it into my mind:
6 Therefore, behold, the days come, saith the Lord, that this place shall no more be called Tophet, nor The valley of the son of Hinnom, but The valley of slaughter.

S.S.O.S.s.

Ruins of ancient temples to Baal are still Scattered allover earth's landscape—for example, the temple of *Baalbek*. Ancient peoples would travel from far and wide to offer their babies to the fire of Baal, in hopes for financial windfall, power over other men, and good fortune.

The temple of Baal at Palmyra Syria—aka The Iraqi City of Nimrod—was named after King Nimrod of Babylon who built the Tower of Babel. This imposing temple stood for 2000 years before making news when it was destroyed by Isis in 2015. The world community was devastated by the demise of the evil structure, and the temple has recently made its way back in the news circles, with on again *off again* **talk of recreating the structure in New York City,** and other major cities around the world.

The swastika, an auspicious symbol, is plastered upon the stone which constructs this synagogue of satan—this is ironic, since Ancient peoples incinerated live humans as offering to Baal, and Hitler also burned the remains of millions of individuals in his ovens, while his soldiers wore the same image.

As you can see, use of the swastika during Nazi Germany was nothing new. The swastika had been used for centuries in Ancient India too, by the North American Indians around the time of the Indian slaughter on the continent, and even long before these events in other ancient cultures.

Baalzebub—A Biblical name for satan (synonymous with "Baal"—see Baal, last entry), is **also known for human sacrifice—especially of the child variety.** In The Bible the spelling is, Beelzebub, and *he* was the god of the Philistine City of Ekron—a

S.S.O.S.S.

Canaanite god who demanded human sacrifice. Beelzebub represents gluttony.

2 Kings 1 King James Version
1 Then Moab rebelled against Israel after the death of Ahab.
2 And Ahaziah fell down through a lattice in his upper chamber that was in Samaria, and was sick: and he sent messengers, and said unto them, **Go, enquire of Baalzebub the god of Ekron** whether I shall recover of this disease.
3 But the angel of the Lord said to Elijah the Tishbite, Arise, go up to meet the messengers of the king of Samaria, and say unto them, **Is it not because there is not a God in Israel, that ye go to enquire of Baalzebub the god of Ekron?**

Again, these are *all* the same-exact deity as Nimrod.

Interestingly, George "Dubya" Bush was never issued a Bones name and remains known simply as, "Temporary," to his demonic colleagues. George W. Bush's lack of a nickname is likely due to the leaks of Skull & Bones information to the public. Also, the internet has made it easier and easier to link The Order to the dastardly deeds which followed their elections and held offices. Now, virtually nothing is leaked.

Is it not becoming clear that these Nimrods believe to become gods upon their knighthood into the "brotherhood of merchants of death?"

s.s.O.s.s.

1 Corinthians 10:20-21

King James Version

20 But I say, that the things which the Gentiles sacrifice, they sacrifice to devils, and not to God: and I would not that ye should have fellowship with devils. **21 Ye cannot drink the cup of the Lord, and the cup of devils: ye cannot be partakers of the Lord's table, and of the table of devils.**

Magog—goes to the Skull & Bones member with the most sexual experience.

Gog—goes to the new member having had sex most recently.

Known Magogs, "well-known wild sex havers," are President William Howard Taft (S&B founder—1833), Robert Taft (S&B 1910), and George Bush Senior (S&B 1948).

Other Rituals

—New Members of the Order are issued a grandfather clock with which to constantly remind of the finite amount of time one has on this planet by which to enjoy one's flesh. In a first ritual for the group, human skulls are placed next to a jester's cap, to remind the recruit that he would be foolish to waste his time here being kind to others rather than serving one's self. The church of satan shares this Skull and Bones belief:

s.s.O.s.s.

"There is no heaven of glory bright, and no hell where sinners roast. Here and now is our day of torment! Here and now is our day of joy! Here and now is our opportunity! Choose ye this day, this hour, for no redeemer liveth!"

—Anton Lavey—

"So, if "evil" they have named us, evil we are-and so what! The satanic age is upon us! Why not take advantage of it and LIVE!"

—Anton Lavey—

—**Kissing the feet of the Pope**—Ron Rosenbaum, author and columnist for the New York Observer, managed to hide out in a building, and covertly filmed an official Skull and Bones ceremony from afar. Rosebaum's secret film features a devil figure and the Pope. Also, there was a special type of slipper that rested on a skull. Investigators have confirmed that during this particular Skull and Bones ceremony 'Knight-X' is forced to kiss the slipper of the Pope. Many have speculated that this ritual symbolizes a secretive alliance with the Pope.

—**The "tomb,"** is a dark, windowless crypt in New Haven Connecticut. The roof of the Tomb doubles as a landing pad for the society's private helicopter. Once they enter the structure, and are sworn to silence, they are informed that they must forever deny their membership to the organization. While being initiated as Skull and Bones members, they are subjected to brutal psychological conditioning, the juniors wrestle in mud and are physically beaten (this ritual is shared by the cartels, mafia, and even street gangs)—this stage of the ceremony represents their 'death' to the world as they have known it.

—**The new members then lie naked in coffins**, masturbate, and reveal to the others their darkest sexual secrets. After this "cleansing," current members give the new recruits robes to represent their new identities as individuals **with a higher purpose. George Bush Senior is said to have watched and presided over Junior as he masturbated.** A quick google video search will produce a glimpse of the sinister ceremonies carried out at Skull and Bones.

—**Bones Favoritism**—Most of the students at Yale hold the arrogant Bonesmen in very low regard. Below is another outtake from Antony C. Sutton's book:

> **The Favoritism Shown To Bones Men**
> "Are not we coming to a sad state when open injustice can be done by the Faculty, and when the fact that a man is a member of Skull and Bones can prejudice them in his favor? Briefly, the case which calls forth this question is this: Two members of the Senior class, the one being a neutral, the other a Bones man, returned at the beginning of the college year laden with several conditions, some of which, upon examination, they failed to pass. Up to this point the cases were parallel, and the leniency, if there was to be leniency, should have been shown to the neutral, who has done all that lay in his power to

further the interests of the college, rather than **to the Bones man, who has, during his three years at Yale, accomplished nothing that we wot of**."

"But, strange to say, the former has been suspended until the end of the term and obliged to leave town, not being permitted to pass another examination until he returns. The Bones man, on the contrary, is allowed to remain in New Haven, attends recitation daily, is called upon to recite, and will have a second examination in less than six weeks. Why is this distinction made? 'O, Mr. So-and-so's is a special case,' said a professor (a Bones man)—**the specialty, we presume, being the fact that Mr. So-and-so wears a death's head and cross bones upon his bosom.** We understand that Mr. So-and-so claims to have been ill during vacation and offers the illness as an excuse for not passing the examination; but the neutral gentleman was also ill, as the Faculty were expressly informed in a letter from his father."

"The circumstance has caused a very lively indignation throughout the Senior class. It is certainly time for a radical reform when the gentlemen who superintend our destinies, and who should be just if nothing else, can allow themselves to be influenced by so petty a thing as society connections."

S.S.O.S.s.
—The Germanic Chapter of The Order of Skull & Bones, known as *Totenkopf* (which literally translates to *dead's head*), is the German word for the skull and crossbones. The Totenkopf symbol is an old international symbol for death—the defiance of death, danger, or the dead, as well as piracy, or to warn one of a poisonous substance. The special forces branch of the US Army Rangers commonly uses the Skull & Bones death head insignia on patches, equipment, and other related regalia.

—*The Group* is England's Chapter of the Order of Skull & Bones—it is located on the campus of Oxford University, and is, ironically, where Bill Clinton was sent away to attend school. I have not confirmed any Clinton involvement in the secret society, but, I haven't looked very hard, either.

Supposedly a Rhodes Scholar, word is, Clinton never even finished the program. Clinton did, however, attend Oxford through the program. Later, Bill attended the evil Yale University, where he met his wife and current Democratic Presidential Candidate, Hillary Rodham Clinton. Clinton had a quick stint in the CIA, from there attending a Bilderberg meeting, after which Bill became US President number 42. *Clinton is confirmed to be a 33 degree Freemason.*

> ***Note***: *Special thanks to Alexandra Robbins for her work, much of which was paraphrased, to write this section. The work was taken from her book 'Secrets of the Tomb,' a great read! Also much thanks to Sutton and kris Millegan—their books are mentioned in the reading list at the end.*

S.S.O.S.s.

Fun fact: In a great triumph for The Order, **John Kerry (S&B 1966) (Democrat)** faced off against George W. Bush **(S&B 1968) (Republican)** for the office of the President of the United States of America, in 2004. Two Skull and Bones members, who are cousins and Frat Bros in the most exclusive club in the world, both competing for the same office, would leave The Order of Skull and Bones in a win-win position. If this doesn't prove to you that both sides of the aisle have the same agenda, nothing will.

s.s.O.s.s.

11. Thor's Hammer

Thor's hammer was claimed to have been discovered in 2013, by men working on the Citybanan tunnel project in Stockholm. (Story found on thelocal.se.) Workers were stunned to find what they believe to be Mjölnir, the hammer of Norse lightning god Thor (King Nimrod), **partially encased in granite bedrock!** The hammer which weighed more than 60 Kilos (**132 POUNDS**) was covered in Rune writing. Authorities have refused to release any information concerning the meaning of the words written upon the object. The hammer was found at an astonishing depth. Quotes concerning the found object:

> "I reacted instead to the object being made of metal and heavily engraved, beautifully so, in fact," **Engineer, Rav Pidertni** told Swedish archaeology trade publication Stenarna, *The Stones.*

> "I at first thought it was piping sticking out of the ground," added engineer Rav Pidertni. "It was a case of shock and awe when one of my engineers recognized engravings on the object to be Norse runes," Citybanan project manager Johan Leber told The Local.

> "I don't think my colleagues understand the empirical implications of this," **Lhodgeec N'Dreesun** told *The Local.*

s.S.O.S.s.

"It's easy for us scientists to slip into atheism by some kind of default, a work hazard of sorts, but *I have no idea how to explain this." —Again, Lhodgeec N'Dreesun—

Note*: I know how to explain it....We have been lied to concerning the rate at which our planet was created; it seems granite forms quite a bit faster than what we have been told. When you have time Google search 'out of place objects.' The items which will follow are absolutely astonishing, and you will quickly realize that something definitely stinks about the bedtime stories which have been touted as *fact*.

"As we're going straight through the bedrock, we never expected to encounter anything down here," said Leber.

12. Illuminati & The Age of Enlightenment

The Satanic Bible

Though there is a large faction of 'The Order' deemed, the 'Bavarian Illuminati,' this section concerns itself with the common term, which most simply associate with 'satanism.'

While it was *no fun* delving into the chronicles of satanism, it was key to understanding these monsters—it was an eye-opening experience. I will bring attention to the areas of interest to save you the despair of the fecal matter betwixt its covers. The first section of the satanic bible, entitled '**Enlightenment**,' is where the whole 'Secret Society,' 'Illuminati,' and '**Age of Enlightenment**' conundrum, came into focus for me. Before that, these words were all just a mystery to me, and no one seemed able to paint me a clear picture of the glowing monikers.

On April 30, 1966, Anton Szandor Lavey founded the Church of Satan, and proclaimed 1966 as 'Year One,' Anno Satanas, 'the first year of the Age of Satan' (though 'illuminati' of all varieties had been celebrating the *Age of Enlightenment,* since the beginning of the 17th century, when harsh feelings concerning magic, satanism, and witchcraft had again settled down in the public eye). Here is Lavey's version of *Enlightenment:*

(AIR) THE BOOK OF LUCIFER
THE ENLIGHTENMENT

s.S.O.S.s.

The Roman god, Lucifer, was the bearer of light, the spirit of the air, the personification of **enlightenment**.

Here is another section of Lavey's satanic bible, which gives us some direction as to what the word, **"Enlightenment,"** refers to:

THE FOUR CROWN PRINCES OF HELL

SATAN—*(Hebrew)* adversary, opposite, accuser, **Lord of fire, the inferno,** the south

LUCIFER—*[Roman version of the devil]* **bringer of light, enlightenment,** the air, **the morning star,** the east

BELIAL—*[Alternate spelling for Baal, or 'Nimrod'—a name taken by Skull and Bones members]* —*(Hebrew)* **without a master, baseness of the earth, independence, the north**

LEVIATHAN—*[Alternate name for Dagon, or 'Nimrod']*—*(Hebrew)* **the serpent out of the deeps, the sea, the west**

Merriam-Webster's definition of **enlightenment**:

s.S.O.S.s.

The **Enlightenment** : a movement of the 18th century that stressed the belief that **science and logic give people more knowledge and understanding than tradition and** *religion.*

In other words, the *age of enlightenment* represents the emergence from the dark ages for the practitioners of the dark arts. The age of enlightenment is a celebration, by the satanist, since he *or* she must no longer hide in the dark shadows of the fringes of society to practice their magic. It is a celebration of luciferian outwardness, and freely practiced satanism.

Some time when you are bored google video the huge public satanic ritual being enjoyed by a handpicked crowd, to celebrate the 'opening of the *Gotthard Base Tunnel* in Switzerland.'

Here is a list of dedications in the opening of Lavey's evil book (I added the descriptive commentary)....

Howard Hughes—film and aviation tycoon (one of the most successful men of his time) who had a horrible social disorder—*fear of being around others.*

Moody (Edward J. Moody)—anthropologist who worshipped the devil, and claimed satanism was *beneficial for curing social disorders.*

Marcello Truzzi—Marcello Truzzi was a professor of sociology at New College of Florida

s.S.O.S.s.

Adrian-Claude Frazier

Marilyn Monroe—was a famous actress.

Wesley Mather

William Lindsay Gresham—was a renown American Novelist.

Hugo Zacchini—was the first circus act in the form of the 'Human Cannonball.'

Jayne Mansfield—was a famous actress.

Frederick Goerner—writer

C. Huntley

Nathaniel West—was an American author, screenwriter and satirist.

Horatio Alger—was a 19th-century American author known for his many young-adult novels.

Robert Ervin Howard—was an American Author.

George Orwell—was an English novelist, essayist, journalist and critic.

s.s.O.s.s.

Howard Phillips Lovecraft—was an influential writer of fictional horror stories.

Tuesday Weld—was an American actress. [Tuesday means, *'Thor's Day.'* Wednesday translates to, 'Woden's Day,' or *'Odin's Day.'*]

H.G. Wells—was a prolific english writer in all genres.

Sister Marie Koven

Harry Houdini—famous escape artist.

Togare—Anton Lavey's 500 pound pet lion, who lived with the writer of the satanic 'bible.'

and the Nine Unknown Men—explained in their own upcoming section…

Anton LaVey claimed to have cast a curse on some lawyer who then died in a car crash. Unfortunately for him, LaVey's close friend, *Jayne Mansfield* was also in the car, with her children, when Miss Mansfield died.

s.s.O.s.s.

13. The Nine *Unknown* Men

The Nine Unknown Men, to which Lavey ends the dedications in his satanic bible (last section), were a secret society founded by the Mauryan Emperor Ashoka (India, around 270 BC) to preserve and develop knowledge that would be dangerous to humanity if it fell into the wrong hands. The Nine Unknown Men were entrusted with guarding these nine books of secret knowledge.

Just as there were nine original Knight's Templar, there were also *The Nine Unknown Men.* As you read, the Nine Unknown Men had a lot of things in common with the Templar—hoarding of esoteric knowledge; a personal relationship with the Pope; clouds of secrecy, and worship of the dead—necromancy—among others.

>Quote:
>"The most dangerous of all sciences," wrote Talbot Mundy (a member of the British police force in India, as **an employee of East India Company**), "is that of moulding mass opinion, because it would enable anyone to govern the whole world."

The Books of the Esoteric Knowledge of the Nine Unknown Men

Volume One—The first of the super-secret books is said to have been devoted to the technique of propaganda and psychological warfare. The French book, *Tchocotine's Le Viol des Foules*, or, *The Rape of the Masses* (1940), was merely a variation of *Ortega y Gasset's* classic work (1929) by the same name. These books heavily influenced the politics during their times, and if you look at the dates, they were just in time for WWII.

Volume Two—A book on physiology, which outlined things such as, a method of killing a man simply by touching him. Theoretically death came with a reversal of the nerve-impulse. Judo is thought to be the result of 'leakages' from this secret book.

Volume Three—offered a complete volume on the subject of microbiology, and it is said to have mainly served as a discussion of protective colloids. Remember, this was a book which is now almost 1300 years old. *(The smallpox blanket give-away program immediately springs to mind here.)*

Volume Four—This book outlined the alchemical transmutation of base metals into gold. There are legends that in lean times the temples and religious groups (something like UNICEF) were offered large quantities of pure gold from an unknown benefactor. There are many modern myths circulating today which boast the same claims, except, in which case, the benefactors were governments in financial straits—and, instead of it being the Nine Unknown Men who offered the bailouts, it is said to have been the Knight's Templar.

Volume Five—This book is a study of all sorts of communication; language and the working dynamics thereof. This work also includes a study of so-called 'extraterrestrial communication.' One cannot help but speculate that, this technology came about due to the disaster at the Tower of Babel—Genesis 11:9:

> "That is why it was called Babel—because there the LORD confused the language of the whole world."

Volume Six—This volume was written entirely around the topic of gravity. The funny thing is, other than some equations which summarize the physical properties of gravity, today we know virtually nothing of the working dynamics of gravity. Interestingly, many think that the mammoth building blocks of the Great Pyramids were built using antigravity technology, *though this is not what I am implying*.

Volume Seven—This volume is said to be the most comprehensive cosmogony ever compiled by the human race.

Volume Eight—Teaches of light—something we virtually knew nothing of, until the advent of the Industrial Revolution.

Volume Nine—The final volume is an in-depth discussion of sociology, and **is said to outline rules for the rise and fall of societies, and the means of estimating the exact time of societal demise based on a set of metrics** (I would guess that America is running toward the end of the dialectic cycle of volume nine).

    This information, whatever it actually was, has definitely fallen into the wrong hands. There aren't many hard facts about this story, and we don't have a Skull & Bones list of attendees at Yale with which to chase these marauders down, historically.

However, there are three more things which beg for our attention here....First, is the parallel between Skull and Bones and the Nine Unknown Men, as far as establishing a group of men which succeed each other, and are guarding humanity from their own technology. Secondly, the fact that this group was known to operate in India, a country which *East India* Company *owned*, also makes this group worthy of further research. Thirdly, the fact that *all three groups* are composed of a fixed number of men who successively guard their knowledge, implies that, Skull and Bones *is an identical organization to the Nine Unknown Men, who in turn are the same fellows as the 'Knights Templar.'*

Below is a great outtake from, bibliotecapleyades.net:

Examples of the Nine Unknown Men making contact with the outer world are rare. There was, however, the extraordinary case of one of the most mysterious figures in Western history: the **Pope Sylvester II**, known also by the name of Gerbert d'Aurillac. Born in the Auvergne in 920 (d. 1003) Gerbert was a Benedictine monk, professor at the University of Rheims, Archbishop of Ravenna and Pope by the grace of Otho III.

He is supposed to have spent some time in Spain, after which a mysterious voyage brought him to *India* where he is reputed to have acquired various kinds of skills which stupefied his entourage. For example, **he possessed in his palace a *bronze head which answered Yes or No to questions put to it on politics or**

s.s.O.s.s.
the general position of Christianity. [cf. "Max the **Crystal Skull" of current notoriety B:.B:.]

According to Sylvester II, this was a perfectly simple operation corresponding to a two-figure calculation, and was performed by an automaton similar to our modem binary machines. This "magic" head was destroyed when Sylvester died, and all the information it imparted carefully concealed. No doubt an authorized research worker would come across some surprising things in the Vatican Library.

Note*: The Catholic Church has *many* of these 'bronze heads' (most of theirs are gold and silver) which hold the actual heads of people that range from popes to Charlemagne. They worship the head, and pray to it, in the same 'divine' way.

As a matter of fact, the Catholic Church has an untold quantity of dead bodies in their collection of magic relics. They send the long-deceased corpses on worldwide tours like rockstars, so that everyone in the world can share in the necromancy.

One of the most recent and disgusting cases of this necromantic behavior is the 1998 exhumation of the body of Saint Luke. The grave was robbed, his head was stolen, and Luke's cranium is worshipped by the Catholic Church to this day.

The idol of Charlemagne, a gold and silver statue, houses the actual head which the Catholic Church worships. The hair of the statue is hinged to form a hatch from which Charlemagne's actual cranium can be removed and worshipped. (Charlemagne too is related to the Russells, and, therefore *to the George Bush family*.)

s.s.O.s.s.

Note**: These crystal skulls, which have been found scattered *around the world,* were used in the dark arts for 'divination.' The hit History Channel program, Ancient Aliens, has manufactured all sorts of alternative theories for these coveted idols.

Below, is the definition for necromancy:

Merriam-Webster—necromancy:

Simple Definition of necromancy
: the practice of talking to the spirits of dead people

Full Definition of necromancy
1
: conjuration of the spirits of the dead **for purposes of magically revealing the future or influencing the course of events**

Note: It appears that the Catholic Church shares this ritual of skullduggery, divinity, and idol worship. The very word *'Vatican'* derives from the Latin word *vates,* **meaning:** *'tellers of the future.'*

The Order of the Thuggee was a secret society in Ancient India who were known to have killed well-over a million men. The earliest known reference to the 'Thugs' as a band, or fraternity, rather than ordinary thieves, is found in Ziau-d din Barni's *History of Firoz Shah* (written about 1356):

s.S.O.S.s.

In the reign of that sultan [about 1290], some Thugs were taken in Delhi, and a man belonging to that fraternity was the means of about a thousand being captured. But not one of these did the sultan have killed. He gave orders for them to be put into boats and to be conveyed into the lower country, to the neighbourhood of Lakhnauti, where they were to be set free. The Thugs would thus have to dwell about Lakhnauti and would not trouble the neighbourhood of Delhi any more. [Sir HM Elliot, *History of India*, iii. 141]

These killers, whom the Sultan *released*, were perhaps the most dreaded clan in the history of the world.

The signature death move of the Thuggee was a sash of cloth which was tied around their waist. At any time of day these Indian Ninja-like warriors would appear from no where, and throw the sash (which had a coin within it for weight) around the victims neck, strangling the victim to death in the Thuggee's hands. This was one of the most stealthy and fierce factions of *The Order* ever to be created.

India's flag wasn't all that different than the first Jesuit version of the American slave ship flag. It can be seen proudly displaying the Union Jack in its upper-left hand pocket, in the same way it did on *Old Glory.*

Several of the old East India Company flags also displayed *nine* red and white stripes, which muses the question: Does the

s.S.O.S.s.

number of stripes on both of these flags represent the Knight's Templar or the *'Nine Unknown Men?'*

Believe it or not, the Flag of Greece *also displays nine stripes*. It is a spitting image of the East India Company flag, save for the colors, and boasts a templar cross in *its* pocket. These flags are configured very similarly to the American Flag.

If you still aren't convinced that we live in Babylon or Rome, keep reading…

s.s.O.s.s.

14. What is 'The Order?'

Well, according to google…

or·der
ôrdər/
noun
noun: **order**; plural noun: **orders**; noun: **Order**

The arrangement or disposition of people or things in relation to each other according to a particular sequence, pattern, or method.

This certainly puts a whole new ring on the old saying, *Law and Order.* Does it not?

On the History Channel they would have a buffoon explain how the ancient Egyptians were using the Great Pyramid at Giza as a Microwave Generator—to communicate with aliens—or as an ancient power plant. The Order refers to the social order of people which, in Egyptian times too, was represented by the pyramid, in which the peasants and commoners comprised the foundation, and as you stepped up, the individuals made up the more elite (google image Egyptian social pyramid). The next Order Pyramid involved the monarchy and looked like this **(google image 'medieval social pyramid')**.

A google image search for, 'colonial money pyramid perennis 50 dollar bill,' will produce an image of a colonial fifty-

s.S.O.S.s.

dollar bill, which features the pyramid, and the latin inscription above the structure reads 'Perennis,' which literally translates to *'parents.'* Where do you fit-in within 'The Order?' If you were recently passed up for that promotion at work in favor of a guy without your talent, or experience, now you know why. Now you also know why the History Channel's presentation, *Ancient Aliens,* was invented, to further confuse the masses of *The Order's* true intentions to continue to enslave our society.

Our censures, The Order, would rather that we believe in aliens who assisted in the construction of these ruins, rather than to know of the Hegelian technology of the dialectic, which is on course to make America the next Nazi Germany, more likely sooner, than later.

The All Seeing Eye at the top of *our* one dollar bill represents lucifer, or the worldwide elite, who interconnect through their networks to run the entire world—known to Ancient Egyptians as *'the all-seeing eye of Horus.'* In the New Testament of the Holy Bible, and in Yale's satanic *Wollebius Book (Yale's 'Bible'),* the office is simply known as "The Beast."

Bonesmen, or, 'The Order,' as they call themselves, seem to consider themselves to rule all races. In fact, The Order refers to all of us commoners, of all different colors, as, *Vandals* or *Gentiles*.

Many think that the term *Gentile* refers to the *white man*, but, in fact, a Gentile was any Biblical man who wasn't referred to as a 'Jew,' *by a 'Jew.'* So, in other words, the *'Jews'* of The Bible referred to everyone but themselves as *Gentile*. The word Gentile was essentially the first know racial slur.

s.s.O.s.s.

The only other term which describes all other races except the one who speaks that slur, are The Order of Skull and Bones, who, as aforementioned, refer to all of us commoners as *'Vandals.'*

15. The Jesuit Order

Merriam - Webster

Simple Definition for *Jesuit*
    Jesuit: a man who is a member of a religious group called the Roman Catholic Society of Jesus.

    This section should be given special consideration, since I believe this to be the satanic model by which all other factions of The Order operate.
    The Jesuits, informally known as the *'Pope's Marines,'* are an Order of men who serve as the Pope's henchman, a sort of CIA for the Pope. Since the Pope, the leader of the Roman Catholic Church, is wrongly perceived as 'Christ Vicar' ('earthly representative of **God** or **Christ**') by its congregation, the Pope hired a group of fringe 'priests' in order to carry out the more questionable missions of his bidding. Many people do not realize that the Pope reigns with supreme authority, in all lands, and holds the authority to grant life, or death, to any person on the planet. The Order of the Jesuits are the fellows who grant those supreme wishes!
    With a very similar outward appearance to the Knight's Templar of the middle ages (who were supposedly eradicated for their atrocities, pillage and genocide), the Jesuits also serve the very same purpose, which begs the question: were the Knight's Templar ever truly eradicated? We shall see...

S.S.O.S.s.

The formal story of the founding of the Order of the Jesuits is as follows: In 1534, Ignatius and six other men, including Francis Xavier and Peter Faber, gathered *and professed vows of poverty, chastity, and faith to the Pope*, including a special vow of obedience to the Pope in matters of mission assignment (*just like as 'The Templar' did*). Ignatius's plan of the order's organization was approved by Pope Paul III in 1540 by a *bull* (written creed) containing the *"Formula of the Institute."*

When a Jesuit is promoted to a higher level of command, he is led into the Chapel of the Convent of the Order, in the presence of only three other individuals. The principal, or *Superior*, takes his place in front of the altar. A monk stands to either side of the dark fellow—one monk holds a banner of yellow and white—the Papal colors. **The other banner is black, with a dagger and red cross above a skull and crossbones** *(Templar Cross and the Skull and Bones insignia)* boasting the acronym *INRI*—the words *IUSTUM NECAR REGES IMPIUS* are printed below the acronym—the meaning: **It is just, to exterminate or annihilate impious or heretical Kings, Governments, or Rulers.**

The following (below) are outtakes from the text of the *Jesuit Extreme Oath of Induction* as recorded in the Journals of the 62nd Congress, 3rd Session, of the United States Congressional Record (House Calendar No. 397, Report No. 1523, 15 February, 1913, pp. 3215-3216). Reportedly, the pages were later torn out.

The Oath is quoted by Charles Didier in his book *Subterranean Rome* (New York, 1843), translated from the French original. Dr. Alberto Rivera, who escaped from the Jesuit Order in 1967, confirms that the induction ceremony and the text of the Jesuit Oath which he took, matched the outtakes below:

s.S.O.S.s.

Upon the floor is a red cross at which the postulant or candidate kneels. The Superior hands him a small black crucifix, which he takes in his left hand and presses to his heart, and the Superior at the same time presents to him a dagger, which he grasps by the blade and holds the point against his heart, the Superior still holding it by the hilt, and thus addresses the postulant:

The Superior speaks:

My son, heretofore you have been taught to act the dissembler: among Roman Catholics to be a Roman Catholic, and to be a spy even among your own brethren; to believe no man, to trust no man. Among the Reformers, to be a Reformer; among the Huguenots, to be a Huguenot; among the Calvinists, to be a Calvinist; among other Protestants, generally to be a Protestant; and obtaining their confidence, to seek even to preach from their pulpits, and to denounce with all the vehemence in your nature our Holy Religion and the Pope; and even to descend so low as to become a Jew among Jews, that you might be enabled to gather together all information for the benefit ***of your Order*** as a faithful soldier of the Pope. You have been taught to plant insidiously the seeds of jealousy and hatred between communities, provinces, states that were at peace, and to incite them to deeds of blood, involving them in war with each other, *and to create revolutions and civil wars in countries that were independent and prosperous, cultivating the arts and the sciences and enjoying the blessings of peace; to take sides with the combatants and to act secretly with your brother Jesuit, who might be engaged on the other side, but openly opposed to that with which you might be connected, only that the Church might be the gainer in the end*, in the conditions fixed in the treaties for peace and that the end justifies the means. *You have been taught your duty as a spy*, to gather all statistics, facts and information in your power from every source; to *ingratiate yourself into the confidence of the family circle of Protestants and heretics of every class and character, as well as that of the merchant, the banker, the lawyer, among the schools and universities, in parliaments and legislatures, and the judiciaries and councils of state, and to be all things to all men, for the Pope's sake*, whose servants we are unto death. You have received all your instructions heretofore as a novice, a neophyte, and have served as co-adjurer, confessor and priest, but you have not yet been invested with all that is necessary to command in the Army of Loyola in the service of the Pope. *You must serve the proper time as the instrument and executioner as directed by your superiors*; for none can command here who has not

S.S.O.S.s.

consecrated his labours with the blood of the heretic; for *"without the shedding of blood no man can be saved"*. Therefore, to fit yourself for your work and make your own salvation sure, you will, in addition to your former oath of obedience to your order and allegiance to the Pope, repeat after me:

Text of the Oath:

I_____, now in the presence of Almighty God, the blessed Virgin Mary, the blessed St. John the Baptist, the Holy Apostles, St. Peter and St. Paul, and all the saints, sacred host of Heaven, and to you, my Ghostly Father, the superior general of the Society of Jesus, founded by St. Ignatius Loyola, in the pontification of Paul the Third, and continued to the present, do by the womb of the Virgin, the matrix of God, and the rod of Jesus Christ, declare and swear that His Holiness, the Pope, is Christ's Vice-Regent and is the true and only head of the Catholic or Universal Church throughout the earth; and that by the virtue of the keys of binding and loosing given to His Holiness by my Saviour, Jesus Christ, *he hath power to depose heretical Kings, Princes, States, Commonwealths, and Governments, and they may be safely destroyed.* Therefore to the utmost of my power I will defend this doctrine and His Holiness's right and custom against all usurpers of the heretical or

s.s.O.s.s.

Protestant authority whatever, especially the Lutheran Church of Germany, Holland, Denmark, Sweden and Norway, and the now pretended authority and Churches of England and Scotland, and the branches of same now established in Ireland and on the continent of America and elsewhere and all adherents in regard that they may be usurped and heretical, opposing the sacred Mother Church of Rome. I do now denounce and disown any allegiance as due to any heretical king, prince or State, named Protestant or Liberal, or obedience to any of their laws, magistrates or officers. I do further declare the doctrine of the Churches of England and Scotland of the Calvinists, Huguenots, and others of the name of Protestants or Masons to be damnable, and they themselves to be damned who will not forsake the same. I do further declare that I will help, assist, and advise all or any of His Holiness's agents, in any place where I should be, in Switzerland, Germany, Holland, Ireland or America, or in any other kingdom or territory I shall come to, and do my utmost to extirpate the heretical Protestant or Masonic doctrines and to destroy all their pretended powers, legal or otherwise. I do further promise and declare that, notwithstanding, I am dispensed with to assume any religion heretical for the propagation of the Mother Church's interest; to keep secret and private all her agents' counsels from time to time, as they entrust me, and not to divulge, directly or indi-

S.S.O.S.s.

rectly, by word, writing or circumstances whatever; but to execute all that should be proposed, given in charge, or discovered unto me by you, my Ghostly Father, or any of this sacred order. I do further promise and declare that I will have no opinion or will of my own or any mental reservation whatever, even as a corpse or cadaver (perinde ac cadaver), but will unhesitatingly obey each and every command that I may receive from my superiors in the militia of the Pope and of Jesus Christ. *That I will go to any part of the world whithersoever I may be sent, to the frozen regions north, jungles of India, to the centres of civilisation of Europe, or to the wild haunts of the barbarous savages of America without murmuring or repining, and will be submissive in all things, whatsoever is communicated to me.* I do further promise and declare that *I will, when opportunity presents, make and wage relentless war, secretly and openly, against all heretics, Protestants and Masons, as I am directed to do, to extirpate them from the face of the whole earth; and that I will spare neither age, sex nor condition, and that will hang, burn, waste, boil, flay, strangle, and bury alive these infamous heretics; rip up the stomachs and wombs of their women, and crush their infants' heads against the walls in order to annihilate their execrable race.* That when the same cannot be done openly *I will secretly use the poisonous cup, the strangulation cord, the steel*

s.S.O.S.s.

of the poniard, or the leaden bullet, regardless of the honour, rank, dignity or authority of the persons, whatever may be their condition in life, either public or private, as I at any time may be directed so to do by any agents of the Pope or Superior of the Brotherhood of the Holy Father of the Society of Jesus. In confirmation of which I hereby dedicate my life, soul, and all corporal powers, and with the dagger which I now receive I will subscribe my name written in my blood in testimony thereof; and should I prove false, or weaken in my determination, ***may my brethren and fellow soldiers of the militia of the Pope cut off my hands and feet and my throat from ear to ear, my belly be opened and sulphur burned therein with all the punishment that can be inflicted upon me on earth, and my soul shall be tortured by demons in eternal hell forever.*** That I will in voting always vote for a Knight of Columbus in preference to a Protestant, especially a Mason, and that I will leave my party so to do; that if two Catholics are on the ticket I will satisfy myself which is the better supporter of Mother Church and vote accordingly. That I will not deal with or employ a Protestant if in my power to deal with or employ a Catholic. That I will place Catholic girls in Protestant families that a weekly report may be made of the inner movements of the heretics. That I will provide myself with arms and ammunition that I may be in readiness when the

s.s.O.s.s.

word is passed, or I am commanded to defend the Church either as an individual or with the militia of the Pope. All of which I,_____, do swear by the blessed Trinity and blessed sacrament which I am now to receive to perform and on part to keep this my oath. In testimony hereof, I take this most holy and blessed sacrament of the Eucharist and witness the same further with my name written with the point of this dagger dipped in my own blood and seal in the face of this holy sacrament.

(He receives the wafer from the Superior and writes his name with the point of his dagger dipped in his own blood taken from over his heart.)

(Superior speaks:)

You will now rise to your feet and I will instruct you in the Catechism necessary to make yourself known to any member of the Society of Jesus belonging to this rank. In the first place, you, as a Brother Jesuit, will with another mutually make the ordinary sign of the cross as any ordinary Roman Catholic would; then one crosses his wrists, the palms of his hands open, and the other in answer crosses his feet, one above the other; the first points with forefinger of the right hand to the centre of the palm of the left, the other with the forefinger of the left hand points to the centre of the palm of the

s.s.O.s.s.

right; the first then with his right hand makes a circle around his head, touching it; the other then with the forefinger of his left hand touches the left side of his body just below his heart; the first then with his right hand draws it across the throat of the other, and the latter then with a dagger down the stomach and abdomen of the first. The first then says Iustum; and the other answers Necar; the first Reges; the other answers Impious. The first will then present a small piece of paper folded in a peculiar manner, four times, which the other will cut longitudinally and on opening the name Jesu will be found written upon the head and arms of a cross three times. You will then give and receive with him the following questions and answers:

From whither do you come? Answer: The Holy faith.

Whom do you serve? Answer: The Holy Father at Rome, the Pope, and the Roman Catholic Church Universal throughout the world.

Who commands you? Answer: The Successor of St. Ignatius Loyola, the founder of the Society of Jesus or the Soldiers of Jesus Christ.

Who received you? Answer: A venerable man in white hair.

s.s.O.s.s.

How? Answer: With a naked dagger, I kneeling upon the cross beneath the banners of the Pope and of our sacred order.

Did you take an oath? Answer: I did, to destroy heretics and their governments and rulers, and to spare neither age, nor sex, nor condition; to be as a corpse without any opinion or will of my own, but to implicitly obey my Superiors in all things without hesitation or murmuring.

Will you do that? Answer: I will.

How do you travel? Answer: In the bark of Peter the fisherman.

Whither do you travel? Answer: To the *four quarters of the globe*.

> **Note: Revelation 20:7-15**
> **King James Version**
> 7 And when the thousand years are expired, Satan shall be loosed out of his prison,
> **8 And shall go out to deceive the nations which are in the *four quarters of the earth*,**

s.s.O.s.s.

For what purpose? Answer: To obey the orders of my General and Superiors and execute the will of the Pope and faithfully fulfil the conditions of my oaths.

Go ye, then, into all the world and take possession of all lands in the name of the Pope. He who will not accept him as the Vicar of Jesus and his Vice-Regent on earth, let him be accursed and exterminated.

Is it possible that the American Chapter 322 of The Order of Skull and Bones Society is the military command post for the Jesuits, created by the Pope? This would mean that America is simply the military trust for the world's greatest fighting force, the US armed forces, at the sole discretion of the Pope of the Roman Catholic Church. Is our highest office the command post of a beast?
Listen:

> Matthew 24:4-8 King James Version
> **4** And Jesus answered and said unto them, Take heed that no man deceive you.
> **5 For many shall come in my name, saying, *I am Christ (Jesuits: 'Society of Jesus')*; and shall deceive many.**
> **6** And **ye shall hear of wars and rumours of wars**: see that ye be not troubled: for all these things must come to pass, but the end is not yet.

S.S.O.S.S.

7 For nation shall rise against nation, and kingdom against kingdom: and **there shall be famines, and pestilences, and earthquakes, in divers places.**
8 All these are the beginning of sorrows.

The following Bible verse shares with us some nuggets of wisdom for those who are considering taking a secret oath of any kind—this is another reason that The Order has dismissed the Bible teachings as fantasy:

Matthew 5:34-37 (NIV)
34 But I tell you, **do not swear an oath at all**: either by heaven, for it is God's throne; **35** or by the earth, for it is his footstool; or by Jerusalem, for it is the city of the Great King. **36 And do not swear by your head, for you cannot make even one hair white or black. 37 All you need to say is simply 'Yes' or 'No'; anything beyond this comes from the evil one.**

Quote by, Tupper Saussy, from his book Rulers of Evil:

"The East India Company was a major subsidizer of the Jesuit mission to Beijing. The Jesuits, in turn, interceded with oriental monarchs to secure lucrative commercial favors for the company, including monopolies on tea, spices, saltpeter (for explosives), silks, and the world's opium trade. Indeed ... **the company appears to owe its very existence to the Society of Jesus.**"

s.s.O.s.s.

In Don Francis Borgia's (1510-1572) most famous image he poses with someone's dehydrated head upon which a crown rests. Borgia was the great-grandson of Don Alexander Borgia—co-founder of the Jesuits. Borgia's mother descended from King Ferdinand of Aragon. As you can see, like the Catholics, and The Order of Skull and Bones, the Jesuits show strong veneration for the head and bones of the dead.

In an image taken from the book, Societas Jesu apostolorum imitatrix, Illustration on page 315, depicting Father Gerogius Tavora (c. 1555-1599), he and his Jesuit brethren are gathered below a ghostly striped flag (an early version of 'Old Glory'). In the mentioned image, the American, slash East India Company, slash Viking striped-flag configuration, is actually emblazoned with the Skull & Bones insignia. This version of the American flag predates '*Old Glory*' by hundreds of years.

A friendly little figurine which I discovered on the internet, of 'Father Loyola' (co-founder of the Jesuits), boasts the same S&B logo on the forehead of the human head tucked beneath his arm.

The skull and bones insignia is a trademark of the jesuits (as well as The Order of Skull and Bones). This assimilation could go on-and-on—if you get the chance, Google image '*Jesuit Church made of bones*' and see what pops up.

The high priest of The Order of Jesuits is affectionately referred to as…'The Black Pope,' as was Anton Lavey (writer of the satanic bible and founder of the church of satan).

As discussed, the word Jesuit means, *a member of the Society of Jesus*. Since the Ten Commandments clearly state that,

s.s.O.s.s.

'Thou shalt not take the name of The Lord in vain,' the name itself is an abomination. Killing a great swath of humanity in the name of Jesus Christ would certainly qualify as…vain. The same would certainly go for the Pope who deems himself—*Vicar of Christ*—since he implies to have the same power over the church as Christ himself.

16. Unholy Whispers

Due to the telling and haunting nature of quotes from our past, I will commit to you an entire section, for the warnings from the *honest* ones, or, at least, the *semi-honest*....Almost every man who signed the act of treason against the British Crown (known as the American Declaration of Independence) were confirmed, high-ranking freemasons. Those fellows wearing silly wigs likely thought they were on the top of the pyramid. That is, until the Jesuits grew in their shadows.

The truth is, these guys had no clue as to the secret Order of the Jesuits, until it was far too late, and the shadows formed behind them. Let us gaze upon the folly of the Jesuits, in order to gain a higher understanding of their internal workings. Listen with me to the whispers from the past victims of the tell-tale trademarks of the ancient art of the Jesuit rope-a-dope:

—John Adams (1735-1826; High-Ranking Freemason & the second President of the United States)
"My history of the Jesuits is not eloquently written, but it is supported by unquestionable authorities, [and] is very particular and very horrible. Their [the Jesuit Order's] restoration [in 1814 by Pope Pius VII] is indeed a step toward darkness, cruelty, despotism, [and] death. ... I do not like the appearance of the Jesuits. If ever there was a body of men

s.s.O.s.s.

who merited eternal damnation on earth and in hell, it is this Society of [Ignatius de] Loyola."

—**Marquis de LaFayette (1757-1834; French General and statesman. Served in the American Continental Army under General George Washington during the American Revolutionary War.)**
"It is my opinion that if the liberties of this country—the United States of America—are destroyed, it will be by the subtlety of the Roman Catholic Jesuit priests, for they are the most crafty, dangerous enemies to civil and religious liberty. They have instigated MOST of the wars of Europe."

—**Abraham Lincoln (1809-1865; 16th President of the United States)**
"The war [i.e., the American Civil War of 1861-1865] would never have been possible without the sinister influence of the Jesuits."

—**Samuel Morse (1791-1872; American inventor (telegraph); Author of the book Foreign Conspiracy Against the Liberties of the United States)**
"The Jesuits…are a secret society – a sort of Masonic order – with superadded features of revolting *odiousness, and a thousand times more dangerous."

s.s.O.s.s.

Note: The word *'odious' is a derivative of the name *'Odin.'*

—Edmond Paris (Author—The Secret History of the Jesuits)
"The public is practically unaware of the overwhelming responsibility carried by the Vatican and its Jesuits in the starting of the two world wars—a situation which may be explained in part by the gigantic finances at the disposition of the Vatican and its Jesuits, giving them power in so many spheres, especially since the last conflict."

—R. W. Thompson (Ex-Secretary of the American Navy)
"[The Jesuits] are the deadly enemies of civil and religious liberty."

—Fyodor Dostoyevsky (1821-1881; Russian novelist)
"The Jesuits…are simply the Romish army for the earthly sovereignty of the world in the future, with the Pontiff of Rome for emperor…that's their ideal. …It is simple lust of power, of filthy earthly gain, of domination—something like a universal serfdom with them [i.e., the Jesuits] as masters—that's all they stand for. They don't even believe in God perhaps."

s.s.O.s.s.

—F. Tupper Saussy (Author—Rulers of Evil)
"...The Roman Inquisition...had been administered since 1542 by the Jesuits."

—Pope Clement XIV (A man who thought that he had "forever" rid the world of the Jesuit Order in 1773–just as his predecessors believed to have disbanded the Templar)
"Alas, I knew they [i.e., the Jesuits] would poison me; but I did not expect to die in so slow and cruel a manner." (1774)

—Cusack, M. F.—The Black Pope (1896).pdf
M.F. Cusack (Ex-nun of Kenmore, and Author—Black Pope)
"In Roman Catholic circles it is well known that the Black Pope is the term used for the [Superior] General of the Jesuits. As the Pope is always robed in white, and the [Jesuit Superior] General in black, the contrast is obvious. But those Romanists who do not greatly love the Jesuits, and their number is not limited, use the term as indicating that the Black Pope rules the White Pope...even while the former [i.e., the Black Pope] is obligated to make, at least, a show of submission to the latter." (1896)
"...The Jesuits are the only religious order in the Church of Rome...which has lain under the ban of the ['White'] Pope, or which has been expelled from any country because of its interference in poli-

tics. Hence we may expect to find that to obtain political power forms a main feature in the plans of the Society [of Jesus – i.e., the Jesuit Order]." (1896)

—Jeremiah J. Crowley (Irishman; ex-priest in the Roman Catholic Church; Author—Romanism: Menace to the Nation)
"The [Jesuit Superior] General is at the head of this black and mute militia, which thinks, wills, acts, obeys – [as] the passive instrument of his designs. Their whole life must have but one aim – the advancement of the [Jesuit] Order to which they are attached." (1912)

—Friedrich von Hardenberg (German philosopher)
"Never before in the course of the world's history had such a Society [i.e., the Jesuit Order] appeared. The old Roman Senate itself did not lay schemes for world domination with greater certainty of success." (1800)

—Robert Jefferson Breckinridge (March 8, 1800 – December 27, 1871) Politician and Presbyterian minister.
"The Society of Jesus [i.e., the Jesuit Order] is the enemy of man. The whole human race should unite for its overthrow. ...For there is no alternative be-

s.S.O.S.s.

tween its total extirpation, and the absolute corruption and degradation of mankind."

It should be quite clear to you, by now, that these frocked monsters have artificially misshapen the intentionally gnarled branches of all of our family trees.

17. The Phony Express

The Silk Road was a chariot highway system which connected the ancient world for trade. Amazing interconnecting routes allowed a company of delivery boys, something like *The Pony Express*, to traverse the old Kingdoms with amazing speed and efficiency. A series of animals which were genetically suited for specific stretches of terrain were chosen, on top of which, keen animal handlers rode the beasts to the limits of their physical abilities—thus allowing the European Royalty to indulge in drugs, spices, and treasure from far-away lands.

But, did we ever wonder how the Kings of 'Camelot' got their mail? Well, as it turns out, the Pony Express too is a recycled technology which is touted as an *American* invention…The Kings of the medieval times were well-known for sending these same couriers on death rides which threatened, both, the lives of the animals and their handlers, simply to remark upon the fox they bagged in the *morn*.

This is why the documentary networks, news outlets and history books, all make a huge deal out of Pharaohs having cocaine or nicotine in their remains—because it disproves The Order's manure teachings that, 'we all just happened to have evolved on different continents at the same-exact time.' Though, the only 'missing link' which was ever discovered, was a skeleton named Lucy (the feminine for Lucifer). And, she too turned out to be bunk, when it was proven that she was built using a myriad of bones 'found at the site,' some of which happened to have been that of an old primate.

S.S.O.S.s.

The deadly element which prevented large scale international commerce from The East, in ancient times, was the low volume at which the Indian resources could be physically removed by land—the voyage by sea (and by land) was just far too long. These shortcomings hastened the discovery of the East Indies Passageway. The same conundrum sparked the digging of the many canals around the world, which were dug by slave labor.

The *William Russell* who was blessed with the privelage of reincarnating the ancient transportation technology of the Silk Road, on the North American continent, was, William *Hepburn* Russell (1812–1872), who created the Pony Express. And, yes, *Katherine Hepburn* (the famous actress) was related to this same royal family.

The man who was chosen to create the Federal *Express* is another *'rags-to-riches'* story for the Order of Skull & Bones—this one shows some of the dirty ways in which The Order gifts money to their upper-level corporate kings.

Fed-Ex founder Fred Smith **(S&B 1966)** supposedly took the company's last $5,000 to a Las Vegas blackjack table, after the shipping giant was denied a vital business loan. Smith 'won' the cash he'd desperately needed, with which he paid the fuel bill, and which supposedly *saved* the company, making it what it is today.

This one might make you think twice about hitting up that local casino, huh?...You're welcome!

Fun fact: Beware of the man with the hidden hand, for they are magicians among men **(google image 'pope hidden hand')**.

18. Slave Ship Flag

A slave en route to America, having the good fortune of witnessing the daylight upon a schooner deck, surely beheld this banner snapping from her creaking masts (google image 'East India Company Jesuit Flag').

East India Company's pirate flag (above) was put into service on East India buildings and ships in 1707 (nearly seventy years prior to the "birth of our nation"). The very same pirate flag also became America's first flag, which was adopted on January 2, 1776. The 'new' flag was unveiled as the "Grand Union Flag." I must beg the question, if Britain was so tyrannical that we organized a war effort, which spilled American blood on American soil, then why is the Union Jack printed on our very first 'American' Flag?

A quote from the book Rulers of Evil, should clear up much of the confusion—the outtake below will provide unique insight as to America's adoption of the East India Company pirate flag:

> At the evening session, [Benjamin] Franklin turned the meeting over to "his new-found and abundantly honored friend." (who was also called "the professor" and who was very likely the retired Jesuit General Lorenzo Ricci) The subject was a flag. Addressing the committee as "Comrade Americans," the Professor explained that, since the colonies were still dependent upon Great Britain, "we are not expected to design or recommend a flag which will

represent a new government or an independent nation," but instead one "that will testify our present loyalty as English Subjects," a flag that was "already in use," a flag that had been recognized by the British government for "half a century," a flag having a field of alternate horizontal red and white stripes with the Grand Union Flag of Great Britain in the upper left corner. "I refer," he said, "to the flag of the East India Company." To hide the fact that Americans would be fighting under the private flag of an international mercantile corporation controlled by Jesuits, the Professor provided a plausible cover whereby the flag could be "explained to the masses:"

"The Union Flag of the Mother Country is retained as the union [upper left corner] of our new flag to announce that the Colonies are loyal to the just and legitimate sovereignty of the British Government. The thirteen stripes will at once be understood to represent the thirteen Colonies; their equal width will type the equal rank, rights and responsibilities of the Colonies. The union of the stripes in the field of our flag will announce the unity of interests and the cooperative union of efforts, which the Colonies recognize and put forth in their common cause. The white stripes will signify that we consider our demands just and reasonable; and that we will seek to secure our rights through peaceable, intelligent and statesmanlike means–if they prove at all possible; and the red stripes at the top and bottom of our flag will declare that first and last—and always—we have the determination, the enthusiasm, and the power to use force—whenever we deem force necessary. The alternation of the red and white stripes will suggest that our reasons for all demands will be intelligent and forcible, and that our force in securing our rights will be just and reasonable."

The Professor reminded the committee that "the masses of the people, and a large majority of the leaders of public opinion, desire a removal of grievances, and a rectification of wrongs, through a fuller recognition of their rights as British Subjects; and few of them desire and very few of them expect – at this time – any complete severance of their present political and dependent relations with the English Government." That severance would occur "before the sun in its next summer's strength" – indicating that the Professor foreknew, as Lorenzo Ricci would have foreknown, a July declaration of independence. At that time, the East India Company flag could be "easily modified" by replacing the Union Jack with stars against a blue background, "to make it announce and represent the new and independent nation."

S.S.O.S.S.

Washington and Franklin lavished the Professor's idea with "especial approval and unstinted praise." The committee formally and unanimously adopted the East India Company's banner, known as "The Thirteen Stripes," as the "general flag and recognized standard of the Colonial Army and Navy." Just before midnight, they adjourned.

On January 2, 1776, at a formal ceremony attended by the Flag Committee, George Washington personally hoisted the East India Company flag "upon a towering and specially raised pine tree liberty pole," unfurling it to the breeze and displaying it for the first time "to his army, the citizens of the vicinity, and the British forces in Boston." **The British officers at Charlestown Heights perceived the event to mean that General Washington had thus announced his surrender to them. At once, they saluted "The Thirteen Stripes" with thirteen hearty cheers.** They immediately followed this spontaneous outburst of British Enthusiasm with the grander and more dignified official salute of thirteen guns, the thirteen gun salute being the highest compliment in gunpowder, the military "God speed you."

By so colorfully equivocating both his enemies, the Professor had made himself God of Confusion. The redcoats were toasting RULERS

s.s.O.s.s.

OF EVIL the good health of the rebels, who in turn were fighting for the East India Company. One of the few places in the world where such ludicrous phenomena are considered standard and routine is in the pages of Lorenzo Ricci's Thirteen Articles: "The General decides everything; he knows how to shape, at will, not only the army he is commanding but also that of his enemies."

To go along with the slave ship flag theme, I have chosen a quote about slavery to close out this section. The satanic bible:

> "If anything, we are enslaved more as human beings now than at any time, probably, in man's history. But it is so sugarcoated, it's so slick, it's so polished."
> —Anton LaVey—

19. Salty *Tea Time*

As bad as I hate to be the one who makes Miss Honey (at school) out to be a liar, the 'No Taxation Without Representation' happened, and is catchy, but, it certainly wasn't the true reason all of that tea went into the harbor. Though, it may have been the reason those sailors were given. What history doesn't tell us about that giant cup of tea is that, the East India Company was behind that brew too!

Three years prior to the Boston, 'Tea Party,' Britain had allowed East India Company a monopoly of the tea hustle in early America (I am sure EIC had a monopoly on all trade and industry in The Colonies, but, again, you could get lost in the misery this Company caused America, and the world). This EIC tea monopoly was referred to as the *Tea Act of 1773*. While the Tea Party was taking place, EIC's other brand—*The people of India*—were documented to have had their own domestic products monopolized *and price-fixed* for around a hundred and seventy years, by East India Company. That isn't what the History Channel says, but the holocaust-like pictures of the disaster say differently (google image 'famine in India').

After the tea monopoly was put into place in The Colonies, Britain and The East India Company began rotating Britain's moldy stock of surplus tea into The Colonies' economies. This went on for three years (17 million pounds of the stinky stuff). East India Company's chartered ships, from which the tea chests were thrown into the harbor, were quite apparently staged—the fed

S.S.O.S.s.

up 'secret' society, *The Sons of Liberty,* would have been burned at the stake, had EIC *not* been in on the fiasco.

Moreover, my point is, by playing games with those who were soon to become the *American People,* East India Company was able to blame the British Crown for 'taxing' the tea and forcing it down our throats, when they were simply imposing the same rules upon The Colonies by which India had been forced to engage for over 170 years—East India price fixing goods and forcing product into stores.

This all happened in the same slow manner at which we modern Americans have seen every small business gobbled up by corporate pestilence over the last hundred years—business practice originally born at EIC. The local business owner in today's America will soon be completely obsolete; so will the rags to riches success story, also known as The American Dream.

To finish our brief visit with The Revolutionary War, I would like to bring some very disturbing news to your attention, hot off the press 240 years ago. Excerpt from Wikipedia describing who Captain William *James* Russell, Sr, was:

> **William Russell** (1735 – January 14, 1793)—son to Lt Col William *"The Ranger"* James Russell (known for Knights of the Golden Horseshoe Expedition), was an army officer and a prominent settler of the southwestern region of the Virginia Colony. He led an early attempt to settle the "Kentuckee Territory" (then part of Virginia). He was a justice of Fincastle County, Virginia. **Russell aided in the drafting of the Declaration of Independence. Dur-**

S.S.O.S.S.

ing the American Revolutionary War he fought in the Battle of Point Pleasant (1774) and the Battle of Yorktown (1781).

Note*: Russell's assistance in "the drafting of the Declaration of Independence" can be confirmed in several sources. But namely, a book by the name of 'Russell County,' which outlines the history of the area:

Russell County was formed in 1786 from a portion of Washington County. It was named for Col. William Russell, **who assisted in the drafting of the Declaration of Independence. Early settlers, who were mostly English and Scotch-Irish,** *endured geographic isolation* as *they shaped the ways of life, attitudes, products, legends, and realities that would ultimately usher Russell County into the information age of the 21st century.*

The family who founded *The Order of Skull & Bones Chapter 322*, located at High Street (on the Yale Campus), are a tribe of the most deadly killers that this world has ever known. The Russell family was responsible for the deaths of hundreds of millions (more-likely billions) of innocent people, and they also '*helped* draft the Declaration Of Independence.' As usual, however, Russell hid behind the men who he manipulated into the act of treason, and, Willy himself didn't even sign the contract.

s.s.O.s.s.

William Huntington Russell's cousin, *Samuel Huntington*, did sign the treasonous document, and also became the 8th President of the Continental Congress *(the prior office of the Presidency of the United States of America)*. Most if not all of the signer's of the Declaration of Independence were related in one way or the other.

The original copies of the Declaration of Independence were printed at *Russell relative, Ezekiel Russell's*, printshop.

The Dark Russell creed had devastated every country it had laid its creepy hands on, throughout history, but this red demon wouldn't make the same mistakes in his new country, America. The demon would draft our very constitution, and structure *America's* governmental, and commercial corporate compartments, so that the United States government and commerce could be manipulated indefinitely, through time, from within.

One area of industry could be completely devastated, without the entire Beast crumbling as it did in India, and, through the Hegelian dialectic, could be reborn. The same elitists who starved, murdered, poisoned, enslaved, and looted, the entire world in the name of financial gain, incorporated the early American Colonies —a stage from which to manipulate the markets of the entire world. Colonist John Andrews wrote the following about the Boston Tea Party in 1773:

> "They say the actors were *Indians…Whether they were or not to a transient observer, they appear'd as such, being cloth'd in blankets with the heads muffled and copper color'd countenances, each being arm'd with a hatchet or ax, and pair pistols, nor was

their dialect different from what I conceive these geniuses to speak, as **their jargon was unintelligible to all but themselves."**

Note*: At the Boston Tea Party Ships & Museum, happy re-enactors proudly toss 'tea' bales, which are printed with East India Company's insignia, into the harbor.

These supposed 'New World Order' preachers *didn't* hijack America, they themselves founded and incorporated it! The cold reality here is, the leaders of the Colonies, who settled in America, were escaping religious persecution, but it definitely *wasn't* a Christian religion from which they did.

Fun fact: A good portion of the city of Alexandria Virginia (named after another ancient city which The Order destroyed) was "donated" as the designated hub of the United States government, ***Washington DC***.

20. Russell Military Academy

The American Civil War gives us a unique perspective of the working dynamics of The Order, in times of war, since we are offered a view of both sides of their evil wealth-generating machine.

William H. Russell, founder of The Order of Skull & Bones, and heir of the evil East India Company, had originally planned on joining the ministry, but bought a defunct military academy in 1836 from Stiles French, and converted it into a terrorist camp, instead. William H. Russell renamed the academy, formerly known as *New Haven Collegiate and Commercial Institute*, the *Russell Military Academy*. Russell Military Academy was located in New Haven, Connecticut.

Around the year of 1840, William Huntington Russell instituted a very thorough, and disciplined, military drill program at the Russell Military Academy, since he somehow *'foresaw'* the coming of the American Civil War (remember, this was 1840, 21 years prior to the beginning of the American Civil War). I am sure that Will H. Russell was well equipped with know-how in the way of teaching others to murder, since his family's company (East India Company) had been responsible for killing over 100 million humans in the country of India, prior to founding his small, domestic terrorist camp.

Russell wanted to ensure that his boys were 'prepared to fight for the Union,' for his self-predicted, long impending conflict, the American Civil War. Later on, during the actual times of the American Civil War, William Russell's military school, which only

s.S.O.S.s.

taught as many as 160 students at a time, groomed as many as 300 boys to serve as *officers* for the Union Army. Russell Military Academy also produced many of the drill masters for the Union side of the conflict, many of them were little more than children.

As the *story* goes, another relative of Russell's, Governor William Alfred **Buckingham,** took quite a shine to William Russell. The Governor realized Russell's military prowess and leadership potential, and, therefore, 'appointed' Russell to assemble the *entire* Connecticut Militia. William H. Russell was later appointed to Major General by the Connecticut Legislature, of which Russell himself *served as a whig (1846-47).*

Controlled conflict, when conducted in secret, is extremely good for business. When you control both sides of a conflict, in essence, you can tell the future, since you created it. Secrecy is mandated when the dialectic is applied to the creation of 'opposing forces' which are manipulated into engaging in a 'controlled conflict.' Secrecy is also necessary so that the opposing forces do not realize that the same banks are providing funds to both sides of said conflict. Think about all areas of industry which were manipulated when Russell planted the evil seeds of war in the heads of our people.

S.S.O.S.s.

21. The Order Founded the KKK

The *KKK* (Ku Klux Klan) was also a Freemasonry spinoff from the, previously discussed, *Knights of the Golden Horseshoe*. In fact, the first two words of the society's name, *Ku Klux,* are derived from the Greek word *kyklos*, meaning circle. *Klan* is a derivative of the English word, clan, meaning family. KKK literally means, 'Circle Family,' in English, which is a Greek wordplay on the previous Order, *The Order of the Knights of the Golden Circle* (founded by William *The Ranger* Russell, of Virginia).

General Albert Pike, 33 degree Sovereign Grand Master of the Ancient and Accepted Scottish Rite of Freemasonry, was a founding member of the Ku Klux Klan. Pike was also a founding member of the Palladian Order of Skull and Bones. The Palladian Order of S&B is, get this, the Arkansas Chapter of S&B, located on the campus of the University of Arkansas at Fayetville! Below is a quote from the Grandmaster of Freemasonry, founder of the Palladian Society of the Skull and Bones, and, co-founder of the KKK—from Pike's book, *Morals and Dogma*:

> That which we must say to a crowd is—We worship a God, but it is the God that one adores without superstition. To you, Sovereign Grand Inspectors General, we say this, that you may repeat it to the Brethren of the 32nd, 31st, and 30th degrees—The Masonic Religion should be, by all of us initates of the high degrees, maintained in the purity of the Luciferian Doctrine. If Lucifer were not God, would

s.s.O.s.s.

Adonay whose deeds prove his cruelty, perdify and hatred of man, barbarism and repulsion for science, would Adonay and his priests, calumniate him? Yes, Lucifer is God, and unfortunately Adonay is also god. For the eternal law is that there is no light without shade, no beauty without ugliness, no white without black, for the absolute can only exist as two gods: darkness being necessary to the statue, and the brake to the locomotive. Thus, the doctrine of Satanism is a heresy; and the true and pure philosophical religion is the belief in Lucifer, the equal of Adonay; but Lucifer, God of Light and God of Good, is struggling for humanity against Adonay, the God of Darkness and Evil...

Many dispute the fact that Pike helped found the 'social club' which has come to be known as, the KKK, but...Here...In 1905 the Neale Publishing Company published the book: *Ku Klux Klan Its Origin, Growth and Disbandment*, written and edited by *Walter L. Fleming*. In this work Fleming incorporates earlier work by JC Lester and DL Wilson. Here are a list of claims which are made by Dr. Fleming in the book:

—Fleming claims that he was given, 'information in regard to Ku Klux Klan, by many former members of the order, and by their friends and relatives.'

—'General Albert Pike, who stood high in the Masonic order, was the chief judicial officer of the Klan.' Pike is mentioned in the

s.S.O.S.s.

book which was scanned and uploaded to the internet—page 27. Pike is mentioned in the 'index' of the damning little KKK manual: 'General Albert Pike, chief judicial officer.'

—In another publishing of the same book, a page of the work includes important founders of The Order of the KKK, on which Dr. Fleming places Pike's portrait in the center (Albert's being the largest of them all). The Order disputes these facts—*for obvious reasons*—but a google book search of the title will quickly reveal the image, if you scroll down to page 19....Look at the fellow in the center. There is another photo which features an image of Pike in full 33 degree regalia.

—As an appendix to the book, Dr. Fleming attached a KKK 'prescript' (secret constitution), which had recently been discovered (in 1909). The document sets forth the regulations of the Klan's 'judiciary' department over which Albert Pike had 'ruled.' The 'judiciary department' is the internal disciplinary, or counterintelligence department, for the KKK. The fact that Pike was in charge of the 'judiciary' department, also corresponds with Pike's (and the Klan's) influence over the public legal profession in the post-civil War southern states.

The Order of the KKK was originally formed in 1865 (the end-year of the American Civil War) in Pulaski, Tennessee. The aftermath of the American Civil War left trained domestic terrorists with no place in society, and so the KKK was said to comprise the misplaced underground militia army of The Order of the Knights of the Golden Circle.

s.S.O.S.s.

The Order of the KKK is an American terrorist organization, and the atrocities which the Klan commits (or committed), came in extremely handy for creating chaos, and confusion, during post Civil War America, as well as creating a distraction post-WWII (and Vietnam) during the intense clashes between American government and Civil Rights activists.

The KKK logo, which is branded on the chest of the satanic Klan, features a Templar cross. The clan often burned *their* human sacrificial offerings alive (remember this, as it will prove important when we study human sacrifice).

Believe it or not, former Confederate General John B. Gordon testified in 1871 to the Joint Congressional Committee on Affairs in the Insurrectionary States that: 'The first and main reason (for the Klan) was the organization of the Union League.' Below is an outtake from that debacle:

> "The first Union League formed in Ohio in 1862, when Confederate military successes coupled with political unrest in the North caused many to doubt a Union victory in the war. The Ohio Union League thrived and soon similar leagues spread to more than 18 northern states. According to historian Clement M. Silvestro, Union Leagues proposed 'to combat and crush the Knights of the Golden Circle, Sons of Liberty, The Order of American Knights, and similar clubs associated with the Democratic Party.'"

s.s.O.s.s.

The Union League was formed in desperation to gain Union support for a Civil War that no one on either side had wanted. The Union League was formed by Frederick Law Olmsted, Brother to Skull & Bones member, John Hull Olmsted **(S&B 1847),** along with Henry Whitney Bellows, George Templeton Strong, and Oliver Wolcott Gibbs. (Though I don't have the time to chase every darting rabbit, Strong, Gibbs, and Whitney, are all prominent Bonesmen surnames as well.)

The most notable of the founders of the Union League was George Templeton Strong. Strong was the son of a prominent attorney, who was partners with **Henry Waters Taft**—a named partner at Cadwalader, Wickersham & *Taft (S&B 1880).* The firm was the largest in New York, and is still in operation to this day—it is the nation's oldest law firm. Strong also *funded* a Union regiment during the Civil War.

Below, is former Confederate, General John B. Gordon's testimony, in 1871, to the Joint Congressional Committee on Affairs in the Insurrectionary States:

> "The first and main reason (for the Klan) was the organization of the Union League." Gordon, who later became Governor of Georgia and then a U. S. Senator, also stated that even the burning of Atlanta and the devastation of Georgia during the war did not create a tenth of the animosity created by the Union League's treatment of the Southern people. Former Confederate General Nathan B. Forrest, a reputed founder of the Klan, testified before the same committee that: "The Klan was intended en-

tirely as a protection to the (Southern) people, to enforce the laws and protect the people from outrages." Both men realized, however, that after a few years, the Klan, formed in a people's desperate cry for survival and justice, had itself become a lawless outrage. But it was the federally sponsored Union League that ranked first in time and violence.

Albert Pike, who was commissioned as a brigadier general on November 22, 1861, was given command of an Indian territory (despite his racist beliefs). This, to me, sounds a whole lot like the tactics which were used for the Boston Tea Party—remember, they too were 'dressed like indians.' They also spoke an 'indistinguishable language.' *Perhaps they were indians who were entered into 'The Order.'*

After the Battle of Pea Ridge, Pike faced charges which stated that his troops had scalped soldiers on the field. Maj. Gen. Thomas C. Hindman also charged Pike with stealing cash and property, and ordered his arrest. Pike, who now faced arrest, fled into the hills of Arkansas, and sent-in his resignation from the Confederate Army. Pike was apprehended on November 3, under charges of insubordination, and treason. Pike was briefly detained, in Warren, Texas, but, after his resignation was accepted, and, like Harry Truman the ***Terrorist (upcoming terrorist for The Order)***, he was allowed to return to home, to Arkansas.

Despite the lack of any overt evidence of heroics, and the charges of treason which were brought forward against the man, Albert Pike is the only Confederate military officer with an outdoor statue in Washington, D.C. (google image 'Albert Pike Statue

s.S.O.S.s.

D.C.). 'The commemorative plaque on the statue, commemorates the date on which Pike was 'coronated a 33 degree Mason and Inspector General Honorary.'

Is it not obvious that lower-ranking Masons take an oath which they swear-to before ever even knowing the purpose that the club serves, and at the beckoning of their superiors, controlled conflict can be called upon of the men on a moments notice? One wouldn't buy a car without knowing the price, and in this case, these men swear to serve without even knowing they are buying an automobile at all.

The Russell's trademarked brooch gift was issued to KKK members too, just like the previous Orders mentioned in an earlier section. A google image search will quickly turn them up.

22. Opposing Horses

Below are the Bones Posts for the Confederate forces during the American Civil War:

—**John Perkins Jr (S&B 1840)**—US representative from Louisiana, and then a senator in the confederate states congress, is another dope-dealing and slave-trading family. Perkins, himself, served in the Confederate States Senate from 1862-till the end of the Civil War. **Perkins served as *chairman* of the state secession convention in 1861.**

—***William Taylor Sullivan Barry (S&B 1841)**—Willy was a US Representative from Mississippi, and a **member of the Provisional Confederate Congress. Willy served as president of the State secession convention in 1861**, and then enlisted in the Confederate States Army. Barry **raised the Thirty-fifth Regiment of Mississippi Infantry, at times acting as brigade commander.** Barry was later captured at the Battle of Vicksburg, and broke parole. He was seriously wounded at the Battle of Allatoona.

—***Richard Taylor (S&B 1845)**—Louisiana State Senator, Richard Scott "Dick" Taylor, was a Confederate general. After the first shots of the American Civil War were fired, Taylor joined the Confederate States Army, as a brigade commander in Virginia, and later as an army commander in the Trans-Mississippi Theater. Taylor commanded the District of West Louisiana and was responsible for successfully opposing United States troops invading Louisiana

S.S.O.S.S.

during the Red River Campaign of 1864. Dick was the only son of Zachary Taylor, the 12th President of the United States.

> **Note***: 'Dick' and William Barry's ancestors were the ones who helped with the ill-gotten Louisiana purchase. Their early ancestor was 'James Taylor' who rode in the original Order of the Knight's of the Golden Horseshoe.

—**John Donnell Smith (S&B 1847)**—Smith served as a Captain in the Confederate Army.

—Albert Pike (founder of the Fayetville Chapter of Skull and Bones)—Al, who we just learned about in the last section (a founder of the *KKK*), was a major instigator of the Civil War on the Confederate side. This outtake from Wikipedia, which, though I stray from quoting Wiki, it is all cited, and shows the working dynamics of The Order, brilliantly:

> In 1847 Pike became disillusioned when the Whig Party refused to take a stand on slavery. At the Southern Commercial Convention of 1854, Pike said the South should remain in the Union and seek equality with the North, but if the South "were forced into an inferior status, she would be better out of the Union than in it." His anti-Catholicism stand led him to join the Know Nothing movement when it was organized in 1856, but was again disappointed when it refused to adopt a strong pro-

S.S.O.S.s.

slavery platform. He joined the other Southern delegates and walked out of the convention. His stand was that state's rights superseded national law and supported the idea of a Southern secession. This stand is made clear in his pamphlet of 1861, "State or Province, Bond or Free?"

Skulll & Bones Union involvement in the Civil War—

—**Orris Sanford Ferry (S&B 1844)**(August 15, 1823–November 21, 1875) was a Republican American lawyer and politician from Connecticut who served in the United States House of Representatives and the United States Senate. He was also a brigadier general in the Union Army during the American Civil War. Ferry, praised for his ability as a leader and military strategist, was later promoted to brigadier general on March 17, 1862, upon the start of the Civil War.

—**Abraham Lincoln**—After forming his domestic terrorist training camp, William Huntington Russell *formed* the Republican party. Willy's good friend Abraham Lincoln became the nation's very first Republican President (in the book titled, *Proceedings of the Connecticut State Medical Society,* penned by *William Whitney Hawkes M.D. of New Haven,* Hawkes describes William H. Russell as a *"friend* of Abraham Lincoln").

—Abraham Lincoln, in turn, appointed **John Thomas Croxton (S&B 1857)** to the position of Union Brigadier General, for the Civil War.

S.S.O.S.s.

—**John Brown**—In order to spark the bloody American Civil War, William H. Russell became a strong 'abolitionist' and a friend to John Brown, who *claimed* the same. Russell was even named as a trustee in the will of John Brown, which came in particularly handy since he would soon need Russell's services in the matter of his trust—*Brown was lynched for leading a slave liberation movement in which his followers killed several supporters of slavery, in the 1850s.*

Brown was involved in the 1856 conflict in Kansas, the Battle of Black Jack, and the Battle of Osawatomie—all of these clashes were considered terrorist attacks, at the time, since they preceded the war by over a decade. Brown's followers killed several supporters of slavery. No credible historian will argue the fact that these events *caused* the cauldron of death, known as the Civil War, to boil over (though, I too agree that slavery was a worthy reason to fight, money and an expansion of power was their true motivation).

In 1859, Brown led a multi-racial group, which included run away slaves, who were captured in an unsuccessful raid on the federal armory at Harpers Ferry—a stunt which Brown hoped would arm his band of trained killers for the events which would unfold. Brown's failed armory mission resulted in his conviction and him being sentenced to death.

John Brown's descendants profited handsomely from the Civil War, and went on to financially manipulate WWII, with the help of Bush family patriarch, Prescott Bush, who became a partner of their firm, Brown Brothers Harriman Company. Remember Averell Harriman **(S&B 1913)**, who also took on the S&B nick-

s.s.O.s.s.

name Thor? Yup! This *Willy* is from the same Harriman Brown clan. In fact, many of the Harriman boys were also Skull and Bones members, as were many of their high-ranking representatives at BBH. *13 Browns were also known as Skull and Bones members.*

After WWII the US Federal Government seized a great number of assets from the group, through the Trading with the Enemy act. Brown Brothers Harriman also funded a great amount of pre-Civil War slave activities, and was heavily invested in strategic investments on both sides of the conflict, from military armament to steel, to the railroads. Shockingly, Brown Brothers is still in business today.

These two juxtaposed executive Bones Posts gave The Order both interior vantage points from which to order the destruction of key man targets in the American theater of war, ensuring the prosperity of their many financial interests.

A book titled *William Russell and His Descendants* also describes Russell family involvement on both sides of the conflict.

s.S.O.S.s.

23. *Civil* Terrorism

Two separate Orders, one for each side of the Civil War, were formed in order to jumpstart the event—an example of Civil War Terrorism.

According to the Columbia Daily Tribune:

Harry Truman, an '*alias*' for a man named JW Terman, also spelled Torman, and, Truemann, in some records, had been authorized to recruit a small force, **dress them in civilian clothes, and lead an 'undercover hunt for guerrillas.'**

Here is some more of The Order's signature crap; hmmm, isn't that a coincidence? Is it possible that this *is* President Truman's blood relative? Remember, Truman ordered the A-bombs which were dropped on Japan, just a few weeks after Franklin Delano Roosevelt....Died!

The historic blurb (below) follows the torture and hanging of a young farm boy. The lynch mob was looking for the boy's father, James Stark Senior. Chariton County records explain:

"Determined not to be disappointed in their evil purpose, they took the boy James to the woods and hung him to a tree to make him tell the whereabouts of his father. They hung him several times, but the boy protested, telling them that he did not know. They finally determined to take his life and after swinging him up the last time they went off and left him hanging." Harry Truman and his men had been in Chariton County, Missouri, for a week. The county history sums up his visit this way:

"If a horse was pressed into service, if a dwelling with its contents was burned to the ground; if a man was robbed, if a woman was raped, if an unoffending citizen was killed; in fact, if all the crimes known to the catalogue were perpetrated by this band of heroes, **they were committed by them in the name of patriotism.** They fought aged and maimed men, and little boys, from principle, and not from a desire to shed innocent blood; they robbed and plundered from principle, not that they had any desire to possess what did not belong to them."

As I did a little more research, I found this, which occurred during the same week of terror:

THE CIVIL WAR
written by James S. WALLACE, of Brunswick

Horatio Philpott, one of the pioneers of Chariton County, who came to the county in 1837 and opened a mill on the east fork of the Chariton, was known as a southern sympathizer, as were many of his neighbors. In October 1864, he was taken from

s.s.O.s.s.

his home by a company of militia under the command of *Captain* **Trueman** and this aged pioneer, **seventy-five years old**, was shot a few yards from his home. When found by his family he had on his person five gunshot wounds and two bayonet thrusts. Two of the gunshot wounds were in the head and the others, with the bayonet thrusts, were in the breast. Dr. James Brumall, living in the same neighborhood, was killed the same day by the same company of militia. It is said that among the soldiers who committed the bloody deeds were one or two of his neighbors who boasted they killed old Dr. Brumall. Jesse Rogers, **an old man of more than seventy years of age, was shot the day by the same soldiers after they had partaken of his hospitality and they refused to allow the family to bury him.** As a result, his body lay two or three days before it was buried. He was a quiet, peaceable citizen and a most humble and devout Christian, whose only crime was that he was a southern sympathizer. Theophilus Edwards, **aged seventy years**, was another victim of this same lawless band, who left a trail of blood along the line of march through the county.

With a little more poking around I discovered some amazing telegraphs between officers who were trying to put out the many fires which 'Harry Truman' had blazing in the area:

S.S.O.S.S.

BROOKFIELD. Mo., June 14. 1864.

General FISK :

I have made a good deal of inquiry and find that the taking of horses, arms, and other property by H. Truman has been indiscriminate, from any and all who did not approve his peculiar way of traveling. I met one of H. Truman's lieutenants on the train yesterday. He was on his way to Quincy with a young lady, as prisoner, whom he was banishing from the State. I asked by what authority. He says their own. He came up to Macon on the train today, and had an old man prisoner he had arrested near Palmyra. He requested me to take charge of him to Brookfield. I told him I should turn the old man over to the provost-marshal at Macon, and he kept him, saying they did not turn over prisoners. I have had application from one or two men for saddles, bridles, and a wagon, who are Union men. Said property was taken by H. Truman. I had conversation with a couple of volunteer aides of H. Truman this p. m., who say they do not know what they will do if H. Truman is taken out of the service, as they cannot make anything in the militia. The provost-marshal got, I think, 2 recruits from the negro brigade brought in by H. Truman. The balance have left. I have sent a guard to look after the property at Bucklin, and shall have it moved to this place in the morning. I will send a scout to Keytesville, to inquire into affairs there, in the morning. **The cause of the trouble has been from acts of citizens who have**

s.s.O.s.s.

gone with H. Truman and done all kinds of devilment to men who are considered sympathizers, and also to men who have been Union men from the start, but they have been reported as copperheads because some neighbor was mad at them. All seems to have been conducted with perfect looseness and, in all cases, a total disregard of the rights of anybody. If we go in for depopulation and devastation, his course is right; for it is driving every man who has been suspected of secession proclivities to the brush, and many who have [not] been engaged, good men, have come in for protection. I tell them to go home; that no more plundering will be permitted in this county by any party, and in all cases when men are known to commit depredations they must be reported forthwith, and that rebels and sympathizers in each district will be held responsible for all depredations committed by bushwhackers, and they must watch out for them; that they (the rebels) have the peace of the country in their own hands, and if they do not want to be annoyed by soldiers they must assist in putting down all acts of lawlessness on the part of friends and be ready at all times to report any breach in their districts.

E. J. CRANDALL,
Captain, Commanding.

Another telegraph transmission:

s.s.O.s.s.

GLASGOW, June 14, 1864.

General C. B. FISK,

Saint Joseph, Mo.:

DEAR SIR: There is much trouble in Chariton County, just north of us. A Captain Truman, Federal scout, as I am informed, has recently been through this section, and the latter part of last week shot and hung some 5 or persons. I know nothing of his orders or the persons shot, only the fact that the people were killed. They may have deserved killing, as I learn they were generally rebels. Last night, however, another party, claiming to be a portion of his command, but who were bushwhackers, killed 5 Union citizens, about twelve miles north of this place. The people of all classes are fleeing from the county, and it is feared retaliation will follow retaliation until there will be no one left to kill. I know you have been advised of these proceedings by telegraph, but I have thought proper to write to you and ask of you to send some discreet man, with a proper escort, to look into the whole matter and reassure the terror-stricken inhabitants. Respectfully, your obedient servant, CLARK H. GREEN.

The Union troops captured the undercover terrorist, and Jacob W. Terman, alias *Harry Truman*, **worked as a 'Federal scout'**—a spy. He terrorized Chariton County, Missouri, in the name of Civil War. The terrorist robbed and killed men women and children, indiscriminately. In mid 1864, the Union Captain

s.s.O.s.s.

'Harry Truman' was convicted of murder, arson, and larceny, and sentenced to be hanged. *US Secretary of War* (the highest office in wartime next to Lincoln) *Edwin M. Stanton had him *released and reassigned to DC, even though he was caught plundering, abusing women, killing unarmed civilians, etc.* He continued his exploits after the war, being arrested for drunk and disorderly behavior in Huntsville, Missouri, after *claiming he was there with Federal authority to restore civil law.*

'Harry Truman' never served a day as a convicted murderer! Stanton turned him loose, and he was *still* poking around the state of Missouri, which he had previously terrorized, long after the war.

Below is an outtake from **Dr. *Taft's*** 'notebook' titled, *Lincoln's Last Hours*, where the same Stanton would have had the opportunity to hasten Lincoln's death. *(Taft was Lincoln's personal Doctor.)*

Listen:

"The room having become speedily filled to suffocation, the officer in command of the provost guard at the theater **was directed to clear it of all except the surgeons**. This officer guarded the door until relieved later in the evening by General M.C. Meigs, who took charge of it the rest of the night, *by direction of **Mr. Stanton**.*"

Note*: Lincoln's Secretary of War—the same Stanton from the 'Harry Truman' telegrams—himself was a high-ranking Freemason!

s.S.O.S.s.

President Harry Truman, was born in Missouri in 1884, less than twenty years after this 'Harry Truman' caused havoc. Truman, who pulled the trigger on two 'A-bombs' which killed a total of 220,000 people, was born only *124 miles* from Chariton County, where *these* terrorist attacks took place. I am inclined to believe, according to the facts, as opposed to Forbe's and Disney's rendition of these events, that this *was* a direct ancestor of President Harry Truman himself.

If you're interested in learning more about this Truman fellow, there is much more interesting telegraph correspondence, between officers involved in the conflict, on the internet.

S.S.O.S.s.

24. The Lincoln Rope-a-Dope

There is plenty of evidence to also suggest The Order's involvement in Lincoln's assassination, such as Lincoln's primary care physician being another Taft (prominent S&B family). But the amount of ground which we need to cover in this conversation is infinite, and the time we have in which to tell the story, finite. Again, there will be a reading list at the conclusion of this paper— it will make many more details clear. I will only start the unfurling of the golden thread of culpability. The President's wife had this to say:

> "...that, that miserable inebriate Johnson, had cognizance of my husband's death—Why, was that card of Booth's, found in his box, some acquaintance certainly existed—I have been deeply impressed, with the harrowing thought, that he, had an understanding with the conspirators & they knew their man... As sure, as you & I live, Johnson, had some hand, in all this..." Letter to her friend, Sally Orne, March, 15 1866. [SOURCE: *Mary Todd Lincoln: Her Life and Letters* by Justin G. Turner and Linda Levitt Turner (New York, Alfred A. Knopf, 1972), p.345.]

After Lincoln's assassination in April 1865, confirmed Freemason, President Andrew Johnson (google image Andrew Johnson 'hidden hand') enacted a lenient Reconstruction policy for the defeated South. Johnson granted near-complete amnesty to ex-Confederates. Johnson also restored U.S.-state status for the se-

s.S.O.S.s.

ceded Southern-American states, and the approval of new local Southern governments, which immediately legislated *'Black Codes.'* These *'Black Codes'* preserved slavery in every which way but its old name—'slavery'—it was simply an evolutionary step toward what we see *now* in America. **Johnson was *impeached* for these unfavorable postwar policies. The House of Representatives voted 11 articles of impeachment against Johnson, 9 of which cited the removal of his Secretary of War, Edwin M. Stanton; the man who released the Civil Terrorist, *'Harry Truman.'***

John Wilkes Booth (assassin of President Abraham Lincoln) was a known member of The Order of the Knights of the Golden Circle, and the Freemasons (google image 'John Wilkes Booth hidden hand'). After firing that infamous shot in Ford's Theater, Booth shouted, 'Sic Semper Fidelis,' which translates to 'thus always to tyrants.' This is a shortened version of what is paraphrased as 'Death to Tyrants,' which is also Virginia's State Motto. The same motto has been adopted by the United States Marine Corps.

If you will recall, the earliest form of *this* 'motto' is as follows, in ***the Jesuit Order***: *INRI*—the words *IUSTUM NECAR REGES IMPIUS* are printed below the acronym—the meaning: **It is just, to exterminate or annihilate impious or heretical Kings, Governments, or Rulers.**

Before we move forward with this topic, please allow me to share with you a couple of quotes… Before we move forward with this topic, please allow me to share with you a couple of quotes…

Quote 1:

S.S.O.S.S.

"The favorite policy of the Jesuits [is] that of assassination." [U.S. Army Brigadier General, Thomas M. Harris; *"Rome's Responsibility for the Assassination of Abraham Lincoln"*; 1897; Page 19]

Quote 2:
"It is of faith that the Pope has the right of deposing heretical and rebel kings. Monarchs so deposed by the Pope are converted into notorious tyrants, and may be killed by the first who can reach them. "If the public cause cannot meet with its defense in the death of a tyrant, it is lawful for the first who arrives, to assassinate him." [Defensio Didei, Jesuit Suarez, Book VI. C 4, Nos. 13, 14]

On *Virginia's State Flag* the motto boasts a dead 'tyrant,' with whom to accompany the latin phrase. The assassin *and* the tyrant on Virginia's flag are dressed in the era of Ancient Rome. Remember, Virginia was the home state for the founder of the Knights of The Order of the Golden Horseshoe. Virginia, William 'The Ranger' Russell's home state, also became the home of our nation's Capitol—*Washington, DC.*

After his assassination, a group of grave robbers were caught in the act of attempting to steal Lincoln's body. The heist was 'thwarted,' and the President's dead body was supposedly 'laid to rest in a steel cage, under 10 feet of concrete.' There is a story involving ransom which surrounds the 'failed' attempt at skullduggery, but, I would again have to point out The Order's affinity for skull and bones of dead historical figures. And, if I had to guess, I would place heavy speculation upon the notion of Abraham Lincoln's remains taking up residence under that giant manmade brick.

Mary Todd Lincoln was embedded into the occult. The First Lady was a Rosicrucian, and famously conducted occult activities and witchcraft in the White House. Rosicrucianism is a secret society of satanists which became popular in the early 17th century.

Below are a pair of quotes from the Great Emancipator— the first comes from a letter written to William Elkin.

Quote 1:

> "I see in the near future a crisis approaching that unnerves me and causes me to tremble for the safety of my country. As a result of the war, **corporations have been enthroned and an era of corruption in high places will follow, and the money power of the country will endeavor to prolong its reign by working upon the prejudices of the people until all wealth is aggregated in a few hands, and the Republic is destroyed.** I feel at this moment more anxiety for the safety of my country than ever before, even in the midst of war."

And, quote 2:

s.s.O.s.s.

"I have two great enemies, the Southern Army in front of me and the bankers in the rear. Of the two, the one at my rear is my greatest foe."

President Lincoln was shot four days following the end of the Civil War, after which, the working dynamics of the American Banking System changed forever. (As with every conflict around the world, over the past couple of centuries or so, The Order's designated bankers backed both sides of this event too.)

The Order created the thesis, slavery, the antithesis, the American Civil War, and the Emancipation Proclamation, the synthesis of a healing nation, and from it profited handsomely in every way possible.

The Order's involvement in the American Civil War also points to the fact that the people of America were most certainly manipulated into fighting, brother against brother, in order to poison America with a mammoth opium dependence.

Perhaps the sickest thing about both the American Revolutionary War, and the American Civil War, is the tactics which these warlords taught the American Revolutionary Army and their home country of Britain, to engage in during combat...If you will remember, during both of these wars, both sides simply caught cannon fire with their faces, mercilessly, while these tactical guerrilla groups of The Order (on both sides) took out strategic financial targets. Particularly disgusting is the fact that, during the American Civil War, many times, the enemy actually *were* brothers.

We are taught in school that this was simply a lesser-evolved way of engaging in combat. But any armchair military historian can tell you that intelligence during war and savage

S.S.O.S.S.

stealthy military techniques long outdate this American conflict. The East India Company had been engaging in the most stealthy and brutal combat that the world had ever seen, and EIC predated these events by well-over a hundred years. America, and Britain, both, taught this new more-evolved method of fighting to be 'Gentlemanly.' (This is quite obviously why Willy H. needed his own military 'academy' for the side which The Order chose to win— *The Union Army.*)

Following the conclusion of the American Civil War, Alphonso Taft (co-founder of Skull & Bones and father of President Taft), became the Secretary of War under Ulysses S. Grant— Grant was later elected as US President. Online there is an image of Grant's 'Hidden Hand' of Freemasonry.

It is also notable that Taft's resumé has a dead spot between the years 1861-1866, the time period of the Civil War. This could indicate that, Bonesman, Taft, also conducted covert terroristic operations during the domestic conflict. Also, as previously mentioned, Alphonso Taft was the only person to ever serve as Secretary of War *and* US attorney General—Taft supposedly had no experience in combat.

We will finish our brief soiree with the American Civil War with a quote —*source* Thomas M. Harris (U.S. Army Brigadier General; Author of the book Rome's Responsibility for the Assassination of Abraham Lincoln):

"It would seem that the Jesuits had had it in mind, from the beginning of the war [the American Civil War of 1861-1865], to find an occasion for the tak-

s.s.O.s.s.

ing off [i.e., the assassination] of Mr. [Abraham] Lincoln."

The Order is famous for producing articles, books, *and or* other popular media with similar themes as The Order's current events. The book *Johnny Tremain* seems to be one of those cases. Johnny Tremain was written by *Ester* ***Forbes (prominent Bones family)***. The book won the 1944 Newbery Medal and is the 16th bestselling children's book in the US, as of the year 2000, according to *Publishers Weekly*. Walt Disney Pictures released a film adaptation of *Johnny Tremain*.

A new video game titled *East India Company* pollutes searches for the original East India Company—not surprisingly, the game revolves around world dominion and plunder. The catchline for the interactive game is, '*Fight, Manage & Rule! Build your own Trading Empire.*' The makers of the new game also thought it would be cute to incorporate the mark of the beast—666—into the letters of the logo **(google image 'East India Company video game')**.

If you google *Civil War Skull and Bones*, or any number of events mentioned in this text, you have to dig fairly deep, since certain keyword searches have been littered with pictures of so-called *superheroes*. A Google image search using key words *Skull and Bones Civil War* turns up a fellow named 'Crossbones.' *Crossbones,* is a villain in the movie, *Captain America—Civil War* **(google image 'Civil War skull and bones')**.

25. The Prescription *is* War

As a profitable byproduct of the Civil War, The Order freely injected the horrible plague of morphine upon we trusting American People. This was the beginning of the prescription madness of taking Xanax, Prozac, Zoloft, or the dependence on any other poison having the properties to chemically enslave Americans. These powerful chemicals are still killing Americans today in the very same disgusting way—a trap which was set forth by the same East India Company thugs, long ago.

Russell & Company—

The Russell family's East India Company had already established its mob territory throughout Asia during the Opium *'Wars.'* The Order's signature structure of men employs systems with which to corrupt leaders of the countries in which they have established control, and to *keep* them in *control*. This style of controlling government from within has corrupted every single country and civilization, throughout time, and comes in handy when descendants are looking for a dishonorable way to become a king on earth.

With EIC's key relationships in place throughout Asia, the stage was set for future Russells to receive, and run with, the wicked baton. Enter, Samuel Wadsworth Russell (1789-1862).

Samuel Russell was the cousin of William Huntington Russell, *the founder of The Order Skull & Bones*. This next chosen Russell followed in his East-India-oppressing ancestors' footsteps, nearly print-by-print. The history books say Sam was orphaned

s.S.O.S.s.

penniless (an age old tactic of these raptors), but Sam's affiliations and business contacts say differently. It is easy to see why the Russells made such great efforts to keep the subsequent heirs' genealogy at arms-length, considering their conquest of most of their known world, and the atrocities committed in their wake. But, you decide:

Samuel Russell's, Russell & Company, was established in 1823 for the purpose of acquiring opium in Turkey and smuggling it into China. But, Sam also introduced the ugliness to the US.

R&C became the premiere trader in China during the Qing Dynasty. By premiere, I mean that Samuel Russell had a high-handed monopoly on trade, just as Russell's famous ancestors had been doing for millennia.

Russell & Co. were a band of ruthless dope dealers, among other ventures. But, remember, Opium, like all drugs, was legal in America. Other than the industrial, monetary, and commercial tyranny, America *was* actually *free* in Colonial America; well, I suppose you would've had to have been white, and rich too. Okay, drugs were just legal, but, with the dialectic, that too would change.

Warren Delano, President Franklin Delano Roosevelt's Grandfather, first went to China at age 24 and was chief dope hustler for Russell & Company, for a decade, before returning to New York as a wealthy aristocrat who was looking for love. While in China, Delano wrote home that opium had an 'unhappy effect' on its users, but argued that its sale was 'fair, honorable, and legitimate.'

Warren Delano lost his ill-gained fortune in the Great Panic of 1857, but returned to China, and quickly rebuilt his cache by

s.S.O.S.s.

shipping Opium from Turkey, to **supply the US military during the Civil War.** Given Delano's ruthless reputation of deceit, I am certain that the directions on the bottles came something like that which came on the Oxycontin bottles of our modern Opium War: **Take a lot!** Delano knew how to ease Americans into the dope game because he and his boss Sam Russell's ancestors had already been spreading that *disease for eons.*

The Order has been secretly killing our children with their prescription poisons ever since. To read a detailed essay describing the method with which The Order has been killing Americans with legal prescription *opiates*, it is on the homepage at TheWindows*Of*Reality.com. Below is a list of dope-dealing individuals who deserve an honorable mention, especially since their descendants still terrorize the world today. There are rabbles more—these are just the few listed on Wiki…

—Warren Delano, Jr., the grandfather of Franklin Roosevelt (32nd President of the United States) served as the Chief of dope-hustling Operations at Russell and Company in Canton.

—Robert Bennet Forbes was the head of Russell and Company.

—John Murray Forbes, brother of Robert Bennet Forbes and the **great-granduncle of 2004 presidential candidate John Forbes Kerry (S&B 1966), was an executive dope hustler at R&C.**

S.S.O.S.S.

—Abiel Abbot Low, founder of trading company A. A. Low & Brothers, served as a partner. This guy was the head of the New York Chamber of Commerce, among many other prestigious positions held.

—Augustine Heard, who later founded Augustine Heard & Company, a large trading house in China was a cartel boss at R&C. Augustine is the nephew of Albert Farley Heard (**S&B 1853**).

—Russell Sturgis, who later became head of Baring Brothers in London, was a dope-dealing exec.

—John Cleve Green (1800-1875), who was a Philanthropist and **benefactor of Princeton University, too was a dope-dealer.**

At least eight of the Ivy League colleges were funded by the same-exact band of East India Company dope dealers.

These clowns were hard at work after WWII, also, look:

Great Article From (http://www.naturalnews.com/054092_Monsanto_acquisition_Bayer_Nazi_origins.html):

Dr. Fritz ter Meer, a director of IG Farben who **was directly involved in developing the nerve gas, Zyklon-B, which killed millions of Jews**, was sen-

s.S.O.S.s.

tenced to seven years in prison but was **released after four years** through the **intervention of Rockefeller** and J.J. McCloy, then U.S. High Commissioner for Germany. An unrepentant Fritz ter Meer, **guilty of genocide and crimes against humanity, returned to work in *Bayer where he served as Chairman for more than 10 years, until 1961.**

Don't forget, the fellows at Bayer are the geniuses who brought heroin to the market as the 'miracle' cure for morphine addiction. Bayer is an old friend of The Order, and *Yale* now actually owns Bayer Medical Complex in New Haven.

In more recent news....Bayer brought us AIDS infected medications, and they have since paid considerably for the misdeed.

This same 'ter Meer,' a convicted Nazi war criminal, **went on to become one of the initiators of the Codex Alimentarius Commission in 1962, an organization that was nurtured by the World Health Organization (WHO), the Food and Agriculture Organization (FAO), and latterly the World Trade Organization (WTO).**

Now, according to bloomberg.com:

> **Bayer has been "exploring a potential bid for U.S. competitor Monsanto in a deal that would create the world's largest supplier of seeds and farm chemicals."**

s.s.O.s.s.

Bloomberg seems to celebrate the idea of combining the evil of Nazis with the Satanic death and destruction of Monsanto, explaining, "Putting the world's largest seed maker together with the German company that invented aspirin would bring together brands such as Roundup, Monsanto's blockbuster herbicide [Roundup], and Sivanto, a new Bayer insecticide."

Just to clarify, **The Order brought us *Heroin following the Civil War*, AIDS infected medicine, *and, the gas chamber.***

Bayer's original logo is a Templar Cross. The Order brought you the round up of people, and now they fittingly own Monsanto, the company from hell who brought you weed *Round Up.*

On May 30, 1879, Society Kappa Psi, which later became Kappa Psi Pharmaceutical Fraternity, was started on the campus of none other than, *Russell Military Academy (the previously discussed Civil War Terrorist Camp)* by F. Harvey Smith.

The same group of corrupt men then regulated, and cornered the market on, prescription drugs. FDR's cousin, Teddy Roosevelt, approved the Food and Drug Act, which led to the FDA. Reagan, who was a smiley face at Bohemian Grove (upcoming), approved the slow-motion drug commercials which now play generously, during your favorite *'reality'* show.

Kappa Psi now consists of 106 collegiate, and 74 graduate chapters organized into 11 separate regional provinces—*and we all sit around wondering why America's drug problem nearly matches that of the rest of the entire world.*

s.s.O.s.s.

Note: As mentioned in the beginning of this book, America, India, and China (three of The Order's greatest settlements, two of which double as the theater for the *Opium 'Wars'*), are *still* the top three opiate users in the World today. And, our opium epidemics are being caused by the exact same band of dope dealers—*the dope is just in different form.*

#1—America—for painkiller abuse
#2—India
#3—China

26. Dirty Showers

The atrocities which have been committed, throughout the annals of human history in the name of eugenics, have become far less acceptable in our time. But, thanks to modern technology, The Order has developed far more clever ways with which to thin the herd. The current model for our FDA and DEA are doing the exact same job as the gas chambers and ovens of Nazi Germany, and the famines and butcherings in India before that.

Any dietician, professional athlete, or even armchair trainer, will tell you that the amount of carbohydrate intake prescribed by our government, for someone who is not a professional athlete, is a death sentence. But we continue to allow this nonsense to be taught in our schools. Your government knows this to be true, also. The food *pyramid* feeds the medical industry, and the fires of the Molech, with vigor. Most of us already know, despite the lies told to us by the people who are paid to protect us, that this pyramid should be flipped upside down—*most pyramids look better that way*.

Another great example is the DEA's drug scheduling Chart which is topped by Marijuana, the greatest all-natural pain reliever on the face of earth. Marijuana is portrayed by the DEA as one of the most dangerous, highly addictive drugs on the planet, for 'having no medical value.' The Order's new gas chambers—wars, prescription opiates, antidepressants, and who knows what else are wiping us out by the millions. Benzodiazepines (Xanax-type drugs), are readily handed out by the double-handful, and they are

s.S.O.S.s.

virtually impossible from which to withdraw. Meanwhile, the cure to opiate addiction, *Ibogaine*, remains a Schedule I illegal drug.

Stadium-loads of us die every year as a result of the intentionally confused information we are given by William Huntington Russell's frat bros, and our government simply views our deaths in the same manner as a rancher thinning his herd, or the way Hitler viewed his camps. Hitler would be so proud of what his old financiér, Prescott Bush, has accomplished.

Below is the transcript of a presentation given at the July 23-24 National Conference of the Citizens Electoral Council by CEC Chairman Ann Lawler. As you read this account I would like for you to remember that Wells is a prominent name of the known member lists of both Bohemian Grove and Skull and Bones. But the damning evidence that Wells himself was in bed with these creeps, is the fact that, H.G. was one of the fellows to whom Lavey gave a shout out in the opening of his satanic bible.

Enjoy:

H.G. Wells: Fabianism, Imperialism and Eugenics:
Parson Malthus was Darwin's hero. But to situate the importance of this Malthus/Darwin duo in British imperial ideology, let's listen to H.G. Wells (1866-1946) in his 1901 book, *Anticipations of the Reaction of* **Mechanical and Scientific Progress Upon Human Life and Thought,** upon which he later said that his entire life's work was based.

s.S.O.S.s.

Wells was at the very center of the British imperial priesthood. He had been a prize student of the man known as "Darwin's bulldog," T.H. Huxley; he co-founded the Fabian Society (Crowley's satanic cult during the late 1920s) with Bertrand Russell and Sydney and Beatrice Webb; he was a fierce advocate of eugenics, like Russell (also, from the William Russell merchants of death squad) and the rest of the Fabians; and, along with Julian Huxley and a couple of others, *he personally invented the modern cult of "environmentalism."* If you understand Wells, you understand the real import of Charles Darwin and of today's cult of environmentalism.

In his book's first chapter, "Locomotion," Wells lamented that the American Revolution had caused a worldwide explosion of railways, and that this "had changed the intellectual life of the world."

Indeed, Lincoln's victory over the British-backed Confederacy in the U.S. Civil War of 1861-65 had unleashed an astonishing growth of nation-states in Germany, Russia, Japan, and elsewhere, which copied the "American System" methods of public credit, intercontinental railways, the advocacy of science and technology, and the creation of a literate citizenry. World population growth surged. Anchored on transcontinental railways, all of this posed a strategic threat to the British *maritime* world empire. **The British responded by unleashing World War I, and by proposing to murder entire sections of the world's population via the new doctrine of eugenics.**

In 1924, *60,000 Americans* who were prisoners, or who were deemed mentally ill or deficient, were sterilized so they could no longer reproduce. **Gas chambers were another proposed method with which to extinguish the undesirable citizens of the United States.** *Chemical and alcohol addiction were among the undesirable traits which were considered worthy of human euthanasia.* Among the American Eugenics Society founders were, **Irving Fisher (Yale attendee and Skull & Bones 1888), and Madison Grant (Yale attendee).**

The American Eugenics Society still exists. The name was changed twice (for obvious reasons), first to the Society for the Study of Social Biology (after Roe vs Wade in 1972), and finally, today, it is still known as the Society for Biodemography and Social Biology. **Biodemography** is a new branch of human (classical) demography concerned with understanding the complementary biological and demographic determinants of and **interactions between the birth and death processes that shape individuals, cohorts and populations.**

s.S.O.S.s.

Darwin's book in which he describes 'survival of the fittest' is only a lie, and a desensitization mechanism for those who choose to manage these manmade disasters of humanity. Now science proclaims there is no God, and Darwinism is the accepted creation theory—a major victory for The Order.

Fun fact: In the recent breakout, interactive video game hit, *Pokemon,* an evil guy is waiting for you at one infamous Skull and Bones member, Adolf Hitler's, death camp, Auschwitz—**(google image 'Auschwitz Pokemon,' it will reveal a purple demon with a 'Skull and Bones' on his chest)**. The sign above the demon's head says, *'Work Sets You Free,'* in German. I can only assume that, the dirty little clouds surrounding the creature represent the poison gas which was pumped into the shower rooms, making skull & Bones of great groups of people in a disturbing fashion.

S.S.O.S.s.

27. World War Too

I may as well mention that The Order started WWI too. Prescott Bush's father, George Dubya's great grandfather, was a key player in initiating *that* bloodbath.

In 1901, 'Samuel Bush' became General Manager of Buckeye Steel Castings Company. The company manufactured railway parts; as we've already learned, an industry which does *quite* well in times of war. Frank Rockefeller was initially in charge of the company, and he and his brother, oil tycoon, John D. Rockefeller (among countless others), profited very handsomely from *that* war. One of Buckeye's longtime clients were the railroads controlled by E. H. Harriman (yes, *more* of the same warmongering Bonesmen).

The following is the most damnatory evidence of Skull and Bones's initiation of WWII: Shortly after Prescott Bush was enthroned at Brown Brothers Harriman, a new associate, Fritz Thyssen (who doubled as the Patriarch to the leading industrialist family on the German side), had bought the Barlow Palace on Briennerstrasse, in Munich (in 1928), which Hitler quickly converted into the **'Brown House,' the headquarters of the Nazi party.** (Prescott doubled as a 'Captain' in WWI.)

As stated in the opening chapters of this book, William Russell identified with the Hegelian creed of the German Totenkopf (German Chapter of Skull & Bones) well, but despite what we are told, William H. Russell did *NOT* learn his hateful and murderous ways from the German Order of Skull & Bones. As you will learn throughout this volume, this was an age old relationship which William Russell was simply calling-on, in order see to

s.S.O.S.s.

it that the dirty deeds which had been entrusted to Russell by his ancestors were being followed by the German Chapter of The Order.

The dialectic was slowly encroaching upon the collapse of Germany, and Russell was simply there, in advance, to begin to groom the beginning of the end for the Germanic civilization as they knew it. Soon after William H. Russell's fateful visit to Germany, he arrived back in the states just in time to harvest *his* inherited Russell windfall, *The American Civil War.*

Not surprisingly, Henry Stimson **(S&B 1888),** who took over the position of Secretary of War in 1911, was appointed by fellow Bonesman, Frat-bro and business partner to William Huntington Russell, *William Howard Taft.* (Just in time for the political climate of pre-WWI!)

Stimson later became Hoover's Secretary of State *and* Secretary of War for the FDR and Truman Administrations, during WWII.

After WWI rampant usury had completely collapsed the economy in Germany, since the world community demanded that Germany pay back the international debt which was accrued, by all nations, as a result of WWI. *This debt was being passed on to the German citizen*—it was an impossible amount to repay—*much like the 18 trillion dollars America owes now.* Hitler, seeing only the tip of this gigantic financial trap, blamed the problem on 'Jewish Bankers.'

Hitler's identification with the German people stemmed from this illusion, which was created by the *American* esoteric warmongers—namely, the prominent Skull and Bones families, the *Bushes, Browns and Harrimans.* As Germany's economy began to

s.s.O.s.s.

collapse as a result of this manmade financial disaster, Hitler began to panic and attempted to isolate his country from the cabalist practices of these so-called 'Jews.' *Hitler began to wage war again, since world domination had become the only way to erase that debt, which had been shoveled upon the heads of German citizens.*

Prescott Bush's banking institutions were among *many* American companies who were lending money and arms to Hitler. This ruse lent to the illusion, among the Germanic people, that Hitler's regime circumvented the *German* 'Jewish Bankers' who had now enslaved the entire country of Germany, when in fact it was American Bankers (which many call 'Jews') who took over the financing of Hitler's new Order. The Order had made *Hitler the savior of German citizens.*

Hitler was desperately throwing *'Jews'* in the fires, as fast as he could, to prevent their financial magic. But what Hitler did *not* realize was, *his* American financiers were key parts to the same exact war machine which had collapsed Germany from the very beginning of WWI. It was a few, rich evil families, who may or may not have been 'Jewish,' that suckered Hitler, not, *'The Jews,'* as Hitler had thought. If you read Hitler's hit book, M*ein Kempf*, it becomes very clear that Hitler caught-on to his frat brothers' tricks toward the end, though.

Adolph Hitler's mother, Klara Hitler (formerly Klara Polzi), was a young, *Jewish* servant girl in the private home of the *Rothschild family's*. There is even speculation that Hitler himself was a blood-linked-lovechild, connecting the family's blood directly to the slaughter of millions of the Rothschilds' supposed own 'people'—another one of The Order's 'rags to riches' stories. Bill Clinton—*William Jefferson Clinton* (three very prominent names

S.S.O.S.S.

combined)—is another one of these tear-jerking success stories; among so many others, as you will soon learn.

These same bloodlines who hoard gold, political power, and the ancient technology in the art of confusion (with their combination of military might when confusion gives way to reason within the masses), is the same conglomerate who overtly enslaved the entire country of India before that—the bloodline of the original Directors of *East India Company.*

The Order's outcome in Germany couldn't have been better. Using the technology of confusion, The Order was able to seize control of the minds and politics of Germany, to coax ordinary citizens into gassing their own neighbors, and then incinerating them in a great offering to Molech. These bankers convert everything that a society works for into worthless paper, and, now, simple bank entries. The evildoers then gallop into the sunset as God's people, once again, explode into flames, famine, and devastation.

The Order had again positioned themselves, not only to strong-arm Germany back into financial oppression and social submission, but, this time The Order had clinched the win for the whole supposed 'New World Order'—the international network which actually *runs* the interwoven fabric of governments, banks, and corporations, which we now call the United Nations.

The UN, or *United Nations,* which was known prior as the '*Legion of Nations*' (a legion is defined as a group of demons), was *also* created by *The Order.* The UN was initially known as the 'Judicial Settlement of International Disputes,' in 1910. The first Chairman of the JSID was none other than, *William Howard Taft,*

S.S.O.S.s.

the son of William H. Russell's frat brother and co-founder of the American Chapter of the Order of Skull & Bones.

Hopefully, by now, you are realizing that there is nothing *'New'* about this, *'World Order.'*

The banking families involved in WWII *all* had connections with *'Patriarch'* Prescott Bush (who profited handsomely from their immense banking empire and international steel holdings), throughout the lengthy worldwide battle—The Order even funded the production of the chemical gas which was loaded into the gas chambers and did away with the supposed 'Jewish Bankers' of Germany. *And,* Hitler's army was found to be operating, almost in toto, using American Firearms. (The art of confusion is a hell of a thing.)

Hollister Bundy **(S&B 1909)** was Stimson's special assistant for the Bohemian Grove's precious Manhattan Project (explained later), which supposedly ended the war. (Two of Bundy's sons also went on to be fellow Bonesmen, and were *very* involved in governmental and foundation affairs.)

After WWII Prescott Bush hired Allen Dulles, an attorney, to hide their assets, which would prevent further financial loss under the Trading with the Enemy Act. Many assets *were* seized from this group of elites, and *no one* was executed or imprisoned for the heinous acts of murder and treason. As a matter of fact, it is believed that Prescott himself would have served as president were it not for the whole 'Trading with the Enemies' thing. *But,* that didn't stop 'Pat' Bush from winning a bid for U.S. Senator, representing Connecticut (the evil home of Yale University) from 1952 until January 1963. Prescott Bush also took *full* credit for enthroning Nixon; attendee of Bohemian Grove (devil-worshipping club),

s.s.O.s.s.

and he was architect of both the 'War' on drugs *and* the shameful watergate scandal.

With the war's end Hitler was *also* discovered to be heavily involved in The Order's trademarked, dark activities of magic, channelling, and the occult. Surprise, surprise. Actually that doesn't do Hitler's love affair with satan justice. Hitler had his own satanic church, and was a blasphemous, open antichrist.

You may also remember that there was some confusion as to where Adolf Hitler's corpse went after his inevitable demise. Many even speculate that Hitler had changed his appearance and simply vanished into another country, due to the absence of a body. I think it is clear, now, that the Bonesmen again reaped their evil bounty, and that Hitler's skull *must* make its home in *'The Tomb,'* on *High Street*, right next to *Geronimo*, as just another leader who was duped into the slaughter of his own people, by…*The Order.*

World War II began as a political feud in Germany, which was being fought to prevent the same ancient esoteric financial strategies, with which the people of America are being abused today. These are the same Cabalistic practices which had plagued and destroyed the Biblical cities, over-and-again.

Thousands of other societies, for ages, have been scammed by the same tactics with which *we* have now been enslaved, through *our* materialistic corporate America. These practices have been carefully disguised, throughout The Bible, by the evil ones who peddle their false teachings for money. (Another reading of the ancient chronicles will clear things up entirely.)

11 million humans were turned to *'Skull & Bones'* in the death camps of the holocaust. Of those, six million were of Jewish descent, and the others were a mix of, financially strategic targets,

s.s.O.s.s.

political prisoners, Jehovah's witnesses, homosexuals, the disabled, and the insane.

A total of over *60 million people* (about 3% of the 1940 world population) were killed in WWII, between combatants on both sides and the holocaust. That being said, 12 Nazi Germans were hung for war crimes in Nurumburg *(which was highly publicized pageantry)*, following the Holocaust. Only 406, out of around 800 Nazi's who were sentenced to death, were actually carried out. Another minuscule 5000 Nazis were sentenced to prison —*there were 20,000 work camps.*

This means that, had we merely executed only the Warden of each camp, *they would have had to hang 20,000 Nazis*—only 5000 of those *hypothetical death-camp wardens* even set foot through the gates of a prison, themselves.

We will end this section with a quote:

> "If you tell a big enough lie and tell it frequently enough, it will be believed."
> —Adolf Hitler—

s.s.O.s.s.

28. Muggy Whisperings

Winston Churchill was Britain's Prime Minister during the second World War (the equivalent to our American President). That being said, one would assume that Winston Churchill would strongly oppose euthanasia, right? Wrong! Churchill, the guy who took up arms with the whole world to dethrone that terrible guy with a funny little mustache, hates the killing of innocent, poor, and crippled people, right? Wrong....The following quotes were made by a man who The Order considers to be one of the greatest minds of yesteryear—Winston Churchill:

—From his Great Contemporaries, 1937
"One may dislike Hitler's system and yet admire his patriotic achievement. If our country were defeated, I hope we should find a champion as admirable to restore our courage and lead us back to our place among the nations."
— Winston Churchill—

—Churchill to Asquith, 1910
"The unnatural and increasingly rapid growth of the feeble-minded and insane classes, coupled as it is with a steady restriction among all the thrifty, energetic and superior stocks, constitutes a national and race danger which it is impossible to exaggerate...I feel that the source from which the stream of mad-

s.s.O.s.s.

ness is fed should be cut off and sealed up before another year has passed."
— Winston Churchill—

—Speaking in the House of Commons, autumn 1937
"I will not pretend that, if I had to choose between communism and nazism, I would choose communism."
— Winston Churchill—

—In a letter to his mother, 1896
"(India is) a godless land of snobs and bores."
— Winston Churchill—

—Churchill to Palestine Royal Commission, 1937
"I do not admit... that a great wrong has been done to the Red Indians of America, or the black people of Australia...by the fact that a stronger race, a higher grade race...has come in and taken its place."
— Winston Churchill—

—Quoted in the Boston Review, April/May 2001
"(We must rally against) a poisoned Russia, an infected Russia of armed hordes not only smiting with bayonet and cannon, but accompanied and preceded by swarms of typhus-bearing vermin."

S.S.O.S.S.
— Winston Churchill—

Writing in The World Crisis and the Aftermath, 1923-31
"The choice was clearly open: crush them with vain and unstinted force, or try to give them what they want. These were the only alternatives and most people were unprepared for either. Here indeed was the Irish spectre—horrid and inexorcisable."
— Winston Churchill—

—Addressing the London Polish government at a British Embassy meeting, October 1944
"You are callous people who want to wreck Europe—you do not care about the future of Europe, you have only your own miserable interests in mind."
— Winston Churchill—

—Illustrated Sunday Herald, February 1920
"This movement among the Jews is not new. From the days of Spartacus-Weishaupt to those of Karl Marx, and down to Trotsky (Russia), Bela Kun (Hungary), Rosa Luxembourg (Germany), and Emma Goldman (United States)...this worldwide conspiracy for the overthrow of civilisation and for the reconstitution of society on the basis of arrested development, of envious malevolence, and impossi-

ble equality, has been steadily growing. It has been the mainspring of every subversive movement during the 19th century; and now at last this band of extraordinary personalities from the underworld of the great cities of Europe and America have gripped the Russian people by the hair of their heads and have become practically the undisputed masters of that enormous empire."

— **Winston Churchill**—

29. Famous Supporters of Eugenics

To give you an idea of the popularity of these beliefs I will provide a short list of the many people in America who openly supported the eugenics movement:

President Theodore Roosevelt—President 26 of the USA—and another member of the Warren Delano East India Company dope clan

Margaret Sanger—Founder of planned parenthood was a supporter of killing less desirable people.

Below is a quote by Presidential Hopeful, *Hillary Clinton*:

> "I Admire Planned Parenthood Founder Margaret Sanger."

Hillary Clinton supports 'late term abortion,' which means that she supports the extermination of children who are as developed as the one you drove home from the hospital on that special day.

Alexander Graham Bell—Bell was credited with the invention of the devices on which you currently rely, to send and receive information of any kind, and too was a supporter of the practice of euthanasia.

John Harvey Kellog—When you are slurping milk from the bowl of your corn flakes in the morning think about the fact that, the

s.S.O.S.s.

gentleman who invented those crispy little flakes of cardboard probably wanted you dead. I suppose it comes as no surprise that a man (a "physician") who invented the carbohydrate *rich*, and nutritionally *void* breakfast cereal, Corn Flakes, was a staunch advocate of eugenics. He even had his own sanatorium in which to experiment on people who were deemed inadequate human beings during his times (I am guessing that most of them were simply poor and not in bloodline with the Russell's).

Many of Kellog's relatives were members of The Order of Skull and Bones:

Charles Poole Kellog—S&B 1890
Fred William Kellogg—S&B 1883
Stephen Wright Kellogg—S&B 1846
W.W. Kellogg—S&B 1939

Henry Ford—Ford even purchased a defunct newspaper in order to circulate his antisemitic beliefs. At its peek, the paper delivered a half-million copies.

Charles Lindbergh—The man who solo-piloted his famous transatlantic flight was a believer in eugenics. BTW: Lindbergh was not the first to fly solo across the pond. He wasn't the second either—nearly eighty brave pilots had traversed the Atlantic, before Lindbergh enjoyed his ticker tape parade.

So, what did Lindbergh do first, then? Well, he was the first person to become an international celebrity, from the live coverage of mass-media, and the first to fly solo, nonstop, from New

s.S.O.S.s.

York to Paris—*that is all*. But, our kid's history book still credits "Lucky Lindy" with the redundant achievement.

Woodrow Wilson—was the 28th President of the US, and also was a supporter of the death head creed of eugenics.

Poor, poor, pathetic, little Hitler....This was clearly a case of....C'mon Bro....Everyone's doin' it!

This list of clowns who promote euthanasia of the poor, weak, and handicapped, could easily fill several volumes. But, for the sake of posterity we will end it here, incase these peoples' relatives don't share the views of the flawed individuals. Don't kid yourself though, these beliefs are still strongly held, in many circles, most of which run our country.

30. Grandpa Bush's Human Zoo

For this section we have an outtake from the book, *Fleshing Out Skull & Bones*, by Kris Millegan:

These were exciting times for Prescott (President Bush family patriarch), with the exception of one terrible tragedy: his mother, Flora was killed in a car crash in 1920. Sadly, she would not see her "war hero" son climb the ladder of power and fortune. Perhaps she was better off. The Bush Walker marriage was more than a doubling of powerful families; it was the creation of the next generation of Bush criminals. The Bush seed, like an infection or a virus, would grow stronger than the previous generation, masking themselves would grow stronger than the previous generation, masking themselves as serving for the betterment of humanity, while they plotted to enrich themselves on huge profits made from the misery and suffering that came from the wars they fueled. Each future generation, nourished by the blood of those less fortunate, drew from an ever deepening well of sociopathic behavior.

Walker and several of his cronies had an interest in horse breeding. (It had most certainly crossed Walder's mind that breeding Prescott with his own

S.S.O.S.S.

Dorothy would prove to be a winning combination for offspring.) The idea of breeding only the strongest male would lead to a much more dangerous idea with humans replacing horses as breeding material. During the 1904 St. Louis World's Fair, which by the way was organized and funded by Walker, Brookings, and Missouri governor David Francis, they featured a "human zoo": live natives from backward jungle regions. These poor souls lived and were shown in cages under the supervision of an anthropologist, William J. McGee."

Prescott Bush, father to President George Bush Senior, and Grandfather to George W. Bush, kept humans from all around the world, in cages, to entertain the masses at the 1904 World's Fair. Exotic men were exhibited like livestock in the year of our Lord 1904, *THIRTY-NINE YEARS AFTER THE CIVIL WAR!*

Human zoos continued to operate long after Grandpa Bush kept his exotic pets. Human Zoos, which are exactly what they sound like, were popular around the world, through the 1950s. Horrific tales hide deep within the archives of mankind, if you dare look, but much of the details have been swept from the stoop of history, long ago.

The last human zoo, for which I could find record, was in Belgium—it closed its doors in 1958. Jardin d'Agronomie Tropicale, which translates to Garden of Tropical Agronomy, was the name for the Human Zoo of Paris. The Paris Zoo is in disrepair and grown-up in weeds, but has been recently reopened to the public without the exhibited humans, as a curiosity. It has been esti-

s.S.O.s.s.

mated that a half-billion gawkers viewed exotic peoples through the gates of human zoos during their infamous existence, until 1958.

Fun fact: Prescott Bush's pal and Germanic frat bro, Adolf Hitler, had this to say about the 'subjugated' (enslaved by conquest) races:

> **"The most foolish mistake we could possibly make would be to allow the subjugated races to possess arms.** History shows that all conquerors who have allowed their subjugated races to carry arms have prepared their own downfall by so doing. Indeed, I would go so far as to say that the supply of arms to the underdogs is a sine qua non (an indispensable and essential action) for the overthrow of any sovereignty. So let's not have any native militia or native police."

This quote is usually paraphrased in our times to:

> "To conquer a nation, you must first disarm its citizens."

s.s.O.s.s.

31. Segregation of Judah

Louis Armstrong recorded this famous song in 1958, first sung by *Fisk Jubilee Singers in 1862—the heart of the Civil War*:

"Go down Moses way down in Egypt land
Tell all Pharaohs to let My people go
When Israel was in Egypt land
Let My people go
Oppressed so hard they could not stand
Let My people go
So the God seyeth, "Go down, Moses way down in Egypt land
Tell all Pharaohs to let My people go"

Note: This 'Negro Spiritual' was a popular field song for the African Americans who were more-recently sold into slavery in North America, by East India Company. The old 'Spiritual' is based on this Old Testament verse, from the story of Moses and the Ten Commandments"...

Exodus 8:1 King James Version
8 And the Lord spake unto Moses, Go unto Pharaoh, and say unto him, Thus saith the Lord, Let my people go, that they may serve me.

s.s.O.s.s.

And so, he did…Moses went into Egypt as God had instructed, and after a series of visits and the horrible prophetic plagues which followed those trips, God's Children were surrendered to Moses by the Pharaoh.

Moses's older brother, Aaron, was also on hand for these stately visits, and therefore, helped release the 'Israelites.' (The israelites were being oppressed by the establishment, in much the way we are now.)

Aaron seemed to have great magic and even threw down his staff before the King, which became a serpent that ate all of the other snakes created by the King's great 'magicians.' Aaron, was later appointed as a High Priest (in charge of sacrificial offerings—*animals*). Since his younger brother, Moses, was known as a man of few words, Aaron became Moses's mouthpiece to his people.

Aaron, *The High Priest*, exercised power over the people, and was even a judge over everyday disputes amongst the tribes, of which there were many. The 'Children of Israel' were 'lost in the Wilderness,' and became restless when their new leaders failed to discover the 'Promised Land.' There was little food and water, though God *did* provide for them they were still bitter.

For forty years the 12 tribes wandered alongside the land of Canaan (Canaan was the 'Promised Land'—they were right next to it the *whole time*).

Then the Lord said to Moses, 'How long will they refuse to believe in me, in spite of all the miraculous signs I have performed among them? I will strike them down with a plague and destroy them' (Numbers 14:11). But, Moses talked God out of the act.

After a second hike for provisions and instruction from God, Moses had the famous visions on Mount Sinai. Moses was

S.S.O.S.s.

on the mountain for forty days...Meanwhile, Aaron turned to the Israelite's abominable ways of magic. They even pooled their gold, and built an idol of a 'Golden Calf' with which to worship, to end their suffering in the wilderness.

Aaron betrayed God and Moses. After Moses returned with their new rules (the Ten Commandments), the rest of the group—nearly three thousand people who led the idol worship—were smitten at the hands of their own relatives and friends.

However, somehow with little explanation Aaron's life is spared....Why?

With little research I discovered the 'Golden Calf' to be an idol known as Molech or Baal (one of the S&B 'nicknames'), which this group had been worshipping, long predating those times. *Molech*, required the sacrifice of children, who would be burned alive, in exchange for dominion over men through trickery, and usury, in combination with magic rituals and spells.

We also saw this sort of fire offering with the Jordanian pilot who was burnt alive in a cage by *Isis (another name for satan in ancient Egypt),* in contrast to the Muslim religion's belief system. If you google this: **Warning Extremely Graphic!**

In the middle ages these spooks built bronze statues in which the dissolute would offer live children for offering to Molech. The child would be stuck into the hollow bronze idol, and a hatch would be closed, after which a fire was lit under the chamber of death, and the youngster would be burnt alive **(google image 'how it works the brazen bull')**. Hitler offered this mass sacrifice to Molech as well, to the tune of seven million.

Remember all of those William Russells?...Remember those worldwide dope-dealers, 'conquerors,' and oppressor of the

S.S.O.S.s.

known world? Burnt human offering had been part of the Russell family's culture for millennia.

The mother of a mutilated unborn child told reporter Russell Hunter that, she'd become "a millionaire after offering her child to Molech via abortion" (fellowshipoftheminds.com 2013/03/03 im-a-millionaire-because-i-had-an-abortion-abortion-and-moloch/)

Leviticus 18:21 King James Version
21 And thou shalt not let any of thy seed pass through the fire to Molech, neither shalt thou profane the name of thy God: I am the Lord.

Ex head of Los Angeles FBI, Ted Gunderson, who worked on the Marilyn Monroe case and the JFK assassination, warned of despicable activity by the financial elite and government officials. Below is an outtake from wikipedia.com:

> He also investigated a child molestation trial in Manhattan Beach, California. In a 1995 conference in Dallas, Gunderson warned about the supposed proliferation of secret Satanic groups, and the danger posed by the New World Order, an alleged shadow government that would be controlling the US government. He also claimed that a 'slave auction' in which children were sold to men in turbans had been held in Las Vegas, that four thousand ritual human sacrifices are performed in New York City every year, and that the 1995 bombing of the Alfred P. Murrah Federal Building in Oklahoma City was carried out by the US government.

s.S.O.S.s.

Online is a copy of the video in which Gunderson outlines the felonious activities of the government, and which many claim got him poisoned.

Gunderson's official cause of death was cancer. A doctor friend of Gundersons', whom Gunderson asked to examine his dead body upon his demise (stating to the friend that he was 'sure he would be killed' for his whistle-blowing) had found acute bruising on the tips of Gunderson's dead fingers. To the Dr. friend this indicated poisoning, this video too can be easily found on the internet.

32. *Stoned* with Horror

The owl form of King Nimrod from Babylon—Lilith—is said to hold the Opium poppy highly sacred. This explains The Order's long love affair with killing humans using this method. The rose was also held sacred.

The red rose represents female sexuality, and the white rose is a metaphor for a pure or virginly goddess. In the Ancient Canaanites' ritual sacrifice to Lilith (or, *Baal*), red rose petals were dropped along the altar before the baby's blood was shed. After the sacrifice was final, white rose petals were scattered to represent the new purity which occurred from the human offering.

Before a stone owl, a 'dummy' child is burnt in a fiery ceremony, upon a stone altar surrounded by 'priests' wearing robes. **Among the Redwoods of beautiful northwestern California**, thousands of the world's leaders, governors, CEO's and financially elite, applaud and cheer as they look on romantically upon the finality of the cremation of the 'child.'

This ancient ceremony is called the Cremation Of Care Ceremony (a quick google image search will likely turn up a wealth of unbelievable imagery. **A google video search will reveal** actual video footage of the sacrifice, which is made annually, at *Bohemian Grove*. Also, there is the fantastic piece written by Vanity Fair on the topic of Bohemian Grove. On the upper right-hand corner of the one dollar bill is a rendering of the demonic *Lilith (in the form of a tiny owl)* looking back at Washington, a known Freemason. And the same satanic deity in owl form has been designed into the lawns and sidewalks surrounding our poor

s.s.O.s.s.

Nation's Capitol. Our nation's Capitol Building rests above Lilith's heart.

Here is a prophecy from one of the high-ranking Freemason's who helped scatter this garbage upon the lawn of America:

'The blessed Religion revealed in the word of God will remain an eternal **and awful** monument to prove that **the best Institutions may be abused by human depravity** (depravity meaning corruption or wickedness); and that they may even, in some instances, be made subservient to the vilest of purposes.'

—George Washington—

It appears that this apron-wearing clown knew this scam first hand.

The very Apple Computer on which I am typing this text displays an illuminated apple with a bite taken from it (representing Adam and Eve's sin and rejection)—but, when on default, an icon of the horned owl stares back at me from the monitor, from the login screen. As I'm booting-up my television I see the unmistakable head of the stone owl in Bohemian Grove, and I wonder what despicable acts Vizio committed to sell big-screen TV's in the pole position at Wal-Mart…

Mazda Motor also seems to be cashing-in on the devil brand. The name Mazda, itself, is the Hindu version of Nimrod, and also requires human sacrifice. *Ahura-Mazda* is the form of Nimrod who developed wings as he morphed into Lilith.

s.S.O.s.s.

In ancient times, a sound-dampening drumbeat would rumble as you handed your screaming child over to the red hot arms of Molech. When you back away from the glaring bronze statue your baby's final piercing sounds fade into the beat of galloping drums. The air becomes cooler as you retreat.

As you read just some of the notable names on the *short* list below, remember the cremation of care ceremony, and what it represents.

Look:

Presidents who have enjoyed 'The Grove'

Theodore Roosevelt—26the President of the US

Calvin Coolidge—President 30 of the US

Herbert Hoover—31st President of the US

Dwight D. Eisenhower—34the President of the US/Supreme Allied Commander for WWII

Earl Warren (not a president but honorable mention)—Appointed to chair of what became known as the Warren Commission, which was formed to investigate the 1963 assassination of President John F. Kennedy (President 35).

Most people consider the 'Warren Commission' to be a joke.

s.s.O.s.s.

Richard Nixon—President 37 of the US *'attended the Grove from Time to Time'*—calling Bohemian Grove *'The Gayest GD Place on the Planet'*—*also called it 'fagotty.'* Waged the War on Drugs and key man in Vietnam War

Gerald Ford—President 38 of the US (President for Tail End of Vietnam)/Lieutenant Commander WWII

Nelson Rockefeller—Vice President of the US under Gerald Ford

Ronald Reagan—President 40 of the US who Elevated the War on Drugs and Signed Slow Motion Drug Commercials into Law (they are currently outlawed in nearly every other country).

James A. Baker III—Reagan's Treasurer and Secretary of State

George H.W. Bush—President 41/VP for Reagan/ Director of the CIA (was in Dallas on the day Kennedy was shot)

George W. Bush—President 43 (during 9/11)/War on Afghanistan/War on 'Terror'/Invasion of Iraq

Donald Rumsfeld—Secretary of Defense Under Bush (during 9/11)/Long Career in Military and Politics (too much to list)

s.s.O.s.s.

Dick Cheney—Vice President Under Bush (during 9/11)/War on Afghanistan/War on 'Terror' and Invasion of Iraq

Colin Powell—12th Chair of the Joint Chiefs of Staff Under Clinton/Bush (during 9/11)

Karl Rove—Senior Advisor and Deputy Chief of Staff during the George W. Bush administration (during 9/11)

Politicians who served under multiple Presidencies—

Barry Goldwater—Five Term US Senator and One Time Republican Nominee for US **President**

Alexander Haig—Military and Political Man Under Multiple Presidents

Jack Kemp—Multiple High Political Offices Held Under Multiple Presidents

Media and Public Influence

Christopher Buckley—Political Writer

William F. Buckley—American conservative Author/Commentator/ Founded National Review magazine in 1955

s.s.O.s.s.

Walter Cronkite—Broadcast Journalist—for many years, Cronkite *was* the voice of Lilith the stone owl, for the cremation of care ceremony

Bing Crosby—American Singer/Actor

John E. Dupont—Creep on the Movie *Fox Catcher/Convicted Murderer*

Clint Eastwood—AKA *'Dirty'* Harry/Actor

Merv Griffin—Media Mogul (brought us many TV and game shows)

Charlton Heston—Starred in Over 100 Films Perhaps Best Known for his Role as Moses in *The Ten Commandments*

Henry Kissinger—National Security Adviser and Secretary of State Under Nixon and Ford (Vietnam)

Jack London—Highly Influential Writer and Journalist

Steve Miller—Musician (Steve Miller Band)

Robert Mondavi—Wine Maker

John Muir—Author/Philosopher/Outdoorsman

Charles Schwab—Wealthy Businessman and Investor

s.s.O.s.s.

David Rockefeller—Longtime Chairman and Chief Executive of Chase Manhattan (could possibly be spawn of the devil himself)—The Rockefellers brought you most of the degeneration of today's society through their many financial trusts which support any program promoting rampant evil in our society.

Mark Twain—Famous Writer who was also mentioned by Lavey in the Satanic Bible—My favorite quote by Mark Twain is the following:

> "Nothing so needs reforming as other people's habits. Fanatics will never learn that, though it be written in letters of gold across the sky. It is the prohibition that makes anything precious"

Summary of Bohemian Grove Guests: There you have it…The creeps who continue to worship the same idols as the Canaanites in the bible brought you WWII, Vietnam, 9/11, the modern day Crusades (the Middle East conflicts), The 'War' on Drugs, and then there's Warren who smoothed over the backlash of the Kennedy Assassination, among so many other dreadful events. There are far too many to count. I just wanted to give you a little sample of this wicked group's deeds.

    Nixon, who enjoyed the most disastrous presidency of all (outside of Lincoln and those fellows), and waged the *'War' on Drugs along with Reagan*, was also a beloved member of the child-killing club—a google image search will reveal the Presidential fellows taking in a good chuckle at *The Grove*—perhaps the boys

S.S.O.S.s.

are laughing about all of the people they will kill with chemicals disguised as medicine.

And there are tens-of-thousands more of these creeps. (Many of these people, and or their family members, double as Skull and Bones members.) Unlike the The Order of Skull and Bones, which enables only 15 initiates per year, Bohemian Grove Club attracts thousands of members, and they *still have a fifteen year waiting list*, regardless of a person's socioeconomic status. These are *our* presidents, priests, CEO's, professors, lawmakers, and all of the people who are 'policing' and running the world.

The Bohemian Grove club is supposedly an American revival of the Hellfire Club in Britain, which also had an impressive celebrity roster. *Benjamin Franklin was a notable international satanist, and was a well-known member of the Hellfire Club.* But as you now know, these rituals predate the Hellfire Club by thousands of years—evil is a timeworn industry.

The skeletons of as many as 15 cadavers were found buried under the prior home of Franklin, in London, on North 36 Craven Street. *The bones displayed evidence of brutal torture.* Franklin was a big celebrity back in London, and was even seen whoring around her Streets, immediately following the Revolutionary War. This was a time when the 'Lobster Coats' would surely have lynched him in his silly wig, by his own knickers, had the nonsense in school been factual.

Franklin was the **Grandmaster of Freemasons* in the state of Pennsylvania.

Note*: Nearly every 'Order' discussed in this book —from the Templar to the KKK—refer to their

S.S.O.S.s.

leader as Grandmaster or 'Grand Wizzard.' Many of these cults, including the KKK, have a position aptly titled, 'Grand Dragon.' If you will recall, the word 'dragon' evolved from the word 'Dagon,' another form of King Nimrod.

Bonesmen, Henry L. Stimson **(S&B 1888**—Secretary of War for the Manhattan Project), and Hollister Bundy **(S&B 1909**—Special Assistant for the Manhattan Project), led the famous *Manhattan project,* which was a codename for the United States effort to develop a nuclear *weapon of mass destruction.* The Manhattan project itself began as an idea in Bohemian Grove California, during the annual Cremation of Care ceremony's *'mock'*...human sacrifice.

Here is the proud outtake from wikipedia.com concerning the fateful voluminous fiery offerings to Molech, that would be Hiroshima, and Nagasaki:

> The Grove is particularly famous for a Manhattan Project planning meeting which took place there in September 1942, and subsequently led to the atomic bomb. Those attending this meeting included **Ernest Lawrence, U.C. Berkeley colleague Robert Oppenheimer, various military officials**, the **S-1 Committee heads**, such as the **presidents of Harvard, Yale,** and **Princeton** along with **representatives of Standard Oil** and **General Electric.** At the time, **Oppenheimer was not an official S-1 member due to security clearance troubles with**

s.s.O.s.s.

the U.S. wartime Government, although Lawrence and Oppenheimer hosted the meeting. Grove members take particular pride in this event and often relate the story to new attendees.

The Jewish Talmud texts mention Lilith on multiple accounts, but the Christian Bible only speaks of her once, in Isaiah 34:13:

Isaiah 34:8-14 King James Version
8 For it is the day of the Lord's vengeance, and the year of recompences for the controversy of Zion.
9 And the streams thereof shall be turned into pitch, and the *dust thereof into brimstone, and the land thereof shall become burning pitch.*
10 It shall not be quenched night nor day; the smoke thereof shall go up for ever: from generation to generation it shall lie waste; none shall pass through it for ever and ever.
11 But the cormorant and the bittern shall possess it; **the owl also and the raven shall dwell in it**: and **he shall stretch out upon it the line of confusion,** and the *stones of emptiness.
12 They shall call the nobles thereof to the kingdom, but none shall be there, and all her princes shall be nothing.
13 And thorns shall come up in her palaces, nettles and brambles in the fortresses thereof: and *it*

s.s.O.s.s.

shall be an habitation of dragons, and a court for owls.

14 The wild beasts of the desert shall also meet with the wild beasts of the island, and the satyr shall cry to his fellow; **the** *screech owl* **also shall rest there, and find for herself a place of rest.**

Note*: Assumably, the stones of emptiness (as spoken of in verse 11) would represent stone idols—such as the one at Bohemian Grove (google image 'Lilith altar Bohemian Grove').

The pagan based burning man festival, which is held annually (in the middle of the Nevada desert), now has an attendance of over 70,000. The burning man is not a new practice.

Burning man dates to the Celts, when a Wicker Man was indeed used to offer sacrifices to the 'gods.' The victims were animals and humans, the latter often prisoners taken during wars or convicts found guilty of a 'crime deserving death.' One manifestation of this type of human sacrifice, made by the Celts, is, Caesar's account of the druids in his Gallic Wars.

Caesar describes a ritual in which large, compartmentalized wicker effigies were filled with grains, small animals, and even human slaves, before being burned as sacrifices.

A man killed himself at a Burning Man-style arts festival by offering himself into a towering fire in front of hundreds of horrified onlookers. Police identified him as Christopher Wallace, 30, of Salt Lake City—eyewitness accounts:

s.S.O.S.s.

'Earlier in the day, he had told the other festival goers he planned to jump into the three-story-tall inferno,' police said. 'This is what he was going to do, and it's what he did,' Grantsville Police Lt. Steve Barrett told reporters on Monday.

'He was running out there. He was dancing around a little bit, and then all of a sudden he jumped into it,' Daisey McDonald told KUTV-TV. 'It's like he didn't even know it was fire—it's like he thought it was just a playground. It took not even seconds. He was just through the barricades and into the fire.'

Bohemian Grove's annual Cremation of Care ceremony takes place on the Summer Solstice. Stonehenge has its pagan ceremony on this very same day, on which its circle of rocks is filled with creeps wearing antlers, horns, and hats fashioned as fishheads. Around the world, beams of sunlight creep through outcropping keyholes, and bend into hidden chambers and hidden shafts, which have been carefully placed there, by people celebrating different evolutions of the same event—*King Nimrod 'killing God' in the mountains on a 'hunting trip.'*

If you conduct a simple search, you too will find that child and adult abduction and murders skyrocket during the many fateful dates which these ghouls celebrate.

33. The Flight of Lilith

The country and the world's most elite have been worshipping a forty-foot, moss-covered stone Owl surrounded by Giant Sequoia, for at least 120 years now....A google image search of 'Lilith stone owl Bohemian' will reveal Lilith in the form of a Giant stone owl, in 'Bohemian Grove, California.

Lilith is a female demon of the night, who flies around searching for newborn children either to kidnap or strangle, and is said to take the form of an owl. Also, Lilith seduces men, to trick them into propagating demon sons.

Stories of Lilith are ancient to man. Rabbinical myths of Lilith circulate, in which she became Adam of Eden's first love. These accounts relate to the Sumero-Babyloian Goddess Belit-ili, or Belili; the 'Burney Relief' is a 2000 year old stone relief carving of Lilith, which was found in Ancient Babylon, in Sumer. The same exact Owl of Lilith can be found on the side of a building at Bohemian Grove, in America—if you google the image, notice that the two owls at Lilith's feet, on the Babylonian stone relief, match the one in Bohemian Grove *perfectly*.

Lilith was depicted in the story of the Ten Commandments as represented by Aaron's Golden Calf—which is synonymous with Baal (remember, Baal, was also a nickname for a Skull and Bones member), or *Molech in that case.*

The Canaanites knew Lilith as *Baalil*, or, the 'Divine Lady.' On a tablet from Ur, ca. 2000 BC, Lilith was known as Lillake.

Lilith is mentioned as a myriad of mother figure forms of *enlightenment* and *terror*, around the world, in multiple cultures.

s.s.O.s.s.

From Inana to Isis, Ishtar to Athena, Gorgon-Medusa, Venus, Ashtoreth, Diana, Libertas, and even *the worship* of the Biblical Virgin Mary, all have a genus relationship to the myths of the demonic goddess Lilith.

Hebrew legend states that Lilith was ousted from the Garden of Eden for sleeping with Adam. She then flew into a hidden cave along the banks of the Red Sea and mothered a multitude of demonic races and curses, which were scattered upon the earth.

The same tradition holds that Cain (Adam's son) too was cast from the Garden of Eden for sacrificing his brother, Abel, to the supreme god Yahweh (which *is* in The Bible). And after finding refuge in a cave, he sexually encountered Lilith, and thus according to some researchers, Cain is the father to some very grimy races of men.

Look:

Rosemary Ellen Guiley, states in her book 'Encyclopedia of Witches and Witchcraft'
"In addition to Jewish folklore, the Lilith demon appears in Iranian, **Babylonian**, Mexican, Greek, Arab, English, German, Oriental *and* **north American Indian legends.** She is sometimes associated with other characters in legend and myth, including the Queen of Sheba and Helen of Troy. In medieval Europe she was often portrayed as the wife, concubine or grandmother of Satan. In the late 17th Century she was described as a screech owl, blind by day, who sucked the breasts or navels of young children or the dugs of goats."

s.S.O.s.s.

You now know that the 'screech owl' Lilith dates back to Ancient Babylon, which makes her many thousands of years old!

s.s.O.s.s.

34. Acting Foolish Around San Francisco

Acting out a series of very creepy plays and high production devil-worship is a centerpiece of the Bohemian Grove, in which the participants—all men as in Shakespeare's days—take the stage with elaborate props. The men dress as women to accommodate the necessity of the opposite sex in their creep-sessions—google image 'play at Bohemian Grove,' and remember, these are ALL DUDES!

The Bohemian Grove is just 80 miles from San Francisco, which is quite convenient, since the wannabe thespians (at boys camp) are also known for frequent homosexual behavior while there. (The original church of satan was founded in San Francisco in 1966 by Anton Szandor Lavey, who also wrote the satanic bible.)

The Order of the Freemasons too have a long series of plays which are acted out by its initiates, who are all eager for great positions of influence, or power, in the name of The Order.

In the same creepy fashion, The Order of Skull & Bones practices the same acting out of dramatic scenarios. I cannot help but wonder if Paul Giamatti's talent wasn't recognized while acting-out a satanic ritual, as an onlooker to a creepy frat kid who masturbated in a coffin.

Acting out bizarre rituals, satanic scenarios, and performing chants, all seem to turn these ordinary people into carefree, psychopathic murderers. Relics of the dead are known to be used in the various magic tricks and offerings to the devil, just as the aforementioned societies did.

s.S.O.S.s.

The Jesuits and the Catholic Church use body parts in their creepy rituals too. If you know The Bible, even if you vaguely remember the scriptures from your youth, you should now realize these things to be of evil. For they are the same ancient practices which have turned all societies to dust and weathered stone.

In 2011, in the movie Ironclad, actor Paul Giamatti portrays the villainous King of England, John Lackland (to whom, as aforementioned, all of the US Presidents, but one, are related). Paul's ancestry too traces back to the same royal European blood, and he is *also* said to be related to Shakespeare, who himself wrote the play—King John—in reverence to the evil king.

Paul was born in New Haven Connecticut to *parents who were both Yale attendees. Paul was inducted into the Chapter 322 of Skull & Bones in his senior year. And, Paul himself graduated from the evil *Hogwarts* (Yale) in 1985.

> Note*: Paul's father was A. Bartlett Giamatti. And, yes…He was the same guy who punished Pete Rose so harshly for fixing a game which Rose had bet on (a big no-no). George W. Bush owned the Texas Rangers, and his S&B Uncle owned, and founded, the New York Mets. If that doesn't make you want to stop betting sports then nothing will.

Burning man festival began in San Francisco on Baker Beach with a 9 foot burning human effigy, who like the child who annually goes up in smoke in Bohemian grove, was sacrificed to Molech. With great demand for the event, the pagan festival was

s.S.O.S.s.

quickly moved to its current location on the playa in Nevada near *Pyramid* Lake.

And, finally, East India Company's slave-trader, dope-dealing Jolly Roger flag still infamously flies at the San Francisco City Hall under the notion that it is America's *first flag,* the *'Grand Union Flag.' If you visit Wikipedia, and enter 'Grand Union Flag,' Look at the first flag down on the left (you have to click on 'history' if you are viewing this book on a smaller device).*

Fun fact: After the earthquake of 1906, which nearly leveled the entire city of San Francisco, rampant fires killed many who survived the earthquake. One of these large fires was said to have been 'accidentally started' in a house on Hayes Street by a woman making breakfast for her family. This came to be known as the *'Ham and Eggs Fire.'* **Some fires were started when firefighters, who were 'untrained in the use of dynamite,' attempted to demolish buildings to create 'firebreaks.'**

Not surprisingly, the dynamited buildings themselves often caught fire, further stoking the ugly event.

35. *Bull*-B-Q

Below, is an outtake from a book titled *Libertas,* by, Charles Hatch Smith—printed in 1880:

The "Fourth of July" is the "Festival of Liberty," commemorated in the United States of America by the people assembling for prayer, praise and thanksgiving. The day is always ushered in by national salutes fired in every city, town, village, and, almost, hamlet.

Then also the spirit of 1776 is let off by "Young America" in fire works, the cost of which yearly would build, rig, arm and equip several national ships of war. On this day, wherever, throughout the earth, where there is an American citizen, there will be seen a celebration sui generis.

But the American did not institute the *Festival of Liberty.* The Eleutheria of the ancient Greeks was the first regularly appointed "Festival of Liberty." Even the mode of celebration is substantially copied by the American, Says Anthon. "By decree it was ordained that, 'Deputies' should be sent every fifth year from all the cities of Greece to celebrate it. The ceremonies began with a procession. At the instant of daybreak a 'Trumpeter' sounded the sig-

s.s.O.s.s.

nal of battle. The procession of 'Deputies' forming column, chariots bringing up the rear bearing myrrh, libations, and **a bull for sacrifice of the "Bull to Jupiter and Mercury."**

"At evening the chief officer of the city (equivalent to Mayor) where the Festival happened to be held, going to the place of 'Sepulture,' lured out the libation and drank to 'Those who lost their lives in defense of the liberties of Greece.'"

France didn't invent the festival either, for as mentioned in the prior citation, the American celebration of the Fourth of July (Independence Day) actually began in ancient Greece as Eleuthe'ria.

Below is an outtake from another old book, A dictionary of Greek and Roman Antiquities, John Murray, London, 1875:

Eleuthe'ria (ἐλευθέρια), the feast of liberty, a festival which the Greeks, after the battle of Plataeae (479 B.C.), instituted in honor of Zeus (the deliverer). It was intended not merely to be a token of their gratitude to the god to whom they believed themselves to be indebted for their victory over the barbarians, but also as a bond of union among themselves; for, in an assembly of all the Greeks, Aristides carried a decree that delegates (πρόβουλοι καὶ θεωροί) from all the Greek states should assemble every year at Plataeae for the celebration of the

s.S.O.S.s.

Eleutheria. The town itself was at the same time declared sacred and inviolable (never to be broken or dishonored), **as long as its citizens offered the annual sacrifices which were then instituted on behalf of Greece. (Bohemian Grove's annual sacrificial event comes to mind here.)**

On the internet I found that familiar old Whore, 'Lady Liberty,' seated in the hooker tent at the, *Fete de la Raison*. The banner over the door reads, **To the Love of Knowledge.**

Another source, *A Dictionary of Greek and Roman Antizuities*, by John Murran, London, 1875, also dates the festival back to the time of the Ancient Greeks:

> When the procession came to the place where the Greeks, who had fallen at Plataeae, were buried, the archon first washed and anointed the tombstones, and then led the bull to a pyre and sacrificed it, praying to Zeus (the most powerful of satan's principalities) and Hermes Chthonios, and inviting the brave (but dead) men who had fallen in the defence of their country, to take part in the banquet prepared for them.

So, in essence these men were doing the same thing as every other group we have studied thus far, *worshipping and making sacrifices to their dead and King Nimrod...*

s.s.O.s.s.

Zeus is King Nimrod of the Greek Mythology. In Britannia, Nimrod is referred to as Esus. 'Zeus' and 'Esus' always *demand* bloody human sacrifices.

In Egypt the old serpent appeared everywhere, even on Pharaoh's crown, where he was known by the name Amun-Ra—Amun-Ra, in Egypt, is the equivalent of Zeus in Greece. In India Shiva is the equivalent of the Greek Zeus, but they are all just subjective names for *Nimrod.*

Our celebration of Independence Day (the Fourth of July) corresponds with the European Summer Solstice celebration 'Old Summer's Eve'—this brings new meaning to the word *'douche.'* Remember, the Summer Solstice is the day on which a mass human sacrifice to Molech occurs around the world?

36. *Whoring* Around

New York's statue of liberty is also a pagan god who represents one's freedom to worship satan. *Lux* Libertas (lux being another name for light, **enlightenment**, or, lucifer) was the name of an ancient goddess who was adopted by the Romans, perhaps as early as the 5th century BC, and certainly by the 4th Century BC. She was referred to as the goddess of personal freedom and liberty.

Libertas was the goddess of freedom because she promoted the ideals for the personal freedom to do anything that felt good. **Libertas was the matron goddess of prostitution** because she promoted sexual freedom; in fact, *she had invented the concept.* Slaves considered her their goddess in the hopes of winning their freedom.

Hebrew myths state that Lilith (the owl god worshipped in Bohemian Grove, California, by the world's elite) was cast out of the Garden of Eden for a variety of reasons—prostitution was among them—Lilith is mentioned in more detail in the ancient Book of Enoch, a book which never enjoyed its coveted place in The Bible (for obvious reasons). Lilith has origins within the Kabbalah, the Talmud, and The Bible. Out of all of the forms taken, Lilith (the Statue of 'Liberty') undoubtedly makes her initial appearance as the Sumerian goddess of dark winds, Lil, and the **Babylonian** demoness Lilitu, or *'Lilith.'*

The Lilitu was a handmaiden to the savior goddess Inana, known to stand at the gateway of Inana's temple and invite worshipers to enter the inner sanctum for blessings and *sexual de-*

s.s.O.s.s.

lights. (Temple prostitution was commonplace in ancient Mesopotamia, Egypt, to the Hindus, and to Ancient Babylon.)

Note: My notes are not an attempt to change the book of Revelation. They are merely representative of an interesting take on the scriptures. Please read and verify your beliefs for yourself.

Revelation 17:1-5 King James Version
Babylon, the Prostitute on the Beast—
17 And there came one of the seven angels which had the seven vials, and talked with me, saying unto me, Come hither; I will shew unto thee the judgment of the great whore **(statue of liberty)** that sitteth upon many waters **(Manhattan—Hudson River/East River/Atlantic, all converge)**:
2 With whom the kings of the earth have committed fornication **(cash in trade for slave labor of other countries' people, for wares which are destined for the US, and for allowing for the sacrifice of their people to satan using war, and other means)**, and the inhabitants of the earth have been made drunk with the wine of her fornication **(Wall Street)**.
3 So he carried me away in the spirit into the wilderness: and I saw a woman sit upon a scarlet coloured beast **(Britain)**, full of *names of blasphemy, having seven heads **(countries of the land of Gog and Magog)**, and ten horns **(Google image**

s.S.O.S.s.

'The Queen's Beasts'—there are *10* of them—notice the 'Yale' on the far right and the red dragon of revelation which stands next to the Yale).

4 And the **woman was arrayed in purple and scarlet colour, and decked with gold and precious stones and pearls **(her hatband lights up at night)**, having a golden cup **(gold plated torch)** in her hand full of abominations and filthiness of her fornication **(goes without saying)**: 5 And upon her forehead was a name written:

MYSTERY BABYLON THE GREAT
THE MOTHER Of HARLOTS
AND
ABOMINATIONS OF THE EARTH.

Note*: If you google image the State Flag of New York, there are renditions in which the old whore is pictured on the left dressed in the purple and scarlet which John had described in the book of Revelation. The shield features a pyramid shaped mountain which is being *'enlightened.'*

Note**: 'Blasphemous names' will be described in the next section, titled, *Blasphemous Names of Revelation*.

The seal of the state of New York has two supporters:

S.S.O.S.S.

- Left: Liberty with the Revolutionary imagery of a Phrygian cap raised on a pole. (A google image search will reveal examples of New York's State Seal in which 'Lady Liberty' is dressed up in purple and scarlet just as the Book of Revelation describes.)
- Right: Justice, wearing a blindfold (representing 'impartiality') and **holding *scales** (which represent 'fairness') and a sword.

Revelation 6:5-6 King James Version
5 And when he had opened the third seal, I heard the third beast say, come and see. And I beheld, and lo a **black horse**; and he that sat on him **had a pair of *balances in his hand. (The Roman form of satan named, Justitia, is an evolution of the same deity in Ancient Egypt named,** *Isis—Isis also was depicted holding scales and is said to have represented FAMINE!)*
6 Then I heard what sounded like a voice among the four living creatures, saying, **"A quart of wheat for a day's wages, and three quarts of barley for a day's wages, and do not damage the oil and the wine!"**

Note: New York State Flag—A banner below the shield shows the motto *Excelsior*, a Latin word translated as *"Ever Upward."*

s.s.O.s.s.

Remember the story of the Tower of Babel which began this journey, where God destroyed the high tower, and His people were first scattered to the ends of earth? They too were worshipping the evil one, and were building their brick tower '**Ever Upward!**' **If you have ever been to New York City and looked *up*, it is not hard to imagine that New York City would be described as *Excelsior*, or, *'Ever Upward.'*** Many consider the tower of Babel to be a metaphor for great technology—I think New York has both the, 'ever upward,' and, the 'high technology,' bases covered. Here is the Biblical account again:

Genesis 11:4 King James Version
4 And they said, Go to, let us build us a city and a tower, whose top may reach unto heaven; and let us make us a name, lest we be scattered abroad upon the face of the whole earth.

Below is one of the prophecies in the book of Revelation, in which 'Mystery Babylon the Great' is destroyed, then destroyed completely, once and for all:

Revelation 18:1-21 King James Version
18 And after these things I saw another angel come down from heaven, having great power; and the earth was lightened with his glory.
2 And he cried mightily with a strong voice, saying, **Babylon the great is fallen, is fallen,** and is **become the habitation of devils (google 'Hindu devils New York')**, and the hold of every foul spirit

s.s.O.s.s. (The Tomb at Skull and Bones), and a cage of every unclean and hateful bird (Lilith the Owl).
3 For all nations have drunk of the wine of the wrath of her fornication, and the kings of the earth have committed fornication with her, and the merchants of the earth are waxed rich through the abundance of her delicacies.
4 And I heard another voice from heaven, saying, **Come out of her, my people, that ye be not partakers of her sins, and that ye receive not of her plagues.**
5 **For her sins have reached unto heaven** ('excelsior'—'ever upward'), **and God hath remembered her iniquities.**
6 **Reward her even as she rewarded you, and double unto her double according to her works: in the cup which she hath filled fill to her double** (there is a double portion of *fire* in the Statue of Liberty's 'cup').
7 How much she hath glorified herself, and lived deliciously, so much torment and sorrow give her: for she saith in her heart, I sit a queen, and am no widow, and shall see no sorrow.
8 **Therefore shall her plagues come in one day, death,** and **mourning,** and famine; and **she shall be utterly burned with fire** (WTC *Towers* exploding into flames): for **strong is the Lord God who judgeth her.**

s.S.O.S.s.

9 And the kings of the earth, who have committed fornication and lived deliciously with her, shall bewail her, and lament for her, **when they shall see the smoke of her burning**,

10 Standing afar off for the fear of her torment, saying, Alas, alas that great city Babylon, that mighty city! for in one hour is thy judgment come. **(The first WTC *Tower* was first struck by an *American* Airlines airliner at 8:46 am, it became a raging inferno, and had fallen completely flat by 9:59 am.)**

11 And the merchants of the earth shall weep and mourn over her; for no man buyeth their merchandise any more **(New York's Port Authority had closed New York's waters to trade, and the skies were void of aircraft)**:

12 The merchandise of gold, and silver, and precious stones, and of pearls, and fine linen, and purple, and silk, and scarlet, and all thyine wood, and all manner vessels of ivory, and all manner vessels of most precious wood, and of brass, and iron, and marble (if you've ever been on 5th Avenue, you understand this one),

13 And cinnamon, and odours, and ointments, and frankincense, and wine, and oil, and fine flour, and wheat, and beasts, and sheep, and horses, and chariots (international shipping industry—the buildings that The Order knocked down were called the, '*World Trade Center*'—and

s.s.O.s.s.

they were replaced by the tallest pyramid in the world), and slaves (slave ships holding 10 million slaves sold in America), and souls of men (Skull & Bones - Genesis Chapter 3:22 - stealing souls of men).

14 And the fruits that thy soul lusted after are departed from thee, and all things which were dainty and goodly are departed from thee, and thou shalt find them no more at all (**New York's Port Authority had closed New York's waters to trade**).

15 The merchants of these things, which were made rich by her, shall stand afar off for the fear of her torment, weeping and wailing,

16 And saying, Alas, alas that great city, **that was clothed in fine linen, and purple, and scarlet**, and decked with gold, and precious stones, and pearls!

17 For in one hour so great riches is come to nought. **And every shipmaster, and all the company in ships, and sailors, and as many as trade by sea, stood afar off** (while the Towers smoked, the merchant ships watched in great bunches from the bay),

18 And cried when they saw the smoke of her burning, saying, What city is like unto this great city!

19 And they cast dust on their heads (google image '9/11 dusty people'), **and cried, weeping and wailing**, saying, Alas, alas that great city, wherein were made rich all that had ships in the sea by rea-

s.S.O.s.s.

son of her costliness! **For in one hour is she made** *desolate* **(google image 'ground zero aftermath').** **20** Rejoice over her, thou heaven, and ye holy apostles and prophets; for God hath avenged you on her. **21 And a mighty angel took up a stone like a great millstone, and cast it into the sea, saying, Thus with violence shall that great city Babylon be thrown down, and shall be found no more at all.** (This one hasn't yet occurred, but reminds me of the movie *Armageddon*)

Remember Gog and Magog? The Skull and Bones nicknames? Following the events of 9/11, President George W. Bush made a prophetic phone call to the President of France, Jacques Chirac. After the call, Chirac wanted to know what the hell President Bush had been going-on about in their last conversation. **Bush had reportedly commented that, when he'd looked at the Middle East he saw 'Gog and Magog at work,' and had remarked, the 'Biblical prophecies are unfolding.'**

But who were Gog and Magog? Neither Chirac nor his office had any idea. They knew that Bush proclaimed to be an *'evangelical Christian,'* so they asked the French Federation of Protestants, who in turn asked Professor Römer. Below is who Chirac discovered *Gog* and *Magog* to be, as described by John, from the book of Revelation:

Revelation 20:7-15 King James Version
7 And when the thousand years are expired, Satan shall be loosed out of his prison,

s.s.O.s.s.

8 And shall go out to deceive the nations which are in the four quarters of the earth (Jesuits use same verbiage in their 'oath' - obvious identification with this evil force), Gog, and Magog, to gather them together to battle: the number of whom is as the sand of the sea.

9 And they went up on the breadth of the earth, and compassed the camp of the saints about, and the beloved city (: and fire came down from God out of heaven, and devoured them.

10 And the devil that deceived them was cast into the lake of fire and brimstone, where the beast and the false prophet are, and shall be tormented day and night for ever and ever.

11 And I saw a great white throne, and him that sat on it, from whose face the earth and the heaven fled away; and there was found no place for them.

12 And I saw the dead, small and great, stand before God; and the books were opened: and another book was opened, which is the book of life: and the dead were judged out of those things which were written in the books, according to their works.

13 And the sea gave up the dead which were in it; and death and hell delivered up the dead which were in them: and they were judged every man according to their works.

14 And death and hell were cast into the lake of fire. This is the second death.

s.S.O.S.s.

15 And whosoever was not found written in the book of life was cast into the lake of fire.

If you will recall President Bush **(S&B 1968)** was sitting in a classroom as the second plane struck. The book George was reading was titled, The Pet *Goat. Below is a prophecy listed in the Book of Daniel, which most-likely gave The Order their love for the Goat as an analog for satan:

Daniel 8:5-7 King James Version
5 And as I was considering, behold, an he *goat came from the west on the face of the whole earth, and touched not the ground: and the goat had a notable horn between his eyes.
6 And he came to the ram that had two horns, which I had seen standing before the river, and ran unto him in the fury of his power.
7 And I saw him come close unto the ram, and he was moved with choler against him, and smote the ram, and brake his two horns: and there was no power in the ram to stand before him, but he cast him down to the ground, and stamped upon him: and there was none that could deliver the ram out of his hand.

Skipped verse 7…

8 Therefore the he goat waxed very great: and when he was strong, the great horn was broken;

S.S.O.S.S.

and for it came up four notable ones toward the four winds of heaven.

9 And out of one of them came forth a **little horn, which waxed exceeding great, toward the south, and toward the east, and toward the pleasant land.

10 And it waxed great, even to the host of heaven; and it cast down some of the host and of the stars to the ground, and stamped upon them.

Note**: Definition for 'Yale' as per mythcreatures.co.uk:

Yale is a four legged beast from Ethiopia and India its colour is a tawny brown or black. It is about the size of a horse; it looks much like a deer but has the lower jaws of a boar with its tusks. The Yale has movable horns that it can control.

The Yale can move a single horn forward to use as in a lance like fashion, the other horn moves out of the way to protect it. If one horn is damaged in a fight it moves the other horn in to place to resume the attack.

The Yale is one of 'The Queens beasts,' and is featured on the arms of *'Christ's'* college, Cambridge University.

s.S.O.S.s.

The world's most recognized symbol of so-called 'freedom,' and, 'The American dream,' was built and donated to the US by freemasons. The *Statue of 'Liberty'* was originally intended for Egypt, which ultimately rejected it for being 'too old fashioned.' For the original unveiling of the Statue of Liberty, the poster which hyped the event is touted to be 'Enlightening the World.'

Lady Liberty was originally named, *'Liberty **Enlightening** the World.'*

Fun fact: On the night of Hillary Clinton's first Presidential debate (for this election, anyway), she announced herself with a **scarlet** pantsuit. For the final night of the election, the disappointed Clinton's wore **purple. Revelation 17:4**

s.s.O.s.s.

37. Blasphemous Names of Revelation

Revelation 17:3 King James Version
3 So he carried me away in the spirit into the wilderness: and I saw a woman sit upon a scarlet coloured beast, full of *names of blasphemy, having seven heads, and ten horns.

I am inclined to believe that, with the fall of each great civilization, as they came to the end of their dialectic cycles which caused their destruction, the names of their god and his many forms also had to change. Now much to our chagrin the many names and forms of satan have been plastered upon our money, his statues erected in our town squares, and his many forms are taught in our schools under the ruse of 'Greek' and 'Roman Mythology,' but not a word can be uttered of Christ.

All of satan's alternative forms which he has taken through the ages are literally EVERYWHERE…and every single Christian in the world is running around asking: 'What will be the signs of the coming of the beast?'

Since the nature of the beast specializes in incorporating entire industries within a few manipulative factions, which have tricked us into buying a T-shirt for 100 times more than what one might cost in a third world country, it is logical to think that corporate logos are *a* mark of the beast.

The original definition for the word *logos* according to the online etymology dictionary:

s.s.O.s.s.

logos (n.)
1580s, *Logos*, **"the divine Word, second person of the Christian Trinity,"** (the son of God is the second person in the Christian Trinity—Jesus Christ) from Greek *logos* "word, speech, discourse," also "reason," from PIE root **leg-* (1) **"to collect"** (with derivatives meaning "to speak," on notion of "to pick out words;" see *lecture* (n.); used by Neo-Platonists in various metaphysical and theological senses and picked up by New Testament writers.

Other English formations from *logos* include *logolatry* **"worship of words, unreasonable regard for words or verbal truth"** (1810 in Coleridge); *logomania* (1870); *logophobia* (1923)

The word logo means Christ—this is one of the most blasphemous marks that a person could take, and we pay extra for the feces stain upon our shirt.

Homework assignment: Google image search 'corporate logo 666' and see what appears. Motel 6 is a good example for this—the single six in the center of their logo is represented by three different colors (including the blue background)—red white and blue—representing a total of three sixes.

Among the easy ones to spot while you are in your daily activity, the pyramid, which is everywhere *(Doritos)*. And, the 666 is hidden within many corporate designs. They are also *EVERY-*

s.S.O.S.s.

WHERE! Many are such obvious symbolism of the occult that there is no cryptology involved, and this will only become more overt.

Revelation 13:18 King James Version
18 Here is wisdom. Let him that hath understanding count the number of the beast: for it is the number of a man; and his number is Six hundred threescore and six (666).

Until then, most people will race to the store to buy the overpriced 'golf shirt' having a different color horseman—Jesus (logo)—embroidered upon it.

Again, I am sure that the final beast will mock the exact mechanism which Paul wrote about in the Book of Revelation but, until then, we must be with eyes-open. For the works of The Order are clever.

A quote:

The Satanic Bible
"The real satanist is not quite so easily recognized as such"
Anton Szandor LaVey—

38. *Conquering* the Papacy

William *the Conquerer* was an illegitimate love child of Robert I Duke of Normandy. Will's father, who was also known as *'Robert the Magnificent,'* died in 1035 riding back from one of the Russell House, pre-crusade Templar recon missions, leaving Will his descriptive handle (a Russell custom which predates the Vikings)—as, 'William *the Bastard.'*

As you can likely imagine from this power hungry clan, Willy would have had his hands *full* while clutching to his Dukedom with whitened-knuckles.

Violence plagued the Duke's early reign as the feudal barons jockeyed for control in his powerful father's absence. Several of the child's guards were murdered during the period of civil unrest. Willy's teacher was even killed during the clashes, which was made quite evident, since William the Conquerer was illiterate and spoke no English. Interestingly, many still argue that the ruler contributed more to the English language than any other man before or after his terrible reign. By his teens little Willy had solid control of his Duchy.

Though scarcely spoken of in this work (due to the extensive, unquestionable history which is readily available on the topic), it is noteworthy that William the Conquerer *conquered* Britain in the Norman invasion. But, by doing so, the power hungry king left a trail of blood and tears in his wake which, as you are now quite aware, is a signature of the Russell family.

If you will remember, with the exception of *Scotland,* the countries for which William *'The Ranger'* Russell claimed the

S.S.O.S.s.

Louisiana Territory on his Knights of the Golden Horseshoe expedition, were, **Great Britain, France,** and **Ireland.**

The 'Stone of Scone,' followed William the Conquerer's family trail of victories and tears through said countries also, and the stone was finally used for the purpose of crowning *England's* Kings.

The Encyclopedia of Freemasonry also gives Freemasons the credit for bringing the Stone of Scone from the Holy Lands....However, before offering to you the profound story, I must admit that there was a long pontification disclaiming the story as allegorical. Though I highly doubt that these clowns sit around their temple of solomon discussing fables and myths.

Enjoy:

> Another legend informs us that from Adam the Stone of Foundation descended to Seth. From Seth it passed by regular succession to Noah, who took it with him into the ark, and after the subsidence of the deluge made on it his first thank-offering. Noah left it on Mount Ararat, where it was subsequently **found by Abraham, who removed it, and constantly used it as an altar of sacrifice.** His grandson Jacob took it with him when he fled to his uncle Laban in Mesopotamia, and used it as a pillow when, in the vicinity of Luz, who had his celebrated vision (Jacob's Ladder).

s.S.O.S.s.

Here there is a sudden interruption in the legendary history of the stone, and we have no means of conjecturing how it passed from the possession of Jacob into that of Solomon. Moses, it is true, is said to have taken it with him out of Egypt at the time of the Exodus, and thus it may have finally reached Jerusalem. Dr. Adam Clarke repeats, what he very properly calls "a foolish tradition," that the stone on which Jacob rested his head was afterward brought to Jerusalem, thence carried after a long lapse of time to Spain, from Spain to Ireland, and from Ireland to Scotland, where it was used as a seat on which the Kings of Scotland sat to be crowned. Edward I., we know, brought a stone to which this legend is attached from Scotland to Westminster Abbey, where under the name Jacob's pillow, it still remains, and is always placed under the chair upon which the British sovereign sits to be crowned; because **there is an old distich which declares that wherever this stone is found the Scottish Kings shall reign.**

There was a large stone beneath the throne on which the Kings of England were crowned, until 1950. This was the date on which the *Stone of Scone* was stolen by a group of Scottish students who wished to replace the stone in their home country, where it had been immediately prior to the Norman Invasion led by William the Conqueror (another member of the Russell crew).

s.S.O.S.s.

In 1996 the stone was returned to Britain from Scotland (though having had been broken into two pieces), at which time the stone was set alongside the crown jewels in Edinburgh Castle for safe keeping.

Willy's conquest of Britain, won through the Battle of Hastings, was key to the establishment of the axis around which evil now rotates. Willy's ancestors clutched onto power, in every country, along the fateful route of the Stone of Scone.

On the apocalyptic Christmas Day of 1066, Willy crowned himself King of England. The dynasty of Dan had begun. The Order had closed a breadth of conquest, up and around the Mediterranean, finally settling in and around the waters' of the United Kingdom—we will refer to this land as *Magog:

> **Revelation 20:7-9** King James Version
> **7 And when the thousand years are expired**, Satan shall be loosed out of his prison,
> **8** And shall go out to deceive the nations which are in the four quarters of the earth, **Gog, and *Magog**, to gather them together to battle: the number of whom is as the sand of the sea.
> **9** And they went up on the breadth of the earth, and **compassed the camp of the saints about, and the beloved city (The Russells migrated around the Scandinavian countries, and settled in France and Britain, before shape-shifting into the 'Knight's Templar' and traveling back down to *re*-conquering Israel during the Crusades)**: and

s.s.O.s.s.

fire came down from God out of heaven, and devoured them.

*In 999 Pope Sylvester II (Gerbert of Aurillac) became the first French Pope on April 2, **and the last pope of the first millennium of Jesus Christ.** This is the guy ('Pope') mentioned in our previous brush with the Nine Unknown Men mentioned in Lavey's satanic bible?

As with all of The Order's shade-casting goons there are swirls of legend surrounding this evil Pope. But what is for certain is that, 'Sylvester' practiced sorcery and was heavily involved in the dark arts. Remember, Gerbert was supposed to have built a brazen head which was 'robotic,' and which would answer his questions with 'yes' or 'no' answers.

Gerbert was also reputed to have had a pact with a female demon named *Meridiana, who warned him harshly to NEVER visit the Holy Land of Jerusalem. The Pope gave Meridiana, who is simply another name for the same 'Lilith demon,' full credit for his rise to popedom.*

Word has it that Gerbert was also in possession of a book of spells stolen from an Arabic philosopher in Spain.

In 1001 the Romans revolted against the government, forcing Otto III ('Holy' Roman Emperor at the time) and Sylvester II to flee to northern Italy. Otto III led a pair of unsuccessful sieges to try and regain control of the city, but died on a third try in 1002. Sylvester II returned to Rome soon after the Emperor's death, never to regain power, and perished shortly after—his death is clouded by deceit in the form of 'legend,' so we will leave that to personal research.

s.s.O.s.s.

Seven Roman popes followed Sylvester's defrocking and his physical removal from the Catholic throne. After which, another Sylvester, *Sylvester III* took office under a haze of corruption, which left him too to be known as an 'antipope.' Hmm...By the Catholic's own confused philosophy, which mistakenly recognizes the Pope as Christ, the word anti-Pope can certainly be translated to mean 'antichrist.' This means that the Catholic Church, over the years, have themselves referred to the throne of their own kingdom to be both the office of the Christ *and the Antichrist.*

Another amazing ten popes later (a total of 17 popes into the first millennium), Pope Alexander II took office; this Pope is who authorized the Norman invasion of England, in which the very first Willy Russell of the clan, *William the Conquerer*, completed The Order's beastly dominion of the UK. The Pope always made the final decision when it came to the path of conquest around the globe, until fairly recently (in historic terms). In other words, the Pope overtly ruled the world with a tight fist, then, as he does covertly now.

The next 'antipope' of interest to this story would be Pope Urban II, *the second French Pope.* Let us not forget William the Conquerer's affiliation withFrance.

This second French Pope would sound the trumpet which kicked-off the First Crusade (the Crusade which initiated the siege on Jerusalem).

I will not speculate on the timeline, the mechanism, or the order of the events which were written about in Revelation. In fact, it should be known that this is a study of history, which *led* me to a Bible Study, and that my added commentary (as it pertains to the scriptures) is a result of my own research. Every individual is responsible for fact-checking their own beliefs against the 1611 King James Version of the scriptures. But, again, I really don't view any of the minute details surrounding these events as being all that necessary to the narrative.

We've discussed the significance of Gog and Magog (the demonic persona whom Bush Senior summoned and became possessed with during his frat boy ritual at Yale). And now I would like to identify one last point of interest. As every Christian looks to their right and to their left for Gog and Magog, two giants named *Gog and Magog* are the 'patron saints' or 'protectors' of the City of *London* (google search 'Gog and Magog London Patron Saints').

Every year (on the second Saturday in November) the two evil-looking fellows who are featured in this article (http://hisheavenlyarmies.com/gog-and-magog-are-the-protectors-of-the-city-of-london/) are paraded through the streets of the City of London. Notice that, 'Magog' has a phoenix ('rising-up' from 'the ashes') on his shield. This indicates that these Nimrods believe that they will *win* the final battle of Armageddon described in Revelation, and that, *they* (and not the good guys) will found the 'New Jerusalem.'

As I finish this account the GOP Republican Convention is unfolding on TV. Below is the still frame on which the so-called 'news' network exited to commercial break. Notice that the premiere seating on the floor of the colossal event is arranged in the design of the *British Union Jack Flag*.

The entire United States was saluting the flag of Britain for our Presidential Election, in the Year of our Lord 2016:

s.S.O.S.

MELANIA TRUMP DELIVERS KEYNOTE SPEECH
FOX NEWS ALERT

In the wake of 'Brexit' (Britain leaving the European Union) this is particularly disturbing. Voting for Brexit officially began on Thursday, June 18, the night of the *Blood red Moon,* which marks the night of satan's mass human offering—*the Summer Solstice.*

Revelation 6:12 King James Version
12 And I beheld when he had opened the sixth seal, and, lo, there was a great earthquake; and the sun became black as sackcloth of hair, and **the moon became as blood**; **13** And the stars of heaven fell unto the earth, even as a fig tree casteth her untimely figs, when she is shaken of a mighty wind. (This is why that particular date was chosen.)

William the **'*Conquerer*'s'** descendants have been very successful in ruling the world. And, in an unbroken chain, every English monarch who followed William, including Queen Elizabeth II, descended from the king. The same can be said for the Presidents of the United States of America. Every single president, including the George Bushes **and Barak Obama**, are *all* descendants of William the Conquerer.

America's *'Birther Movement'* was a group who demanded to see Obama's birth certificate, in a failed attempt to remove him from office, based on the premise that Barack *wasn't* born in the US—a requirement for a Presidential Candidate. Barack tiptoes around the topic with reluctance.

But Barack's reluctance is not due to his birthplace; now we both know that it is his *royal blood* which he truly intends to hide.

39. Bohemian Trap City

The Order's greatest roadblock to world domination was the necessity for control over the artery of ancient commerce, which connected Europe to the East. Located at the crossing of north-south and east-west trade routes, the *Silk Road* would be a major prize for The Order.

Spices, silk, opium, and all other valued rarities coming from the Middle East and China had only this route to the West at the time. But especially close to the hearts of the House of Russell was the pursuit to retake the epicenter of their homeland, *Jerusalem*.

In the book *Memoirs of the House of Russell,* the Russell family proudly takes responsibility for the waste which was lain to the poor unfortunate pilgrims (and inhabitants) of the cities along this route during the 'Pope-ordered' Crusades of the middle ages.

But before the The Order could reclaim the city of Jerusalem, they would first have the opportunity to lay claim to Antioch, which was the gateway to the Silk Road. These military clashes along the Silk Road were the forerunner to the Opium Wars which took place *following* the discovery of the water shortcut to the East Indies. The discovery of this small water passage allowed vast resources, *belonging to the people along these routes*, to be plundered and shipped back to Europe.

The Crusades were a call to arms by the Pope, to supposedly 'protect' pilgrims along this route. But if that indeed was the Pope's intention there would have been no need for conquest along

s.s.O.s.s.

the way to the Holy Land, by The Order. But that isn't even close to what had happened.

Listen to the boisterous whispers from the past, in the documentation of the first Knight's Templar, from the *Russells'* proud family book:

> The declaration of the this 'Holy War' (the quotations added to the words "Holy War" suggest that The Author himself knew this war to be motivated by greedy factors) at the council of Clermont in November 1095, operated, as is well known, upon the youth of Western Europe **like the sound of an inspiring trumpet.** The two brothers, ***Hugh and Roger** embraced the cause with ardor (passion), and hastened to receive upon their habits the consecrated cross (Templar Cross). Upon the deeds which the former may have wrought in this romantic enterprise, **the page of history is altogether silent. But his brother was more fortunate; and the monkish writers, who were eye-witnesses of his exploits, are eloquent in their praises of the Lord of Barneville. To aid, perhaps, in furnishing his A.D. 1096 array for the voyage, he made over to the church, like many others, for a trifling valuation, a portion of his patrimonial inheritance, selling to the abbot of St. Stephen's, with the consent of his son Robert and the Duke of Normandy, the lordship of his fief at Rosel for the sum of 15/. 1.

s.s.O.s.s.

Joining then, with his brother Hugh, with his two sons, Robert and William, and a vast number of other knights from Normandy, Bretagne, and England, the banner of Duke Robert (William the Conquerer's Father), he set forward in the month of September 2 for Palestine, by the route of Rome and Durezzo, which, wintering in Apulia, they did not reach till the April of 1097. [Historical Memoirs of the House of Russell: From the Times of the ..., Volume 1, By Jeremiah Holmes Wiffen, Pages 31-32]

Note*: The person whom Wiffen hints to as 'the latter' *(Roger de Barneville)* ended up wearing his head upon a stick during The Order's successful siege at Antioch. And **Hugh** went on to become wildly infamous by committing horrific acts which, like other Russells, had banished him from their cherished bromantic memoirs.

Roger was then deified by The Order's monks of Tyre, who followed the Russell family around so not to lose their proud connection to their conquerings of the Holy Land.

Note**: So, what was the reason that, **'the page of history went silent'** for this *Hugh* guy?

Well, *Brace yourself*....Hugh, went on to be Hugh de Payens, or *Payns (in English)* (c. 1070 – 24 May 1136), and with Saint Bernard of Clairvaux, Hugh went on to co-found, and became *first Grand Master* of, **the Knights Templar.**

s.S.O.S.s.

Hugh the Pagan is also credited with the creation of the ***Latin Rule,*** the code of behavior for The Order.

Among the Templar rules of engagement called the *Latin Rule* (written by Hugh himself) is rule #56:

'**Rule #56**—It is the truth that you especially are charged with the duty of giving your souls for your brothers, as did Jesus Christ, and of **defending the land from the unbelieving** *pagans* who are **the enemies of the son of the Virgin Mary.**'

My point here is….Hugh, who wrote these rules of engagement for the Templar, himself, was supposedly only *known* as **Hugh the** *'Pagan,' and, 'pagans', were the very people from whom Hugh was now pledged to 'protect' Jerusalem.*

Below is what wiki has to say about the first Grand Master of the Knights Templar:

No early biography of Hugues de Payens exists, nor do later writers cite such a biography. None of the sources on his later career give details of his early life. Information is therefore scanty and uncertain; embellishments depend partly on documents that may not refer to the same individual, partly on histories written decades or even centuries after his death.

The Order did a relatively good job of hiding Hugh's *true* identity, except for several undeniable facts….

s.s.O.s.s.

—**First**, obviously, is the name *Hugh,* which, as far as my research goes, was exclusive to this family at the time—*the Russells invented the name just decades earlier.*

—**Secondly**, the accounts for the Hugh in question *do* tell from where he came—*Troyes France*—it's only miles from the House of Russell's French fiefs; these residents were *all* royal Russell family members *in one way or the other.*

—**Thirdly**, this group of *'Croises'* were all well-documented members of the *missing Hugh's* family.

—**Fourthly**, the departing Hugh in question left for the Crusades *with* the group, and the arriving Hugh turned up randomly with the group, during *THE SAME EXACT TIMES!*

According to the Russell Memoirs, the group of *to be* Templars sieged, and took possession of, the Capital of Bithynia on June 20, 1097.

And, nine days after the capture of *Nice*, they pursued their march to Antioch.

Several damaging clashes with the 'Turks and Arabs' were at the cost of the life of Robert Count of Paris, along with *many* of the 'Norman Knights' of the House of Russell.

The bloody victory produced a wealth of provision, armor, gold, silver, horses, and camels:

s.s.O.s.s.

The victors, after chanting hymns of devout thanksgiving for their triumph, and devoting three days to the funeral obsequies of their slain friends, recommenced the march toward Antioch. [Historical Memoirs of the House of Russell: From the Times of the ..., Volume 1, By Jeremiah Holmes Wiffen, Page 36]

It would be another grueling 500 mile march to Antioch, from where the group had clashed with the 'muslims.' (This stretch toward Antioch had already been lain waste by the Sultan.) In order to reach Antioch The Order suffered another long bloody conflict while crossing the bridge of nine arches, which spanned the Phar Phar (the River Orontes).

An iron gate covered with metal plates guarded passage over the bridge. Under the command of Barneville and Pusey, the knights found the gate guarded and another long bloody conflict ensued. The group overtook the bridge, continuing toward Antioch, and on November 11 the group reached the city.

'Bohemond' (another Russell who is highly celebrated in the Russell Memoirs), *persuaded* an insider, within the city of Antioch, to open the gates *(The Order seems to have had comrades hiding within the walls of the city of Antioch)*. The Templar filled the city immediately, butchering thousands of soldiers and civilians. Bohemond was given kingship of Antioch as a reward for his cunning.

Antioch was established in 300 B.C. by Seleucus I, king of Syria—the City was named for his father Antiochus, a Macedonian general. The city soon became a great commercial and cultural center, waxing the city wildly rich, making it something like Las Vegas is today.

s.S.O.S.s.

As implied, Antioch was an important win in the name of international trade which would turn to the world's waters several centuries later, eventually leading to the enslaving and famine in India, which ultimately led to the founding of the United States. During the middle ages, after the East Indies waterways were discovered and maintained by East India Company, Antioch no longer held its economical value as a trade center and began to lose its citizens.

Radulph of Caen wrote this account of the Russell's siege on Antioch:

'In Ma'arrat our troops boiled pagan adults in cooking pots; they impaled children on spits and devoured them grilled.'

Fulcher of Chartres, wrote:

I shudder to tell that many of our people, harassed by the madness of excessive hunger, cut pieces from the buttocks of the Saracens already dead there, which they cooked, but when it was not yet roasted enough by the fire, they devoured it with savage mouth.

Below is an outtake from a book titled, *The Collected Works of Sir Francis Palgrave, K.H.*—it is from this work that we can draw solid insight as to the source of the veneration which the Bohemian Grove creeps hold for *Bohemond*—veneration enough

s.s.O.s.s.

to revive Bohemond *Russell's* name in honor of a horrific place which they now find so sacred.

Listen:

> The vast extent of the fortifications, and the want of discipline amongst the Crusaders, rendered an assault impracticable. Bohemond's energies were roused, and here did he display the inexorable cruelty as well as the extreme fraudulence of his character. It was in the camp before Antioch that Bohemond gave the hideous banquets of human flesh, repeated again and again in the course of this war, and excused with faint disapprobation by those who admired, if they did not share, the cannibalism. Most intent upon winning Antioch, Bohemond had fixed his heart on establishing himself in this part of **Syria**, far more important for the prosecution of his designs against Byzantium than Jerusalem: and **he succeeded through a secret league concluded with Phirous the Renegade.**

And to finish this section, the 'secret league' is uncovered. And, just as you and I had suspected, the dreaded Bohemond *did* have a secret alliance which would lead to The Order's brutal signature slaughter of the men women and children of this ancient city.

The History of the Crusades (Complete), By Joseph Francois Michaud Look:

s.S.O.S.s.

To lull the garrison of Antioch in the greatest security, it was agreed that the Christian army should quit the camp, and direct its march at first towards the route by which the prince of Mossoul was expected to arrive, and that at night-fall it should meet under the walls of Ascalon. On the following day, early in the morning, the troops received orders to prepare for their departure. At some hours before night the Crusaders issued from their camp, and marched away, **trumpets sounding and standards flying (Rev 8:7).** After a march of a short distance, they retraced their steps, and returned in silence under the walls of Antioch. At a signal given by the prince of Tarentum, they halted in a valley on the West, and near the tower of the Three Sisters which Phirous commanded. It was there that the leaders revealed to the army the secret of the great expedition which was to them the gates of the city.

The projects of Phirous and Bohemond, however, were near failing. At the moment that the Christian army quitted the camp, and all was prepared for carrying out the plot, a report of treason all at once was spread throughout Antioch. The Chrisians and newly-converted Mussulmans were suspected; **the name of Phirous even was whispered, and he was accused of keeping up an intelligence with the Crusaders. He was obliged to appear before Ac-**

cien, who interrogated him closely and fixed his eyes intently upon him in order to penetrate his thoughts; but Phirous dispersed all his suspicions by his firm countenance. He himself proposed the proper measures to be taken against the traitors, and advised his master to change the commanders of the principal towers. This advice was approved of, and Accien determined to follow it on the morrow. **In the mean time orders were given to load with chains and** *put to death, during the darkness of the night, all the Christians that should be found in the city.* The renegade was then sent back to his post, loaded with praises for his carefulness and fidelity. At the approach of night everything appeared tranquil in Antioch, and Phirous escaped from such threatening danger, awaited the Crusaders in the tower which he had agreed to surrender to them.

The Crusaders then gained access to the city (as the Russell Memoirs account of the onslaught mentioned), and proceeded to butcher its unfortunate inhabitants.

The name, Bohemond, is derived from the Latin word, *Buamundus*, the name of a mythical Gigas (giant), originally given as a nickname to the crusader prince Bohemond I (christened Mark; c. 1058-1111) by his father, ***because he was extremely large at birth*** (behindthename.com).

s.S.O.S.s.

And now that we know how Bohemian Grove derived the *'Bohemian'* portion of its name, below is how the abomination earned the '*****Grove'** part:

2 Chronicles 14 2-6 King James Version
2 And Asa did that which was good and right in the eyes of the Lord his God:
3 For he took away the altars of the strange gods, and **the high places (Babel), and brake down the images,** and **cut down the *****groves*:**
4 And commanded Judah to seek the Lord God of their fathers, and to do the law and the commandment.
5 Also **he took away out of all the cities of Judah the *high places* and the *images*:** and the kingdom was quiet before him.
6 And he built fenced cities in Judah: for the land had rest, ***and he had no war in those years***; because the Lord had given him rest.

Antioch is located on the border of Turkey and Syria—the epicenter of *our* modern-day Crusades.

Fun fact: The Ancient City of Antioch has been a wealth of archeological goodness, and the swastika has been found in abundance on its structures.

s.s.O.s.s.

40. The Du Rozel Code

Wiffen, the amazing man and Poet who wrote the Russell Memoir book, was a hero, *and* an adventurer. While you read the passages below, I would like for you to imagine the Author traveling by schooner to the many castles and chateaus along the route of the conquerers who he was trailing. Imagine long guided trips (on pack animals and wagons) across the terrain between terrestrial locations. Imagine Wiffen unfurling ancient dusty scrolls, and prying open books which were hidden inside tower attics and other secret places to which only the elite had access.

Being almost beyond belief, the Author, of the tales among the *Russell Memoirs,* actually left behind some telling clues, in a secret code which I have only begun to unfold.

Other than a quick scan of 'The Little Book' (which boasts many hundreds of digital pages on my device), the text, by me, has gone virtually un-investigated for these hidden gems of knowledge. Most of my discoveries were found hidden within the Preface, so there should be many more surprises hidden between her covers, *if you too are an adventurer.*

When you finish this section, you too may restore *some* of your faith in humanity. *Though I am sure there are many good men and women among the snakes about which we've until now learned, that, unfortunately....is* **not** *what this book is about...*

The Author was screaming warnings to us from the past. Here, have a listen:

s.s.O.s.s.

"I flattered myself that the survey would, in some degree at least, give back an image of those past ages, manners, and achievements, which at all times strongly excite our curiosity and interest; **and that there might be a value and utility which 'posterity would not willingly let die,'** found couched in the records of a House, **the members of which have born an almost uninterrupted and conspicuous part in British story, from the time of the Norman Dukes to the Tudors, from the Tudors to the Stuarts, and from the domination of that intolerant and repudiated dynasty to the latest constitutional benefits effected under the more congenial scepter of the House of Hanover."** [Historical Memoirs of the House of Russell: From the Times of the ..., Volume 1, Preface]

The Little Book begins with this adventurous disclaimer:

"In the tower of Matignon at St. Loo, I reviled in a perfect mer noire (means 'black sea') of abbey charters, those of the whole department of Calvados **having been safely deposited in the former during the revolution that swept away the abbeys and their riches and those of all La Manche** *being with equal convenience* **gathered in the latter receptacle** *(the author too thinks it strange that the things held sacred were mysteriously saved during the trademark siege of The Order)*. There every bundle which I opened disclosed some note or

242

s.s.O.s.s.

memorial of the surnames most renowned in Norman or in English story: Cliffords, Percies, *Clintons (hmmm…),* Byrons, Mortimers, and Bruces besides those of equal lustre which are now only to be met with in the extinct baronage of England.

The pleasure which I derived from my researches amidst this most interesting mass of deeds of the feudal and chivalric ages, I shall not soon forget: I went upon a tour of four weeks—I stayed as many months. The discovery of upwards of eighty charters, granted by the early De Rosels (Russells), was the result of this visit. The interest which my success naturally awakened, afterwards induced me to pursue their parentage beyond the conquest, through the Bertrands and the Turstains **(name means 'Thor')**, to the times of the Norwegian Jarls; but as the history of this first race, however curious, might appear extraneous to many, *it was not thought advisable to include it strictly within the compass of the present volumes.* **I have therefore embodied their wild achievements in a few separate *sheets, of which a limited number of copies only are struck off for those who may be interested in the annals of this remoter age.** [Historical Memoirs of the House of Russell: From the Times of the Norman Invasion, Volume 1, Preface]

***Note**: The 'limited number' of 'sheets,' of which the Author speaks, is important as they document

s.s.O.s.s.

much of the early *Viking* history of the Russell family, which has been left out of the Author's two-volume chronicle of Memoirs for obvious reasons. The work discussed is titled, *Memoirs of the First Race, or Early Ancestry of the House of Russell, from the **subjugation (see below for definition) of Norway by Harold Harfagre, to the Norman Conquest.* Printed uniform with the present work, in atlas 4 to royal 8 vo, pp. 84 and Co. We shall delve into the Viking portion of this amazing story later in this work.

**Subjugation (dictionary.com)
noun
1. The act, fact, or process of subjugating, or bringing under control; **enslavement**: The subjugation of the American Indians happened across the country.

The Russell historian who researched and recorded the hijinx of this clan was surely tormented by much of what he'd uncovered.

Russell Memoirs Quote Continued…Read on:

This work, with all its *demerits* or merits, I now dismiss from my hands, to undergo the same *frank ordeal of opinion* which I myself have exercised; and to receive, as I venture to hope, that candor which, in speaking of the actions and the characters

s.s.O.s.s.

of others, *I have endeavored to preserve.* Though not indifferent to either censure or approval, the writer has no ambition to gratify, beyond that of leaving some memorials that neither his leisure nor his life have been misspent or unimproved. From those who are habituated to make a strict analysis of sentiment on the prevailing fallacies relative to military practices, the unchristian tendency of which is *not yet so generally unveiled,* or so seriously considered, as it ought to be, I am not quite sure that I have not some indulgence to bespeak; for in narrating the events of history, it has been difficult not to speak of such things under their general acceptation; whilst I deem it personally a duty to assert, in its full force, the justice of the objections urged against them by an increasing number of conscientious and reflective minds. [**Historical Memoirs of the House of Russell: From the Times of the Norman Invasion, Volume 1, Preface**]

At the bottom of this page there is a note which refers to an artist who Wiffen thanks for his help in providing engravings for the depictions of the various shields used by the Russells over the years. The note contains a cryptic message which we will decode:

They are executed by Mr. Clennell and his son, a very young wood engraver of considerable promise. The arms are left unshaded, for the convenience of those who may wish to have the shields coloured, in which case they might be suitably consigned to the

s.s.O.s.s.
skillful care of the designer, ***Hercules Buildings, Lambeth.**

Note*: I read this last sentence a dozen times before I began my research of the topic. Like the many you see in older books, I thought it was merely a *typeset blunder*, but upon the discovery of its meaning I was shocked! The author, who understands symbolism well, was leaving us a clue; a desperate cry from the *past which corresponds perfectly with our conversation!*

This reference to the *Hercules Buildings* of *Lambeth* points to another Poet who lived in London during Wiffen's times, *William Blake*—Blake lived in the Hercules Buildings. Blake's address was, *Mr Blake Engraver, Hercules Buildings, Westminster Bridge*. The probability of this reference actually being a legitimate referral to Blake, for the painting of the shields on the pages of the Little Book, were, to me, far-fetched. Especially since Blake himself was an engraver *and* a printer, and Wiffen used Blake for none of those services for the publishing of His work in question. That being said, I began to research the clues which were given, and you will be surprised at what I found.

Lambeth was a pleasant rural area of Central London when Poet William Blake (1757-1827) first arrived. But with the legislation of the industrial revolution in full swing, many of the disgusting (and unregulated) industries were located across the river from Blake's home. Lambeth began to change into an obnoxiously loud,

s.s.O.s.s.

disease-infested slum, which is, no doubt, the *London* which is described in Blake's *'Eponymous'* poem.

All of that being said, it became obvious that the reference to ***Hercules Buildings, Lambeth,** referred to William Blake's book length poem, *Jerusalem (Blake has a similar short poem)*, in which Albion (England) has been infected with a 'soul disease' and her 'mountains run with blood' **(a Biblical reference from the book of Revelation)** due to the horrific consequences of the *Napoleonic wars—Napolean was a Freemason—*(google image 'Napolean Hidden Hand').

In Blake's poem religion exists merely as a cash generating machine, which is operated by monarchy and clergy, in order to exploit the lower classes. Greed and war have obscured the true message of Christ. If, however, Albion (England) can be as one with Jerusalem, then all humanity will once again be bound together by the ties of love.

Note: The meaning of Blake's Poem (above) was borrowed from tate.org.uk. I would have loved to have given credit to the individual who wrote it, but it was not cited. Another interesting note…On the same page where I found the colorful meaning described (above), there was a photo of some artwork, also by Blake, under which reads the following…

'© *Yale* Center for British Art, Paul Mellon Collection'

s.S.O.S.s.
Below is the passage from the Book of Revelation, to which William Blake's book-length poem refers:

Revelation 21:1-4 King James Version
21 And I saw a new heaven and a new earth: for the first heaven and the first earth were passed away; and there was no more sea.
2 And I John saw the holy city, new Jerusalem, coming down from God out of heaven, prepared as a bride adorned for her husband.
3 And I heard a great voice out of heaven saying, Behold, *the tabernacle of God is with men, and he will dwell with them, and they shall be his people*, and God himself shall be with them, and be their God.
4 And God shall wipe away all tears from their eyes; and there shall be no more death, neither sorrow, nor crying, neither shall there be any more pain: for the former things are passed away.

It appears as if the Author is warning of The Order's plans to counterfeit the 'New Jerusalem' of The Bible. And if so it should be duly noted that, *there are only 144,000 people listed who will take residence in the 'New Jerusalem'* described in the Book of Revelation. So to The Order's version of heaven, most of us would not be extended an invite.

Quote from Russell Memoirs continued:

s.S.O.s.s.

To judge of these and various other subjects, less according to the magic influence of hoary custom, than by the purer principles of our common Christianity. Our statesmen and legislators will then be so truly enlightened as to allow to the divine rules for all human government and conduct their proper place of right, above the shallow expediencies and the hollow maxims of the world, which have but too frequently actuated and guided them. At present, without giving the remark any specific application, there has not been either courage, faith, or purity enough for such a course. ***The iron and the clay in the feet of the prophetic image of empire, is an apt and instructive emblem of the brute force, or of the crumbling policies, which have been constantly employed by the governors of human kind, in every modern division of the old theatre of Roman domination.** But it is consoling to believe that more solid principles are rapidly unfolding; and that under the momentous changes in society which are everywhere silently or obviously developing, **the unchangeable spirit of Christianity, which, surmounting every prejudice, MUST ULTIMATELY BE REGNANT,** *is actively at work, in *"the removing of those things which are (now) shaken, that the things which cannot be shaken remain."* [Historical Memoirs of the House of Russell: From the Times of the ..., Volume 1, Preface]

s.s.O.s.s.

Note: The Bible passages below may seem fairly lengthy, but I included them in their entirety because they are important. Wiffen knew that he was part of something much larger than the recording of a wealthy family's deeds. The passage below prophecies of a series of great empires which would rise and fall successively. The passage also tells of The Order's shape-shifting bloodline. There is a *lot* to learn from these passages, and since I didn't have the time to analyze every nuance, I included the Bible Story in its entirety so that it wouldn't be forgotten. This way you too can be part of the adventure of discovery....

Here is the Bible verse to which the quote at the ending of the above Memoirs passage refers:

Hebrews 12:25-29 King James Version
25 See that ye refuse not him that speaketh. For if they escaped not who refused him that spake on earth, much more shall not we escape, if we turn away from him that speaketh from heaven:
26 Whose voice then shook the earth: but now he hath promised, saying, Yet once more I shake not the earth only, but also heaven.
27 And this word, Yet once more, signifieth the removing of those things that are shaken, as of things that are made, that those things which cannot be shaken may remain.

s.S.O.S.s.

28 Wherefore we receiving a kingdom which cannot be moved, let us have grace, whereby we may serve God acceptably with reverence and godly fear:
29 For our God is a consuming fire.

Note*: This reference—*"The iron and the clay in the feet of the prophetic image of empire"*—is important, as it is another coded Bible reference. It is the Authors way of again trying to send us a warning which had literally risked his head to publish.

Remember, the writer has access to privileged family information if he was entrusted to write this book of Memoirs for the Russells...*He still chose to send us the secret messages from the past!*

King Nebuchadnezzar's Dream

The King was a rotten and immoral man. Like Wiffen, Daniel, the King's Prophet had to choose his words very carefully, since the King was renown for torturous public human sacrifice.

Nebuchadnezzar II was a Chaldean king of the Neo-Babylonian Empire. The king's reign was between c. 605 BC - 562 BC. Nebuchadnezzar was the king responsible for the construction of the famous Hanging Gardens of Babylon, but, he is also credited with the destruction of King Solomon's temple.

Have a look at the passage to which Wiffen refers (*'The iron and the clay in the feet of the prophetic image of empire'*):

s.s.O.s.s.

Daniel 2:31-35 King James Version
31 Thou, O king, sawest, and behold a great image. This great image, whose brightness was excellent, stood before thee; and the form thereof was terrible.
32 This image's head was of fine gold, his breast and his arms of silver, his belly and his thighs of brass,
33 His legs of iron, his feet part of iron and part of clay.
34 Thou sawest till that a stone was cut out without hands, which smote the image upon his feet that were of iron and clay, and brake them to pieces.
35 Then was the iron, the clay, the brass, the silver, and the gold, broken to pieces together, and became like the chaff of the summer threshingfloors; and the wind carried them away, that no place was found for them: and the stone that smote the image became a great mountain, and filled the whole earth.

It would have taken great courage for Daniel to prophecy the divine truth as he deciphered the horrible king's dreams, *listen:*

Daniel's Interpretation of the King's Dream
36 This is the dream; and we will tell the interpretation thereof before the king.

s.S.O.s.s.

37 Thou, O king, art a king of kings: for the God of heaven hath given thee a kingdom, power, and strength, and glory.

38 And wheresoever the children of men dwell, the beasts of the field and the fowls of the heaven hath he given into thine hand, and hath made thee ruler over them all. Thou art this head of gold.

39 And after thee shall arise another kingdom inferior to thee, and another third kingdom of brass, which shall bear rule over all the earth.

40 And the fourth kingdom shall be strong as iron: forasmuch as iron breaketh in pieces and subdueth all things: and as iron that breaketh all these, shall it break in pieces and bruise.

41 And whereas thou sawest the feet and toes, part of potters' clay, and part of iron, the kingdom shall be divided; but there shall be in it of the strength of the iron, forasmuch as thou sawest the iron mixed with miry clay.

42 And as the toes of the feet were part of iron, and part of clay, so the kingdom shall be partly strong, and partly broken.

43 And whereas thou sawest iron mixed with miry clay, *they shall mingle themselves with the seed of men: but they shall not cleave one to another, even as iron is not mixed with clay.*

44 And *in the days of these kings shall the God of heaven set up a kingdom, which shall never be destroyed*: and the kingdom shall not be left to other

s.S.O.S.s.

people, but *it shall break in pieces and consume all these kingdoms*, and *it shall stand f*or ever.

45 Forasmuch as thou sawest that the stone was cut out of the mountain without hands, and that it brake in pieces the iron, the brass, the clay, the silver, and the gold; the great God hath made known to the king what shall come to pass hereafter: and the dream is certain, and the interpretation thereof sure.

Perhaps Wiffen, who I expect is another member of this family, knew exactly what The Order (and the bankers who finance them) were planning for in America—*The Civil War.*

A quick google search for the title will turn up an actual online copy (scanned) of the book in question (Historical memoirs of the house of Russell : from the time of the Norman conquest), which can be perused at your leisure.

Fun fact: On the topic of those 'who wish to have their shields colored,' the Rothschild name literally translates to, *Red Shield.* The Rothschild family (a family known to have financed countless controlled conflicts, allover the world, throughout history) was notorious for changing their surname over the years (a practice which most likely preserved their very existence). The Russells did the same.

The name Russell, aptly, means *'Red.'* The base word for the name *'RUSSia,'* is *'Ru,'* which *ALSO means 'red.' Russia* too was settled by the same family of *'Vikings,'* and *their* army is known as the *'red army.'*

41. British *'Israelism'*

Though we haven't seen anything close to what New Israel will be here on earth, these charlatans (The Order) still attempt to counterfeit anything which is of God, and, therefore, good....**Richard Brothers** (25 December 1757 – 25 January 1824), is credited with the idea of **British Israelism, which is the belief that the British people descend from the 12 Lost Tribes of Israel.**

Furthermore, Brothers proposed that the Capital City of Britain should therefore be redesigned as *New Jerusalem* (from the Book of Revelation) **for the coming Age of Enlightenment (which, as we have discussed, is simply a euphemism for the** *age of satanism).*

Many profess the idea of a 'New Jerusalem' to date back to 6th Century England, ascending its height of popularity during the First World War. Many buildings of the age reflect such sentiment—St Paul's Cathedral is one such building which is said to contain elements of said British *'Israelism.'* I would argue that, *The Order* simply couldn't resist using their native tongue, and symbolism, in and around these structures, just as Yale couldn't resist the mystery which still blows the minds of the public; the inscribing of Hebrew accompanied by Latin on Yale's school seal (discussed further, later).

William Blake, who died a few years before the Russell Memoirs Author published this work, would have most likely been a friend to the Writer of the Russell Memoirs.

s.s.O.s.s.

Blake, though considered as one of the best Poets ever published now, never gained widespread popularity until long after he was dead. Blake's ideas, which were contrary to Britain's charters of world conquest and newfound wealth, were never very popular during the dawn of the 'age of enlightenment.' Blake saw the disturbing signs of the forthcoming apocalypse all around him, though he was one of the few who did. In fact, Blake wrote an entire series of work which are referred to as the Prophetic Books, and which, I am sure hold many surprises for the reader who now does so with eyes-open.

The name of Blake's shorter poem which many know as, *'Jerusalem,'* is known properly as, *'And did those feet in Ancient Times.'* The meaning of which has been misconstrued to mean something *good* for Britain. The short work was set to music long after Blake's death, and is now used as London's de facto Anthem:

And did Those Feet in Ancient Time
('Jerusalem')
BY WILLIAM BLAKE

And did those feet in ancient time
Walk upon Englands mountains green:
And was the holy Lamb of God,
On Englands pleasant pastures seen!

And did the Countenance Divine,
Shine forth upon our clouded hills?
And was Jerusalem builded here,
Among these dark Satanic Mills?

s.S.O.s.s.

Bring me my Bow of burning gold:
Bring me my arrows of desire:
Bring me my Spear: O clouds unfold!
Bring me my Chariot of fire!

I will not cease from Mental Fight,
Nor shall my sword sleep in my hand:
Till we have built Jerusalem,
In Englands green & pleasant Land.

Since, The Order (who conquered the entirety of Europe) *were originally from Israel,* it's not hard to imagine why this poem was made London's Anthem.
Below is the hideous National Anthem of Britain:

God Save the Queen

[Verse 1:]
God save our gracious Queen,
Long live our noble Queen,
God save the Queen!
Send her victorious,
Happy and glorious,
Long to reign over us,
God save the Queen!

[Verse 2:]
O lord God arise,

s.s.O.s.s.

Scatter our enemies,
And make them fall!
Confound their knavish tricks,
Confuse their politics,
On you our hopes we fix,
God save the Queen!

[Verse 3:]
Not in this land alone,
But be God's mercies known,
From shore to shore!
Lord make the nations see,
That men should brothers be,
And form one family,
The wide world ov'er

[Verse 4:]
From every latent foe,
From the assasins blow,
God save the Queen!
O'er her thine arm extend,
For Britain's sake defend,
Our mother, **prince (?)**, and friend,
God save the Queen!

[Verse 5:]
Thy choicest gifts in store,
On her be pleased to pour,
Long may she reign!

S.S.O.S.S.

May she defend our laws,
And ever give us cause,
To sing with heart and voice,
God save the Queen!

[*Verse 6:]
Lord grant that Marshal Wade
May by thy mighty aid
Victory bring.
May he sedition hush,
And like a torrent rush,
Rebellious Scots to crush.
God save the Queen!

Note*: Verse 6 is often omitted. These words were sung when Bonnie Prince Charlie first set foot in Scotland as a "prayer" to save him from the Scottish Uprising, and keep him safe so he could become king.

The gentleman who wrote the first anthem herein, *William Blake,* died in 1827. Russell Memoirs was printed in 1833. And Jeremiah Wiffen (Memoirs Author) died only three years after that, in 1836. When Blake *(whom shared Wiffen's antiestablishment beliefs)* died in 1836, he was only 69…Perhaps the Poets were attempting to thwart the looming American Civil War, which, The Order had, no doubt, *already been brewing*….And Wiffen, *whom had lost His coconspirator right before shoving off on his inves-*

s.s.O.s.s.

tigative travels, for all one knows, *may have just sought revenge for an old mentor and friend.*

And, perhaps it *wasn't* simply a coincidence that Jeremiah Holmes Wiffen died an untimely death, just after publishing a work with so many damnatory hidden messages between its covers.

During the same year that Wiffen published his work in 1833, William Huntington Russell was establishing The Order of Skull and Bones on the campus of Yale University.

Fun fact: There were only 12 original colonies, not 13, as we are taught in The Order's schools.

This lie was likely forged in order to justify using East India Company's former flag, as the flag which today we refer to as 'Old Glory.' The addition of the *'13th colony'* was most-likely an attempt to mask the fact that the Jesuits who formed America were actually trying to found a 'New Jerusalem.'

After all, there were 12 tribes of Israel *and 12* original colonies.

42. The Order's Siege Upon Jerusalem

Following The Russells' successful siege on Antioch, a half-year break was had by The Order. The Order was now rested and prepared to chain-up and take the grand prize, the Holy City of Jerusalem.

In the Russell Memoirs book, before it tells of The Order's siege on Antioch or its siege upon Jerusalem, the book's Author, Wiffen, drops us another amazing clue, which places The Order at the scene of the crime over 100 years before the Crusades.

In the Russell Memoirs book, the author describes this group of Knights as terrorists, and he identifies them and their locations of terrorism, so we can easily identify The Order as the Cause *and the effect* of The First Crusade.

Just as with William Huntington Russell, *the Russell patriarch who made an out-of-the-ordinary visit to Germany, around a hundred years before WWII*, the Russell family also galloped to the Holy Lands nearly 100 years before the 'trumpet' which kicked off the Crusades for the Russells was sounded.

Here is the damning evidence:

"....a daughter Gisela, who, during the government of Duke Richard II, engaged the affections of Giroye, lord of Montreuil and Echauffour, and became the mother of seven sons and four daughters, whence issued, says Ordericus, **a race of hardy knights, who were the *terror* of the barbarians in Apulia, Syria, and Thrace."** [Historical Memoirs of

s.s.O.s.s.
the House of Russell: From the Times of the Norman Invasion, Volume 1, Page 12]

These Russell Knights made a horribly long trip to the Holy lands for The Order, to begin the very conflict which kicked off the *First Crusades.*

The trip in which The Order made to 'terrorize' '*Apulia, Syria,* and *Thrace,'* was over 2700 miles in length! Most of these men were born in the first decade of 1000 AD which would mean that these men would all be well-dead by the dawn of the first Crusade. That terror campaign was kicked off, depending on who you talk to, on or after 1096. These would have been the very 'hardy Knights' of The Order who would 'terrorize' the 'barbarians' *(pilgrims)* on their way to the Holy Lands. This all-important recon trip was key to lending purpose to the future Russell generations' who would desolate the birthplace of most modern religion. This abominable act came to be known as the *'First Crusade.'*

Note*: These are the same-exact geographical areas where The Order is still terrorizing Christians and Muslims today.

As a result of The Order's recon visit to the Middle East, the Holy City of Jerusalem (birthplace of Christianity, Judaism, and Islam) passed from the relatively tolerant Egyptians to the Seljuk Turks in 1071. As the epicenter of all three of these religions, Jerusalem was also at the center of religious pilgrimage in the Ancient World, as it is to this modern day. During its long history, Jerusalem has been destroyed twice, besieged 23 times, attacked 52 times, and captured and recaptured 44 times.

s.s.O.s.s.

In 1096, Jerusalem was sieged by 'Muslims' who grew hostile toward the Christians and 'Jews.' As a result, Christians were being persecuted, robbed, and raped, on their way to the homeland *(again, by the Russells)*. Near the end of the 11th century, Byzantine Emperor Alexius Comenus, also being bullied by the Turks, looked to the West for military help to quail the onslaught. *(Boy, does this tired old story sound familiar?)*

At the height of the terrorism along the road to the Holy Lands, it was said that there were so many pilgrims slain, that many of the roads into Jerusalem were 'littered with skull and bones' of the victims of the evildoers.

Never fear, because In 1095, Pope Urban II (also a Russell relative) publicly called for a crusade to 'aid Eastern Christians and recover the Holy Lands.' Western Europeans, *mainly France,* seemed already to have had a band of devils in mind for the project. Nine Knights were chosen as the managing Order of the ripening conquest, and they took up arms alongside an army of German and French peasants, *against the Muslims*.

The Order besieged the walls of the City of Jerusalem, but the city was well fortified, and well stocked with food and water. The Order's tens of thousands of soldiers were growing weary as there was little food or water outside Jerusalem's walls.

The Order found new zeal for their quest after a fleet of Genoese ships commanded by *Guglielmo Embriaco,* had arrived at Jaffa in support of the land-based crusaders. The Order built two siege towers of the ships timber and tackle which were erected—one on the South wall of Jerusalem, and the other was raised to the Northwest.

s.S.O.S.s.

City guards pelted the South siege tower with flaming arrows and bowls of hot oil until it finally crumbled in flames. The Order was now only left with the Northwest siege tower. Two soldiers on the remaining tower finally reached a weak spot in the wall, after which, the Muslim gate guard retreated. Even for medieval times, the massacre, which took place once The Order passed the guard of the muslim protectors, *was particularly grizzly*.

An account written in the Gesta Francorum, speaking only of the area of the Temple Mount, records:

> "...[our men] were killing and slaying even to the Temple of Solomon, where the slaughter was so great that our men waded in blood up to their ankles..."

Raymond of Aguilers reported this of the Temple Mount area:

> "In the Temple and porch of Solomon men rode in blood up to their knees and bridle reins."

Writing about the Temple Mount area alone, Fulcher of Chartres said:

> "In this temple 10,000 were killed. Indeed, if you had been there you would have seen our feet coloured to our ankles with the blood of the slain. But what more shall I relate? None of them were

left alive; *neither women nor children were spared."*

The Knights then set up shop at the Great City of Jerusalem.

Though having taken a strict vow of poverty, the Knight's Templar introduced usury to the masses. The Knight's Templar, being the problem and the solution for the Holy Land pilgrims being robbed, established the first known international banking system.

The pilgrims could deposit money in their home country and later withdraw from the account at *or along* their destination, lowering the risk of losing their cash. This technology later evolved into the ATM's we use today.

Most other modern lending and banking practices can also be traced back to the Knight's Templar.

Fun fact: Al Qaeda and Isis, both, have called for *Holy War* by different factions within the Muslim nation. In those cases the 'holy' wars were deemed *'Jihad.'* If you study the Pope's official call to action which gave The Order pious authority to rape, plunder, pillage, and torture indiscriminately, you will realize that the similarities between the structure of the verbiage used to call 'Muslims' to Jihad, and that which the Pope used to call 'Christians' to war for The Crusades, were nearly identical.

43. The *Un*-holy *Grail*

After all of the blood was mopped up from the siege on Israel, the Knight's Templar set up shop in Jerusalem. The Order now had control of the Holy City, where they would again shape-shift their DNA into that of their new community *(and ancient homeland)*.

In 1119, the French nobleman from the Champagne region, *Hugues de Payens,* collected eight of his knighted relatives including Godfrey de Saint-Omer (all from the Russell clan), and *officially* began The Order of The Knight's Templar, with the stated mission of protecting pilgrims on their journey to visit the Holy Land. King Baldwin II of Jerusalem allowed The Order to set up headquarters there, on the Temple Mount.

The Dome of the Rock, at the center of the Mount, was understood to occupy the site of the Jewish Temple of Solomon; King Solomon's Temple was known to Christians during the Muslim occupation as the *'Holy of Holies.'* Because the *Aqsa mosque* was known as the *Templum Solomonis,* it was not long before the knights had encompassed the association in their name. The official name of this Order became, the *Pauperes commilitones Christi Templique Solomonici*—the *Poor Fellow-Soldiers of Christ and of the Temple of Solomon*, which was eventually shortened to *'Knight's Templar.'*

Of Hugues de Payens and his original eight knights, two were brothers, and **all of them were *The Pagan's* relatives by either blood, or marriage**: Godfrey de Saint-Omer, Payne de Monteverdi, Archambaud de St. Agnan, Andre de Montbard, Geoffrey

S.S.O.S.s.

Bison, and **two men recorded only by the names of Rossal *(another French variation of the Russell name)*,** and Gondamer.

Most writings have created a cloud of confusion around these mystery Knights, but the Russell Memoirs has identified two-or-three fellows from the Russell family who could have doubled as the dreaded Hugh the Pagan.

Either way, this is of no circumstance, since all of the founding Knight's Templar were known to have been from the same family (some who had married into it, or most of whom were of the *actual William Huntington Russell bloodline—the founder of The Order of Skull and Bones*). The fact is….Hugh De Payens *was* a *Russell*, and so it really doesn't matter which particular Russell of which they spoke (unless you were writing a biography)—all that is important to the narrative of this story is, the connection of the Knights Templar to the Russell family—*and we most certainly have that.*

Like all of The Order's cherished objects and relics of ancient history, the Grail is clouded in secrecy and mystery. The Order has written about the Grail extensively—most of which were fantastic stories having heroic knights who were also saving damsels in distress and, righting the wrongs of the day. But none of this is even close to being accurate. Knights, are satanic cults of heartless marauders who have been commissioned to conquer peoples and their lands.

Many Biblical treasures were robbed and looted from the Templar occupation of Jerusalem, but it is well-documented that the Templar sought something in particular—something special. Many think that whatever the Templar had been searching for had been dug-up from beneath the Temple of Solomon, or even simply removed from the Holy of Holies. But, the fact remains that, something was discovered which the Templar believe held great power. I propose that much of what the Templar found at the temple were hidden scrolls, stone tablets, and or baked clay upon which the esoteric knowledge, with which the Freemasons use to control men, was scribed. But there is certainly a single object which inspired their romantic literature.

The Holy Grail has been written of, and speculated about, perhaps more than any other object in history. An amazing feat for an object which hasn't even been positively identified. That is, until now....

The Holy Grail is considered to be a dish, *plate*, platter, stone or cup, which played an important part in Arthurian literature. According to legend, the Holy Grail has special powers too. Here today I will reveal that ***the Holy Grail was a 'magic plate' of braided gold.*** Feast your eyes on the 'Holy Grail,' (google image 'Urim and Thummim' - or 'Breastplate of Judgment'). Below is the Biblical account which describes how Aaron's Breastplate of Judgement first came into existence:

> **Exodus 28** King James Version
> **28** And take thou unto thee Aaron thy brother, and his sons with him, from among the children of Israel, that he may minister unto me in the priest's office, even Aaron, Nadab and Abihu, Eleazar and Ithamar, Aaron's sons.
> **2** And thou shalt make holy garments for Aaron thy brother for glory and for beauty.

s.s.O.s.s.

3 And thou shalt speak unto all that are wise hearted, whom I have filled with the spirit of wisdom, that they may make Aaron's garments to consecrate him, that he may minister unto me in the priest's office.

4 And these are the garments which they shall make; a breastplate, and an ephod, and a robe, and a broidered coat, a mitre, and a girdle: and they shall make holy garments for Aaron thy brother, and his sons, that he may minister unto me in the priest's office.

5 And they shall take gold, and blue, and purple, and scarlet, and fine linen.

6 And they shall make the ephod of gold, of blue, and of purple, of scarlet, and fine twined linen, with cunning work.

7 It shall have the two shoulderpieces thereof joined at the two edges thereof; and so it shall be joined together.

8 And the curious girdle of the ephod, which is upon it, shall be of the same, according to the work thereof; even of gold, of blue, and purple, and scarlet, and fine twined linen.

9 And thou shalt take two onyx stones, and grave on them the names of the children of Israel:

10 Six of their names on one stone, and the other six names of the rest on the other stone, according to their birth.

11 With the work of an engraver in stone, like the engravings of a signet, shalt thou engrave the two stones with the names of the children of Israel: thou shalt make them to be set in ouches of gold.

12 And thou shalt put the two stones upon the shoulders of the ephod for stones of memorial unto the children of Israel: and Aaron shall bear their names before the Lord upon his two shoulders for a memorial.

13 And thou shalt make ouches of gold;

14 And two chains of pure gold at the ends; of wreathen work shalt thou make them, and fasten the wreathen chains to the ouches.

The Breastpiece

15 And thou shalt make the breastplate of judgment with cunning work; after the work of the ephod thou shalt make it; of gold, of blue, and of purple, and of scarlet, and of fine twined linen, shalt thou make it.

16 Foursquare it shall be being doubled; a span shall be the length thereof, and a span shall be the breadth thereof.

17 And thou shalt set in it settings of stones, even four rows of stones: the first row shall be a sardius, a topaz, and a carbuncle: this shall be the first row.

18 And the second row shall be an emerald, a sapphire, and a diamond.

19 And the third row a ligure, an agate, and an amethyst.

s.S.O.S.s.

20 And the fourth row a beryl, and an onyx, and a jasper: they shall be set in gold in their inclosings.

21 And the stones shall be with the names of the children of Israel, twelve, according to their names, like the engravings of a signet; every one with his name shall they be according to the twelve tribes.

22 And thou shalt make upon the breastplate chains at the ends of wreathen work of pure gold.

23 And thou shalt make upon the breastplate two rings of gold, and shalt put the two rings on the two ends of the breastplate.

24 And thou shalt put the two wreathen chains of gold in the two rings which are on the ends of the breastplate.

25 And the other two ends of the two wreathen chains thou shalt fasten in the two ouches, and put them on the shoulderpieces of the ephod before it.

26 And thou shalt make two rings of gold, and thou shalt put them upon the two ends of the breastplate in the border thereof, which is in the side of the ephod inward.

27 And two other rings of gold thou shalt make, and shalt put them on the two sides of the ephod underneath, toward the forepart thereof, over against the other coupling thereof, above the curious girdle of the ephod.

28 And they shall bind the breastplate by the rings thereof unto the rings of the ephod with a lace of blue, that it may be above the curious girdle of the

s.s.O.s.s.

ephod, and that the breastplate be not loosed from the ephod.

29 And Aaron shall bear the names of the children of Israel in the breastplate of judgment upon his heart, when he goeth in unto the holy place, for a memorial before the Lord continually.

Since Aaron disobeyed God in the story of The Ten Commandments, by building the golden calf idol and offering children to the fire of Molech, his *Breastplate of Judgment* became important to The Order.

The 12 Oracle stones situated on the High Priest's Breastplate represent the 12 Tribes of Israel (all of us humans). The 'Breastplate of Judgement' was accompanied by the Urim & Thummim, which was two rocks—a black rock and a white rock.

I Samuel 14:41 gives us a clue to understanding the Urim and Thummim; the passage describes an attempt to identify a sinner **via divination (magic)**, by repeatedly splitting the people into two groups and identifying which group contains the sinner. The black and white rocks were used sort-of like dice, which accompanied the twelve flashing oracle stones. (Many texts explain that a candle was lit in order to encourage the stones to flash by the dancing flame.) Through the process of elimination, Aaron could 'identify guilty people' or 'make decisions' based on the ephod gear.

I now know that the Templars believed that God and Moses's antithesis was Aaron. The Templars coveted the antithesis to God's Word (which was written on those tablets); the object which governed His People. The ephod was the antithesis to *The Ten Commandments since Aaron had acted so abominably in his*

s.s.O.s.s.

brother's absence. The Templar *must have* considered the sacred relic, Urim and Thummim and Aaron's priestly breastplate (the ephod), to have strong magic.

What historic object would make a better Holy Grail than a *golden* Bible treasure which was used by *The* High Priest, for telling the future and *judging* the many tribes of the world?

There is a lot of controversy surrounding the High Priest of the Ancient Israelites, known as Aaron, the older brother of Moses.

Many point out his many downfalls and abominations before the Lord, to whom the dirty deeds seemed to have gone unnoticed. To me too they are hard to understand. For example, after the building of the Golden Calf (while Moses was on the mountain talking with God and receiving the Ten Commandments), Aaron was certainly sacrificing children to Molech below. (They were burning those children alive.) Thousands of Israelites were put to death by their own people for the mistake, but, again, *Aaron escaped unscathed.*

On another occasion, two of Aaron's son's were struck dead by God, for offering 'strange fire.' Look:

> **Leviticus 10:1-7 King James Version**
> **10 And Nadab and Abihu, the sons of Aaron, took either of them his censer, and put fire therein, and put incense thereon, and offered strange fire before the Lord, which he commanded them not.**
> **2 And there went out fire from the Lord, and devoured them, and they died before the Lord.**

s.s.O.s.s.

To me, these are clear signs that Aaron was using the art of confusion (Freemasonry), even back then, to cover the dirty practices still lingering in their culture.

Many ancient writers associate Hermes with a real person who was 'close to Moses'; I would like to propose today that Hermes is synonymous with Aaron, Moses's Brother (Priest of the Israelites). This alternate theory could be supported by the fact that Hermes holds a staff having two snakes around which it is wrapped. Remember, Aaron and Moses's staffs were thrown to the ground and turned to serpents before the Pharaoh, during their attempt to free the Israelites. Remember, Aaron's snake consumed all of the snakes of all of the Pharaoh's greatest magicians, which rendered Aaron to have powerful magic in the eyes of the King?

The same observation of the art of confusion can be made with Noah's sons when the curse was placed on the descendants of Canaan, and not Ham, the son who was the *supposed* violator. Why did Noah curse Canaan when it was Ham who saw him naked? And, why was Noah so angry that Ham saw him naked in the first place? Some propose that Ham *and or* Canaan actually did something to Noah in addition to seeing him naked.

I propose that they were practicing the dark arts, for which the entire planet had just been drowned. And, again, I propose that there was some Freemasonry taking place here, which allowed Canaan to appear as the violator, when in fact it was Ham. In other words, Ham used his magic tricks of manipulation to put Canaan up to the abomination, and therefore got off scot free.

We have discussed that The Holy Grail is considered to be a dish, cup, stone, ***plate***, or **platter**, as per Arthurian literature cre-

s.S.O.S.s.

ated by The Order. But, what does the word 'grail' truly mean? etymonline.com:

> Grail (n.) c. **1300**, gral, "The Holy Grail," **from Old French** *(France is home of the Russells)* graal, greal "Holy Grail; cup" *(This was the Russells' contrived version of the Grail since, 'grail,' never meant cup or chalice before Arthurian stories created by The Order, listen…)* earlier: "large shallow dish, basin," from Medieval Latin gradalis, also gradale, grasale, "a flat dish or shallow vessel." *('cups' and chalices are not 'shallow vessels.')* The original form is uncertain; the word is perhaps ultimately from Latin crater "bowl," which is from Greek krater "bowl, especially for mixing wine with water" (see crater (n.)). Holy Grail is Englished from Middle English seint gral (c. 1300), also sangreal, sank-real (c. 1400), which seems to show deformation as if from sang real "royal blood" (that is, the blood of Christ) ***The object had been inserted into the Celtic Arthurian legends by 12c., perhaps in place of some pagan otherworldly object.**

Note*: In the above passage, only the bold text within parenthesis is my added commentary. *And, just to clarify, the Arthurian 'chalice' legend wasn't fabricated until the 12th Century.

S.S.O.S.S.

Also, according to legend, the Holy Grail has special powers. This description would far-better fit an object such as the priestly Breast-**'plate'** of Judgement, which could tell the future, or which could be used to make judgements for war, rather than an old *cup made of silver or stone*. Now let us look at the facts....Here we have a magical golden **'plate'** which was used for divinity, like a crystal ball, and, for some reason...everyone continues to be enamored by stories of King Arthur and his Knights of the Round Table. Amazing!

This is just another case of The Order's 'writers' creating torrents of cerebrally-void bedtime stories for which to throw the bloodhounds off of the scent-trail of the actual object of interest.

But, if the Templar found the original Breastplate of Judgment, what happened to it? Well, guess what? Don't worry, because I think that you and I have found it. Google image 'Freemasonry Order Chart' (the one which features a stepped pyramid with men standing on its steps) and look at the fellow standing five steps down, on the right side of this Masonic Order Pyramid, just below the giant 'G' with the all-seeing eye of Horus in its center....And would you look what is strapped around his neck? Now....If you've had a good look at the Holy Grail, look at the same image and notice the symbol above the head of the Freemasons, 'Royal Arch Mason' ***'High Priest.'*** The image inside that little yellow triangle is called a 'triple tau,' which is the symbol for the *Jesuit Order of the Catholic Church! To view the East India Company's version of the darling symbol* **google image *'East India company E. I. Co. emblem.'***

The triple tau is also featured in the most recognizable of Jesuit insignias **(google image 'Jesuit Triple Tau')**. With another

s.s.O.s.s.

quick search, you can see the Jesuit insignia made from actual human skull and bones on the wall of a Jesuit church.

Below is one of The Bible's greatest mystery verses, which I believe you and I *may have solved here today…*

> **Mark 13:14** King James Version
> **14** But **when ye shall see the abomination of desolation,** spoken of by Daniel the prophet, **standing where it ought not,** (let him that readeth understand) then **let them that be in Judaea flee to the mountains**:

With all of the Pope's wealth, and out of all of the getups that he could don, it is a mystery to me that he chooses to wear garments which have nothing to do with the regalia which God himself had commanded the High Priest of his people to wear. And now the ephod is worn by the High Priest of Freemasonry, and the *'Pope'* ('Christ Vicar') *sports the miter of Dagon.*

S.S.O.S.s.

44. Supposed Disbanding of the Knight's Templar

Here is the list of charges drawn up by the Inquisition against the Templars, when they were supposedly dismantled, on 12 August 1308—*The Articles of the Accusations:*

> Item, that in each province **The Order** had idols, namely heads, of which some had three races and someone, and others had a human skull.
>
> Item, that they adored these idols or that idol, and especially in their great *chapters* and assemblies.
> Item, that they venerated (them).
> Item, that (they venerated them) as *God*.
> Item, that (they venerated them) as their Savior....
> Item, that they said that the head could save them.
> Item, that [it could] make riches.
> Item, that it made the trees flower.
> Item, that [it made] the land germinate.
> Item, that they surrounded or touched each head of the aforesaid idols with small cords, which they wore around themselves next to the shirt or the flesh.
> Item, that in his reception, the aforesaid small cords or some lengths of them were given to each of the brethren.
> Item, that they did this in veneration of an idol.
> Item, that they (the receptors) enjoined them (the

s.s.O.s.s.

postulants) on oath not to reveal the aforesaid to anyone.

During The Trial of the Templars in 1307 Brother *Jean Taillefer of Genay* gave evidence.

He,

"was received into the order at Mormant, one of the three perceptories under the jurisdiction of the Grand Priory of **Champagne at Voulaine (House of Russell)**. He said at his initiation 'an idol representing a human face' was placed on the altar before him. ***Hughes*** **de Bure**, another ***Burgundian from a daughter house of Voulaine***, described how the 'head' was taken out of a cupboard, or *aumbry*, in the chapel, and that it seemed to him to be of gold or silver, and to represent the head of a man with a long beard. Brother Pierre d'Arbley suspected that the 'idol' had two faces, and his kinsman Guillaume d'Arbley made the point that the 'idol' itself, as distinct from copies, was exhibited at general chapters, implying that it was only shown to senior members of *The Order* on special occasions."

Noel Currer-Briggs, The Shroud and the Grail—A Modern Quest for the True Grail:

s.S.O.S.s.

"Nearly all the brethren agreed that the head was bearded and had long hair, and the Templars, like the majority of their contemporaries, regarded long hair as effeminate, so the length of the 'idol's hair was remarkable for this, if for no other reason."

According to the *Deposition of Jean Tallefer*, the idol was:

"…about the natural size of a man's head, with a very *fierce-looking face and beard."

Note*: Remember this head with a 'fierce beard' account, since it will be referred-to toward the end of this work.

In other words, the Templar were sentenced to death, and The Order of the Knight's Templar was to be disassembled, based on the fact that they were worshipping the heads of the dead. Necromancy was practiced by the Nine Unknown Men of India, the Catholics, the Jesuits, and even The Order of Skull and Bones; many *if not all them* still worship the heads of the dead, today.

Below is another historic account of the same head worship activities, which *also* puts the Russell's at the scene of another cabal:

Forrest Jackson, The Baphomet in History and Symbolism
"We found indisputable evidence for the charge of secret ceremonies involving a head of some kind.

s.S.O.S.s.

Indeed the existence of such a head proved to be one of the dominant themes running through the Inquisition records. Among the confiscated goods of the **Paris (House of Russell)** preceptory a reliquary in the shape of a woman's head was found. *It was hinged on top*, and contained what appeared to have been relics of a peculiar kind."

Here is another account of the same necromantic ritual (predating 489 BC):

Julian Jaynes, The Origin of Consciousness in the Breakdown of the Bicameral Mind
"Herodotus (4:26) speaks of the practice in the obscure *Issedones* of gilding a head and sacrificing to it. Cleomenes of Sparta is said to have preserved the head of Archonides in honey and consulted it before undertaking an important task. Several vases of the fourth century BC in Etruria depict scenes of persons interrogating *oracular heads. And the severed head of the rustic Carians which continues to 'speak' is mentioned derisively by Aristotle."

As you can imagine, the worship of dead heads and the dirty deeds of those willing to step over to the dark side, both, have moved underground in our society. Well, unless you are one of the 15 plutocratic, *harmless* frat boys at Skull and Bones. But what is the common satanist to do in today's society, when openly wor-

s.S.O.S.s.

shipping a fellow's dead mellon is more frowned upon for the rest of us?

Never fear, the ancients thought of this too, since throughout time devil worship has faded in and out of good taste. This image (google image baphomet star Adam and Eve) demonstrates a 'baphomet.' As you can see, the circle on the left features the words Adam and Eve. This is clearly a celebration of our stolen souls.

The circle on the right contains an upside-down five pointed star in which a goat's head is visible. Featured inside the top perimeter of this circle is the name of the same Babylonian owl demon that our elites and governors serve at Bohemian Grove California—Lilith. On top of the baphomet, the name Samael is written. In some myths, Samael was mated with Lilith, but the two produced no offspring. More importantly, however, Samael is the name of a red dragon named Leviathan:

Red Dragon
Revelation 12:1-4 King James Version
12 And there appeared a great wonder in heaven; a woman clothed with the sun, and the moon under her feet, and upon her head a crown of twelve stars:
2 *And she being with child cried, travailing in birth, and pained to be delivered.*
3 And there appeared another wonder in heaven; and behold a *great red dragon, having seven heads and ten horns, and seven crowns upon his heads.

s.S.O.S.s.

4 And his tail drew the third part of the stars of heaven, and did cast them to the earth: and the dragon stood before the woman which was ready to be delivered, for to devour her child as soon as it was born…

Note*: The 'Great Red Dragon' in this passage most-likely refers to the Welsh Dragon which is pictured on the **flag of Wales**. *Also, the Russell Coat of Arms features the* **'Red Dragon' and a goat!**
The word dragon originates from the fish-head-god version of King Nimrod of Babylon, Dagon. The George Herbert Walker Bush family is also Welsh, as are a multitude of our US Presidents.

This 'baphomet' (or pentagram) is a substitute for a real human head in beginner levels of Masonic and satanic 'knighthood' rituals. These 'pentagrams' are a part of most of the satanic rituals described in the satanic bible too, and will just have to do, since severing heads (or digging them up) isn't entirely feasible for the rest of us mere mortals—*the slaves.*

Regardless of The Order's many publications which claim that the Knights Templar were 'disbanded,' US President John Quincy Adams published a book titled, *'Letters and Addresses on Freemasonry,'* in which he outlines the, *'KNIGHT templar's OATH.'*

In His publication, Adams identifies an 'interesting connection' between the oath taken by the 'Knight Templar' and that which is taken in 'Freemasonry.'

s.s.O.s.s.

Below is a quote from an oath taken by the Freemason in which our Ex-president found the parallels to the Knights Templar so intriguing:

Address of the Master:
Pilgrim, the fifth libation is taken In a very solemn way. It is emblematical of the bitter cup of death, of which we must all, sooner or later, taste; and even the Savior of the world was not exempted, notwithstanding his repeated prayers and solicitations. It is taken of pure wine, and from this cup. Exhibiting a human skull, he pours wine into it, and says: To show you that we here practice no imposition, I give you this pledge. (Drinks from the skull.) He then pours more wine into the skull, and presents it to the candidate, telling him that the fifth libation is called the sealed obligation, as it is to seal all his former engagements in Masonry.

If the candidate consents to proceed, he takes the skull in his hand, and repeats after the Most Eminent, as follows:

This pure wine I take from this cup, in testimony of my belief of the mortality of the body, and the immortality of the soul; and as the sins of the whole world were laid upon the head of our Savior, so may the sins of the person whose skull this once was, be heaped upon my head, in addition to my own; and

s.s.O.s.s.

may they appear in judgment against me, both here and hereafter, should I violate or transgress any obligation in Masonry, or the Orders of Knighthood which I have heretofore taken, take at this time, or may hereafter be instructed in. So help me God. (Drinks of the wine.)

The passage above shows an uncanny resemblance between the Freemasons and the Knights Templar, and it was written by the second President of the United States!

Fun fact: In the Year of Our Lord 2000, George W. Bush's year of election, the three stars on the Republican Party's logo—the elephant—were turned upside-down, forming 'baphomet stars.' Remember, Skull and Bones founder William H. Russell, virtually formed the Republican party. This 'two party system' is a vetting process for the powers of evil, and ensures that only the intended holders of the office are presented to the American public. Prior to Russell's *formation* of the Republican Party he was a member of the 'Whig' Party.

The logo for the 'Modern Whig Party' *also* displays four baphomet stars, and its mascot is none other than '*Lilith*' the horned owl. One could assume the significance of the four stars to represent the *'Four Horsemen of the Apocalypse.'*

s.S.O.S.s.

45. Breaking the Seals

This passage(below) is the single most-amazing Revelation which caused me to begin writing this book—It was, for me, the initial Revelation of the Holy Grail! It all started when I had realized that it wasn't just the secret society of Skull & Bones who were evil, but that Yale was also in on this amazing debacle. But the intense writing and research, for this book, began after I decoded the symbology behind Yale's School Seal. We will decode it together….Enjoy:

A book featured on Yale's Coat of Arms is scrawled with *Hebrew* writing which reads, *'Urim and Thummim,'* and which are synonymous with the, *Breastplate of Judgement*, described in the last chapter. In fact, the Breastplate of Judgment is the only object to which those words were *ever* applied. So we can surmise that the Urim and Thummim *is* the object which is described on Yale's school seal.

Here is the passage describing the words Urim and Thummim, written on Yale's School Seal, from Yale's own website:

> "The two Hebrew words *(Urim v'Thummim)* at the center of the official Yale seal appear eight times in the Hebrew Bible. Jewish sources considered them **oracular gems** worn by the high priest Aaron. And their presence in Leviticus 8:8—the middle verse of the Pentateuch—suggests that **they identify the book on the Yale seal as The Bible itself.**"

s.s.O.s.s.

Urim and Thummim translate to, 'Lights and Perfections' or 'Lights and Truths,' in some texts.

The book on Yale's seal is definitely *not* the Holy Torah, *or* the Holy Bible—it is most certainly the *Wollebius's book!*

The Wollebius's book is a version of The Bible which has been molested for the purposes of the *protestant reformation*—The Wollebius's book was modified into an anti-christian work. Yale's School Seal is from a page of Yale's own website (http://archives.yalealumnimagazine.com/issues/01_03/seal.html), where the statement below is made:

> *"similar to a Harvard seal produced in 1650. Where Harvard had once written, In Christi Gloriam, "For the Glory of Christ." Yale inscribed the familiar, Lux et Veritas—"Light and Truth."*

The name Lucifer consists of two elements. The first part comes from the familiar Latin noun *lux*, meaning light. The second part of lucifer's name is a derivative of the Latin verb *fero*, which means to bring or carry and which exists in Greek as the verb φερω (*phero*); the second part of the Greek name εωσφορος (*eosphoros*)—means, 'light bringer.'

Luxury, root word Lux (n.) (etymonline.com)

c. 1300, "sexual intercourse;" mid-14c., "lasciviousness, sinful self-indulgence," from Old French luxury "debauchery, dissoluteness, lust" (Modern French luxure), from Latin luxuria excess, luxury,

s.s.O.s.s.

extravagance, profusion; delicacy" (source also of Spanish lujuria, Italian lussuria), from luxes" excess, extravagance, magnificence," probably a figurative use of luxes (adj.) "dislocated," which is related to luctari "wrestle, strain" (see reluctance)."

Here is the debacle which Yale describes as 'its biggest controversy to date' (again, taken from Yale's website):

The Urim and Thummim seal may have had religio-political overtones as well. The date on which the trustees first applied for a seal, October 17, 1722, was no random one in Yale history. Meeting in New Haven, **the trustees were likely preoccupied with the greatest scandal in the University's history. Rector Timothy Cutler had just publicly challenged the ordination of virtually every minister in New England**, thereby attacking the foundations of New England society. Cutler's earth-shaking Anglican-Arminian declaration has been compared by Yale historian Brooks M. Kelley to the 20th-century equivalent of a Yale President declaring that Russian communism was superior to American democracy.

Below, taken out From Yale's Bible, the Wollebius's book:

—THE RULES—

S.S.O.S.s.

*The High Priest was a type of Christ, the High Priest. (This Office of Christ is threefold, Prophetical, Sacerdotal, and Regal: His Prophetical office was to **instruct his Elect in heavenly Truths**, the parts whereof are, the **external Preaching of Gods will, and the internal illumination of the mind.** His Sacerdotal office is, to appear for us before God, with full satisfaction, and to intercede for us: the parts whereof are, Satisfaction and Intercession. **His Regal office is, to rule and preserve the Church**: the parts whereof are, the Government of the Church, **and the destruction of his enemies.**)*

I. *The High Priest was a type of Christ the High Priest.*

II *His rich clothing & ornaments, almost equal to regal robes, were types of Christ's dignity, and chiefly of his most perfect justice, See* Zac. 3.5.

III. *The chief ornaments were the Ephod, or cloak and Breast-plate fastened to the cloak: on the Ephod were the names of the twelve Tribes engraven upon precious stones; on the breast-plate were* Urim *and* Thummim; *from whence the Church received Oracles: The Cloak then represented the Church*; **Urim and Thummim, that is, light and perfection, did signify Christ the Word**

s.S.O.s.s.
and Interpreter of *the Father, our light and perfection (this line signifies Lucifer to be the God of Yale);* the Ephod represented *Christ,* as he performed the things that concerned us; *the Breastplate shewed him,* as he performed the things concerning God.

The Levites were they who, being used in stead of the first-born, were to attend the Priests, to keep and to carry the Tabernacle with its utensils (including the Breastplate of Judgment, and, the Ark of the Covenant—the item in question in the movie, *Indiana Jones and the Raider's of the Lost Ark).*

The extraordinary Ministers were the Prophets and *Nazarites.* The Prophets were they, who by divine inspiration teaching and reforming the *Priests and people, were types of Christ,* the great Prophet.

The **Nazarites** were they, who by a special vow abstaining from wine, and consecrating themselves to God, **were types of the holiness of Christ.**

In the holy worship, **we are to observe the instruments, and the manner of it.**

Note: In the satanic religion, the leader of the legion also dons the Biblical ephod, and calls himself a

s.S.O.S.s.

'high priest.' The evil one has stolen Aaron's High Priesthood (what was really the office of Moses in the first place), and has stolen the Breastplate of Judgement.

Just to summarize, Yale removed the words, *'For the Glory of Christ,'* from their seal, in favor of the new words, *'Urim and Thummim.'*

As aforementioned, the words, *Urim and Thummim*, are **only** used to describe *Aaron's Breastplate* in the story of the Israelites—*the object for which 'Judgment Day' of Revelation seems to have been named.*

Fun fact: *'Urim and Thummim'* doubles as Yale's school motto.

s.s.O.s.s.

46. The Nazi Rites

At the end of the last passage, the Nazirites were mentioned in Yale's molested Bible, the *Wollebius's book*. But who were the Biblical Nazirites mentioned toward the end of 'The Rules'? Well, let us break it down....Nazi means, *'Prince,'* in Hebrew. The word *'Rites'* means *'an act that is usually part of a religious ceremony,'* according to Miriam-Webster Dictionary.

Going back to WWII, it is widely accepted that the word 'Nazi' was an abbreviation for the word *'Nationalsozialist.'* The full name of the political party being, the "Nationalsozialistische Deutsche Arbeiterpartei"—or, *the National Socialist German Worker's Party*. I find this theory highly unlikely. Sure, the word, 'Nationalsozialist' employs all of the same letters as the word *Nazi* (though not in a convincing order), but, I know that the word was derived from a Biblical Jewish vow of the combined Hebrew words, 'Nazi,' and 'Rites'—the *Nazirites*.

Just like the Russells, and many more imperial and esoteric, elite Jewish families around the world, The Order seems to hide their Jewish heritage, only leaving faint clues and cryptic signs as to their lineage. Though, these elitists could not resist assigning their offspring with overtly Jewish names—on most occasions the arrogance of this bunch was their folly. These Cabalist, esoteric 'Jewish' elitists likely wanted to harm other 'Jews' for several reasons:

s.s.O.s.s.

—To thin the competition of those who may possess their ancient Cabalist technology of magic: i.e. mass manipulation, confusion through war intelligence, usury, etc.

—By thinning the 'Jewish' population, it would eliminate the possibility of the second coming of the Messiah, or for the Jewish it would technically represent the first coming of the Messiah, which, in any case, could potentially cause problems for this tight group of esoteric satanists which many wrongfully refer to as illuminati or 'Jews.'

These cowards have not the right to be deemed 'Judah,' as the rest of us do.

—By rounding up and killing the common so-called 'Jews,' The Order made their mass offering to the pagan devil Molech (Lilith).

—Finally, by continued oppression and genocide of the 'Jewish,' this small group of openly 'Jewish' (such as the Rothschilds) bankers is offered social safe haven for having been persecuted so often, when it is *they* who have perpetrated the persecution of the 'Jews' and *every other tribe of Judah on the planet.*

By naming the German Order, 'Nazis' (after the Nazirites of The Bible), it was the ultimate form of blasphemy. The Hebrew word 'Nazirite' has come to have its own meaning, 'consecrated,' or 'separated,' which is what the Nazis were in charge of—separating the 'Jews' from the Arian Germans....Though, for the Nazirites it meant they were separated in a Holy way for keeping a vow with God.

s.S.O.S.s.

In the book of Numbers, The Lord commands Moses to tell Aaron (the High Priest) to inform his people to themselves become, 'Nazirites,' **by *restricting their contact with the dead.*** One can only assume that the group which God deemed 'Nazirites,' had been practicing the same art of grave-robbery, and necromancy, as Skull and Bonesmen *still do* today.

We also see the same necromantic behavior from the Catholic Church, with their act of collecting and worshipping 'relics.'

God offered this vow to the Nazirites as a second chance to abandon their old ways of skullduggery, human sacrifice, and magic.

Animal sacrifice was the penalty for violating these Rites, but by actually killing *people* by their own hands, burning the bodies in the stead of an animal sacrifice became *the ultimate sin.*

Have a peek:

The Nazirite Vow
Numbers 6:1-5 King James Version
6 And the Lord spake unto Moses, saying,
2 Speak unto the children of Israel, and say unto them, When either man or woman shall separate themselves to vow a vow of a Nazarite, to separate themselves unto the Lord:
3 He shall separate himself from wine and strong drink, and shall drink no vinegar of wine, or vinegar of strong drink, neither shall he drink any liquor of grapes, nor eat moist grapes, or dried.

s.s.O.s.s.

4 All the days of his separation shall he eat nothing that is made of the vine tree, from the kernels even to the husk.

5 All the days of the vow of his separation there shall no razor come upon his head: until the days be fulfilled, in the which he separateth himself unto the Lord, he shall be holy, and shall let the locks of the hair of his head grow.

6 All the days that he separates himself to the Lord he shall not go near a dead body.

The German Nazi Order shaved their own heads in defiance of God's promise to the Nazirites who took this sacred vow.

Also, each Jewish prisoner's head was shaven at the moment they arrived at the concentration camps. This was another way for the evil Order to defile God's Word. For if the Nazirites were not to shave their own heads *or* come into contact with the dead, it most certainly would have been an abomination to shave the head of a human sacrifice to Molech.

Stalin had also practiced the head-shaving practice during his genocide of another seven-million so-called 'Jews' (which is also never spoken of), casting The Order's stinky shadow allover those atrocities too. Today you see 'Neo-Nazi' groups following the same evil orders, as they also shave their heads, deeming themselves, 'skinheads.' Sinead Oconnor, a known devil worshipper, also shaved her head for her performance on Saturday Night Live, at which she shredded a photograph of the Pope to show her loyalty to satan. (Whether or not Sinead knew that the Pope was one of satan's affiliate partners remains a mystery.)

s.s.O.s.s.

Head-shaving for American Soldiers (of all sort) coincided with World War I, which predates the Nazi soldiers only by several years. This would indicate that The Order passed this ritual on (from the American Order of Skull and Bones) to the Nazis, through their affiliate Chapter in Berlin—*Totenkopf.*

Numbers 6:6-11 King James Version
7 He shall not make himself unclean even for his father or his mother, for his brother or his sister, when they die (this could be where Templar head-worship originated), because his separation to God *is* on his head. **8** All the days of his separation he shall be holy to the Lord. **9 'And if anyone dies very suddenly beside him, and he defiles his consecrated head, then he shall shave his head** on the day of his cleansing; on the seventh day he shall shave it. **10** Then on the eighth day ***he shall bring two turtledoves or two young pigeons to the priest, to the door of the tabernacle of meeting; 11** and the priest ***shall offer one (dove) as a sin offering and** *the* **other as a burnt offering, and make atonement for him, because he sinned in regard to the corpse; and he shall sanctify his head that same day.**

*Note: In 2014 the first Jesuit Pope (Pope Francis) allowed two small children to release two white doves, as a peace offering, from a Vatican window. The two doves were brutally attacked, immediately,

s.S.O.S.s.

by two birds of differing species—a seagull, and a crow.

Prior to the release of the two doves, Francis had appealed for peace in Ukraine after three people were killed in clashes with government officials. Animal rights groups protested the event and the ritual was banished by the vatican—it seems that God was still a little salty about the necromantic Pope's blasphemous disregard of the *Nazirite vow.*

The Papal tradition of releasing two doves comes from one place in The Bible, and one place only....The above passage (Numbers 6:10-11). Therefore, the notion that the doves are released for peace, or for any other reason other than to rebel against God's direct order to sacrifice the birds for **the Pope's forbidden handling of the dead**, is a horrible distortion of the truth—*a direct slap in the face of God.*

The Papal tradition is in direct violation with the Biblical Nazi Rites which God himself had mandated.

Not only did the Nazis make bolts of sackcloth from human hair, they also made an assortment of household sundries from the skin and other organs of the human sacrifices to Molech. Google image 'holocaust victim lampshade'....As you view these images, I would like for you to remember that the Nazi Rites were given to The Order because they couldn't keep their hands off of the dead bodies, for their specific use in the dark arts.

The Nazirites were prohibited from having *any* contact with the dead, making a light shade extra-blasphemous, since it com-

s.S.O.S.s.

bines lucifer, the supposed bringer of *light*, with the skin of the deceased—a direct violation of the Pope's agreement with God.

Fun fact —Before the new Jesuit Pope could don his Dagon fishhead miter cap, another Pope had to 'resign.' On the night of Pope Benedict XVI's strange impromptu resignation, lightning struck the dome of Saint Peter's Basilica, not once, but twice, in only hours. The news event can be read about online (http://www.mirror.co.uk/news/world-news/lightning-bolt-hit-vatican-not-1705156).

Revelation 13:13 King James Version
13 And he doeth great wonders, so that he maketh fire come down from heaven on the earth in the sight of men,…

47. The Indian Head Scalping Lie

'Indian' head-scalping, despite what you have been taught, was never a Native American tradition. In fact, there is no known record of Indians 'scalping,' *anyone* on the North American continent, that is until the dreaded Order showed up in supposed 1492, when, '*Columbus, sailed the ocean blue.*' Catchy right?

Although Native American peoples were all too often accused of being the sole practitioners of head-scalping, in reality they did nothing others, throughout history, had not done before.

Orosius reported that the Romans scalped during the battle of the Raudine plain. And Herodotus found the practice among the Pontic Scythians, and, according to the Maccabees.

It is *highly* likely too that, Germanic tribes behaved similarly, for we know that they also assigned magical meaning to a shock of human hair, rendering the skin and wig of an enemy as a symbol of the 'free man.' The ancient Persians have also been known to use the 'scalping' practice on prisoners.

In ancient Germanic law, if a court demanded that a guilty party's head be shaved, it was considered to be a particularly heinous sentence—in very serious cases the court could sentence that the hair of the accused be ripped out *with* the skin.

As mentioned, the Germans exhibited the same practice of shaving bald heads of prisoners held in Nazi *death* camps. But, the same form of scalping was inflicted on the *bochesses* (German-lovers) after the defeat of the *Wehrmacht* in the zones occupied by Germany during World War II.

S.S.O.S.s.

The Vandals instituted the same method of head-scalping (*decalvatio*) as a method of torture; several provisions described in the Sachsenspiegel *(the oldest and most influential legal code of medieval Germany)* reflect the same. (Remember, The Order of Skull and Bones refers to anyone outside of The Order as, '*Vandals.*')

In museums around the US, actual scalps were still on display, even as late as the 1980s.

Museums having 'scalps' in their collections included Harvard's Peabody Museum of Archaeology and Ethnology, the Fort Ticonderoga museum on Lake Champlain, and the Robert S. Peabody Museum of Archaeology in Andover Michigan.

In 1990, the feds passed the Native American Graves Protection and Repatriation Act. This Act mandated the return of *all* sacred Indian artifacts and other remains. **Museums then began to poor through the Colonial human remains in their collections. Their curators returned the Indian scalps to their rightful owners, and, there was but one exception made….*Skull and Bones kept their relic, Geronimo's head*.**

History confirms that many of the early Colonial authorities even offered a bounty on *Indian* scalps.

Hannah Dustin, a Colonial Puritan (the same religion claimed by the 'Yale Bible'), while detained on an island in the Merrimack River in present-day Boscawen, New Hampshire, killed and scalped 10 Native American family members who held them hostage, with the 'assistance of two other captives.' She even collected a monetary reward and a pewter tankard, for her bravery.

In Salem (where the infamous witch flare-ups and 'trials' were held), trophy Indian scalps were proudly displayed along the

S.S.O.S.S.

walls of the town courthouse, in full public view, *until the building was demolished in 1785.*

s.S.O.S.s.

48. American Education

With little research I came upon some more disturbing truth —we are 'dumbed down' intentionally in order to give The Order an unfair advantage over the common man. In fact, the very phrase 'dumbing down' comes from the Hegelian Theory which William Huntington supposedly 'traveled to Germany to learn,' before founding The Order of Skull and Bones on Yale's Campus.

In American schools we are intentionally taught, and tested upon, stupidity such as memorizing dates of events, or birth and death dates of so-called leaders, when the meat of the information lies within the concepts and mechanisms with which changed our world. Every subject we are taught in school follow this same philosophy—they are all taught in confusing, non-essential, and complicated ways, *after* our window of intense learning, at a young age, closes.

Listen:

> "Instruction in world history in the so-called high schools is even today in a very sorry condition. Few teachers understand that the study of history can never be to learn historical dates and events by heart and recite them by rote; that what matters is not whether the child knows exactly when this battle or that was fought, when a general was born, or even when a monarch (usually a very insignificant one) came into the crown of his forefathers. No, by

S.S.O.S.S.

the living God, this is very unimportant. To 'learn' history means to seek and find the forces which are the causes leading to those effects **which we subsequently** *perceive* **as historical events."**

— Adolf Hitler, Mein Kampf

The elite become skilled in attributes leaning toward running our world, and we are destined to remain the foundation of the pyramid—i.e. slaves and craftsman.

Progressives were a new brand of educator who arrived at the scene around the turn of the century. They rejected the literal meaning of The Bible and replaced faith with science, evolution and psychology—the people would now *be their own saviors.* Later this bastardized philosophy was imposed on American education, which transformed the psychology of academic function from one designed for learning, to one devoted to behavioral change. A philosophy which denies one of their individualism and conditions the young of a society to be children of the state, a small brick in a far greater structure.

A man named **James Earl Russell** was highly responsible for changing all of that.

As with his relative, William Huntington Russell, James Earl Russell also was sent away to Germany to get his Hegelian education. Just as his eugenics philosophy of the late 1800s to the mid-1900s was being circulated around the world, today's teaching methods are the result of the legacy of the same German psychologist Wilhelm Wundt and the Rockefeller family's so-called *'philanthropic'* project.

s.s.O.s.s.

Outtake from, *Deliberate Dumbing Down of America, by,* Charlotte Thomson Iserbyt:

Professor at University of Leipzig, Wundt **(James Earl Russell's mentor in Germany)** was the originator of what he termed a "new" or "experimental" psychology that **stripped psychology of any of its potential philosophical concerns with the soul, will, or self-determination of the individual.** In Wundt's reconfiguration of psychology the **mind is merely an apparatus that responds to given stimuli**, and through the measurement and recording of the stimuli and responses of the subject the psychologist in the laboratory (subsequently the teacher—and now the students—in the classroom) can determine the effectiveness of one stimulus-response method over another, as well as the functional capacities of the student.

For Wundt and his followers the human being is the sum total of one's experiences; **devoid of character and essence that might interfere with the ends of the collective unit. This view of the human psyche set the stage for the establishment of eugenics, psychiatry, and the social engineering carried out in public school classrooms.**

This is the very foundation of psychiatry.

s.s.O.s.s.

The reason I shared this excerpt with you was not to bore you to the point of closing this book. Moreover, it was an attempt to bring your attention to *James Earl* **Russell** who inspired the institution of 'change agents,' who then were dispatched by our federal educational agency, in order to delay intensive learning curriculum a couple of years. This strategy closed the window of learning to the child, during the years in which a solid intellectual foundation can be most-readily accepted.

This must be why I hated school. That is as far as I care to regurgitate the boring, dogmatic, enigmatic and historically perverted philosophies behind the stupidity which is being programmed into our American youth (suggested book list at end of work, if one is interested).

Rather, I will break this unbelievable phenomenon down to its absurd simplicity—the excrement with which we program our offspring in their formative years will demonstrate, more basically, how silly we have truly become. I will then spend the remainder of this section (and the next couple of sections) completely undressing and attacking the very credibility of the most respected, lying 'educational' institutions of our land.

Along with the age of 'enlightenment' came the perversion of every Christian holiday. Satanic, puritanic anti-christian zealots, who claim not to be religious, spent the dawn of the nineteenth century mounting a campaign which would remove Christ from the greatest holidays ever honored, and which they've replaced with their fictitious teachings.

With luciferian religious zest these 'new light' crusaders set out to pluck any shred of Christianity from the American culturescape. The result of which is the pagan revival of a 'jolly old elf' who stole Christmas. The Dr. Seuss movie, *The Grinch Who Stole Christmas,* is a very good celebratory analogy for what actually took place with the removal of Christianity in America (and the world) during those times.

The pagan ritual of erecting a 'Christmas' tree replaced the nativity scene. The material-drunk, ritualistic waste of lent credit, which we repay throughout the remainder of the year with interest to the usurious monsters selling us this wagonload of manure, is what followed. It is now virtually unAmerican to not take part in this satanic orgy, and, just as no kid at school cares to be made to feel left out, or to feel different from others, every family in America, and most of the world, followed suit in the invented pagan ritual.

Though this in itself is a worthy topic of discussion, I am merely making a point, which is that, this sword, which has been thrust into the belly of Christianity, has many edges....One edge killed Christianity and moved 'enlightenment' closer to its goal of corruption of every mind on the planet. The Bible went away, along with the true Christmas—our book of Holy Scriptures, at that time, became a collection of myths to the general public.

Another edge of the sword fills the coffers of the banking and retail industries—it could strongly be argued that our very economic engine would seize were it not for the bastardized holiday on which we have come to rely in place of our savior. Christmas has become a form of bondage whose red slave-master we attempt to outpace as he brushes the heels of our work-boots with the tips of his black, buckled clodhoppers.

Think about the perverted nature of this concept....We spend the entire year teaching our children—'don't speak with strangers'—and—'there are very bad people out there who want to cause you harm.' After which, we bus them to the mall and set them upon the lap of a creepy old guy smelling of vodka, whom they don't know; a guy who whispers enamoring fantasies into the ears of our young.

During another holiday they dress like skeletons, and *pirates*, and we shuttle them to random neighborhoods, to indulgently take pounds-and-pounds of processed sugar (poison), from… *strangers*. However, this is not my point, I just couldn't resist—my point is this….Our entire goal in life, if we are good parents, is to offer our children an education which will suit them in preparation for what we call the 'real world.'

Contrary to that premise, we teach our child about fictional anthropomorphic characters, most of whom have replaced the true meaning of Christian holidays, and we choose to have our children believe these things until they are *teenagers*. Our children live in a complete fantasy world where nothing is reality, at all. And then we wonder why they cannot sit still in class, and we cannot imagine how little Johnny developed, *'A-D-D.'*

We then shatter our child's entire reality when we break their tender little hearts with the news that, everything we have ever taught them about every major holiday is complete contrived feculence. I remember making *my* girls cry, it broke *my* heart. But, I think that, the reason it hurt so bad is the fact that, I had deceived them for so long. I felt awful for breaking their confidence. And their little expressions showed me their lack of trust in me, afterward.

This is a dangerous concept; for a human being to be nurtured in such confusion. For a religion who claims to represent

s.S.O.S.s.

'lux et veritas,' or, *'light and truth,'* the luciferian rituals, which have spread like a cancer through our society, certainly are contradictory to everything they teach. It is no wonder we have so many behavioral and educational problems with our children.

At the ages in which our children ought to be rigorously taught to read, write, and solve problems of mathematics, they instead are outlining their hand in crayon; after which they cut the shape out with scissors; to which they attach multicolored construction paper feathers. They then make a construction paper headdress and moronically run around a cafetorium stage as they pound their mouths with their palms; which in turn emits a ridiculous, intermittently muffled noise by the hand with which their mouth is being pounded.

The re-enactment of a contrived holiday of excess, and turkey-eating follows, as we also celebrate a holiday which adds insult to the injury we have caused to an entire continent of people whom we now call, *'Indians.'*

To finish our soiree with the education of our small children, we will review an eighth grade final exam from 1895; from Salina, KS.

The test below was taken from the original document on file at the Smoky Valley Genealogical Society and Library in Salina, KS and reprinted by the Salina Journal.

8th Grade Final Exam: Salina, KS 1895

Grammar (Time, one hour)
1. Give nine rules for the use of Capital Letters.

s.s.O.s.s.

2. Name the Parts of Speech and define those that have no modifications.
3. Define Verse, Stanza and Paragraph.
4. What are the Principal Parts of a verb? Give Principal Parts of do, lie, lay and run.
5. Define Case, Illustrate each Case.
6. What is Punctuation? Give rules for principal marks of Punctuation.
7. Write a composition of about 150 words and show therein that you understand the practical use of the rules of grammar.

Arithmetic (Time, 1.25 hours)
1. Name and define the Fundamental Rules of Arithmetic.
2. A wagon box is 2 ft. deep, 10 feet long, and 3 ft. wide. How many bushels of wheat will it hold?
3. If a load of wheat weighs 3942 lbs., what is it worth at 50 cents. Per bu., deducting 1050 lbs. for **tare**?
4. District No. 33 has a valuation of $35,000. What is the necessary levy to carry on a school seven months at $50 per month, and have $104 for incidentals?
5. Find cost of 6720 lbs. coal at $6.00 per ton.
6. Find the interest of $512.60 for 8 months and 18 days at 7 percent.
7. What is the cost of 40 boards 12 inches wide and 16 ft. long at $20 per >>m?

S.S.O.S.S.

8. Find bank discount on $300 for 90 days (no grace) at 10 percent.
9. What is the cost of a square farm at $15 per acre, the distance around which is 640 rods?
10. Write a Bank Check, a Promissory Note, and a Receipt.

U.S. History (Time, 45 minutes)
1. Give the epochs into which U.S. History is divided.
2. Give an account of the discovery of America by Columbus.
3. Relate the causes and results of the Revolutionary War.
4. Show the territorial growth of the United States.
5. Tell what you can of the history of Kansas.
6. Describe three of the most prominent battles of the Rebellion.
7. Who were the following: Morse, Whitney, Fulton, Bell, Lincoln, Penn, and Howe?
8. Name events connected with the following dates: 1607, 1620, 1800, 1849, and 1865?

Orthography (Time, one hour)
1. What is meant by the following: Alphabet, phonetic orthography, etymology, syllabication?
2. What are elementary sounds? How classified?

s.s.O.s.s.

3. What are the following, and give examples of each: Trigraph, subvocals, diphthong, cognate letters, linguals?

4. Give four substitutes for caret 'u'.

5. Give two rules for spelling words with final 'e'. Name two exceptions under each rule.

6. Give two uses of silent letters in spelling. Illustrate each.

7. Define the following prefixes and use in connection with a word: Bi, dis, mis, pre, semi, post, non, inter, mono, super.

8. Mark diacritically and divide into syllables the following, and name the sign that indicates the sound: Card, ball, mercy, sir, odd, cell, rise, blood, fare, last.

9. Use the following correctly in sentences: Cite, site, sight, fane, fain, feign, vane, vain, vein, raze, raise, rays.

10. Write 10 words frequently mispronounced and indicate pronunciation by use of diacritical marks and by syllabication.

Geography (Time, one hour)

1. What is climate? Upon what does climate depend?

2. How do you account for the extremes of climate in Kansas?

3. Of what use are rivers? Of what use is the ocean?

4. Describe the mountains of N.A.

s.S.O.S.s.

5. Name and describe the following: Monrovia, Odessa, Denver, Manitoba, Hecla, Yukon, St. Helena, Juan Fernandez, Aspinwall and Orinoco.
6. Name and locate the principal trade centers of the U.S.
7. Name all the republics of Europe and give capital of each.
8. Why is the Atlantic Coast colder than the Pacific in the same latitude?
9. Describe the process by which the water of the ocean returns to the sources of rivers.
10. Describe the movements of the earth. Give inclination of the earth.

If this test was a requirement to simply *move on* to High School (only a hundred years ago), and a Yale Grad most-likely couldn't pass it today, *how are we ever supposed to believe in evolution?*

Fun fact: Christmas, 'a celebration of the birth of Jesus Christ,' is celebrated on December 25. There is no known record of the date on which Christ was born. King Nimrod *was* born on this date, and *he* sports a long beard and hair just like 'Santa Claus.'

s.s.O.s.s.

49. The Ordure of Yale University

A little known book titled *William Russell and his descendants* has this to say about what the Russells brought to the North American Continent:

> A large number of the earliest settlers of the Colony of Virginia were cavaliers and younger branches of noble English Houses. **They brought with them education, influence, and wealth; and shared largely the tastes, feelings, and principles of *Their Order.***
>
> The large extent of rich territory to be obtained by patent or purchase offered great inducements to the adventurous youth of the mother country; and **the granting of this in large tracts to many, established at a very early period all the elements of a landed aristocracy.**
>
> The histories of many of the early colonists were doubtless full of interest, and some of them were of a romantic nature, but we are denied the pleasure of obtaining much relating to their deeds and exploits, as at that period, few records were kept, and comparatively little has been preserved for posterity. ***In founding their families in America they seem to have overlooked the importance of keeping an**

s.s.O.s.s.
account of their times and of chief events of their histories, for the benefit of future generations; consequently, tradition has largely to be depended on in gathering the history of colonial families. [William Russell and His Descendant, By Anna Russell Des Cognets, Page 1]

Note*: By now it is very clear to anyone who is reading this with a conscience, why the Russell's *'seem to have overlooked the importance of keeping an account of their times and of the chief events of their histories.'* I believe this may be what the confused (but inspired) conspiracy theorists call, 'The Shadow Government,' on the websites having red letters upon black backgrounds.

As you will see **Yale University was also founded entirely by 'The Order' of the Russell family** whose degenerated values were spread to India by the **East India Company** of Jesuits, long before they were forced upon our American youth. The Jesuits knew they would have to govern the very foundation of education in order to ensure that their clandestine *values* and *traditions* carried on in America. The shape-shifters are now among our educators, which gives The Order control of our government officials, bankers, doctors, ministers in *all* religions, and our highest judges of the land. They all blend together like a giant spiderweb of evil which has now encased, and enslaved, the entirety of America.

The Order has ensured that any challenge to their scientific authority will be vehemently shot down, at the risk of the professional demise of their academic prey. The Order are *not* bringers

S.S.O.S.S.

of *truth,* or *light,* but instead a group of marauders who have murdered the word truth, and who have traded the only light of fact for a simple, sketchy, keychain flashlight which intermittently sparks in a dim fashion.

Here is where this story all comes together....Originally named the *'Collegiate School'* in the Colony of Connecticut, the school was renamed 'Yale' in 1718 in the honor of Elihu Yale. But, before being an intellectual benefactor for the highest school in the land, Elihu Yale was also a high-ranking rapist at East India Company, serving as **President, of the *'Honourable'* East India Company—its *proper* name.**

During his working years at EIC, Yale spent some time in Africa where there was an established Order among African men who, after being overcome by the darkness of the creed, were quite willing to enslave their own African people and pack them up on the slave ships destined for America.

After his stronghold in the slave trade was assured in Africa, Yale himself resided in, and presided over, the country of India for years. But, Yale's corrupt nature, which must have come with the territory of the business of piracy, got him fired by EIC share holders in the end. Yale amassed a fortune while looting for the company, largely through secret contractual *looting* with Madras merchants, which was against the *Honourable* East India Company's less-than-*honorable* business directive.

Yale died on July 8–1721, in London, England, but was buried in the churchyard of the parish church of St. Giles in Wrexham, Wales.

Yale's tomb in Wales is inscribed:

s.S.O.S.s.

Born in America, in Europe bred
In Africa travell'd and in Asia wed
Where long he liv'd and thriv'd; In London dead
Much good, **some ill, he did; so hope all's even**
And that his soul thro' mercy's gone to Heaven
You that survive and read this tale, take care
For this most certain exit to prepare
Where blest in peace, the actions of the just
Smell sweet and blossom in the silent dust.

Note: I take the last line of the feculence above to mean:

For you who survive take care, for Elihu Yale's internment was blessed in peace—but the horrific atrocities which Yale committed on this earth will grow and thrive, as his body turns to dust.

In Boston, Massachusetts, a tablet to Yale was erected in 1927, at Scollay Square, near the site of Yale's birth. Yale president, Arthur Twining Hadley **(S&B 1876)** penned the inscription, which reads:

On Pemberton Hill, 255 Feet North of This Spot,
Was Born on April Fifth 1649 Elihu Yale, Governor
of Madras, Whose Permanent Memorial in His Native Land is the College That Bears His Name.

s.s.O.s.s.

Elihu Yale was an evil man, and even to this day racially charged demonstrations take place on Yale's Hogwarts-like campus of magic.

Recent controversy surrounding Yale's dirty past (namely the sale of over ten-million slaves and untold thousands of shiploads of dope) has stirred up the idea of changing Yale's name. As you can now imagine, that controversy has been met with extremely harsh resistance.

William Huntington Russell (co-founder of Skull and Bones) was, if you will also recall, another sad, sad, hard luck story.

Below is what Wikipedia has to say about Little Willy's tough situation:

> Born in Middletown, Connecticut, Russell was a cadet at the American Literary, Scientific and Military Academy (later Norwich University) from 1826 until graduation in 1828, where he was taught under strict military discipline. **In 1828, William's father died, piling family responsibility on to him. Under severe financial restraints, he entered Yale College. He supported himself throughout his college years.** In 1823 Samuel Russell, his cousin founded Russell & Co.

The reason that none of this holds water? One of the original founders of the college was another patriarch to the Russell family, *Nodiah Russell*. **Believe it or not, Nodiah Russell was the son of yet another William Russell who emigrated to North**

s.s.O.s.s.

America in 1638! (Disturbingly, Nodiah Russell was a renowned minister, as were many of his 9 children.)

If you will remember, Sammy Russell (founder of Russell & Co. which first brought opium to America in great volume) was supposedly an 'orphan' who made all of his money the good old-fashioned way, hard work. Sammy didn't even attend school. But, despite Sam's 'lack of education,' the guy is highly honored at Yale. *'The Samuel Wadsworth Russell House'* is preserved in the dope-dealer's honor to this day. Yes, Samuel Russell, the premiere opium dealer during the Qing dynasty, made his home on High Street, on what is now the Yale Campus, right down the road from the infamous Skull & Bones tomb.

Before my Gramps died, he pointed at a book in his collection which he had held in high regard. He explained to me that it held information which I would need to know for the future. Even years after Gramps died, after even reading the book, I had no idea why in the world Gramps would have had me read that old book—though it *was* interesting.

The Book was titled, *War on Gold*, which was a solid read, but, the following outtakes are from Antony C. Sutton's tell-all Skull and Bones book, *America's Secret Establishment (which you too should read in order to understand what's happened at Yale)*, enjoy:

First, there is a Yale secret society open only to a select few:

"For more than forty years a secret society called Skull and Bones has existed in Yale College. It receives a certain number of men from each class. These are chosen nominally by the members of the class . . ., although **it is understood that a prominent man's influence avails for his friends and relatives through several years after his graduation. By observing the men elected from year to year, we find that they are chosen with a distinct end in view, namely, that of obtaining for the society the most honors.** Some of these honors are given to literary, some to wealthy men. This, then, is the case. Men receive marks of distinction from Yale College or from their entire class, because of which they are taken into this secret society. Since Yale honors men, this fraternity professes to honor them also."

Secondly, the Iconoclast states that The Order has obtained control of Yale, and its members care more for their society than for Yale:

"Out of every class Skull and Bones takes its men. **They have gone out into the world and have become, in many instances, leaders in society. They have obtained control of Yale.** Its business is performed by them. **Money paid to the college must pass into their hands, and be subject to their will.** No doubt they are worthy men in themselves, **but the many whom they looked down upon while in college, cannot so far forget as to give money**

s.S.O.S.s.

freely into their hands. Men in Wall Street complain that the college comes straight to them for help, instead of asking each graduate for his share. The reason is found in a remark made by one of Yale's and America's first men: Few will give but Bones men, and they care far more for their society than they do for the college."

Finally, the Iconoclast calls The Order a "deadly evil" growing year by year:

"Year by year the deadly evil is growing. **The society was never as obnoxious to the college as it is today, and it is just this ill-feeling that shuts the pockets of non-members.** Never before has it shown such arrogance and self-fancied superiority. It grasps the College Press and endeavors to rule it all. It does not deign to show its credentials, but clutches at power with the silence of conscious guilt."

We will finish our brief tour of Hogwarts with a final outtake from Antony C. Sutton's same book:

Just to ensure the official line dominates, in 1946 **the Rockefeller Foundation allotted $139,000 for an official history of World War Two.** This to avoid a repeat of debunking history books which embarrassed the Establishment after World War

S.S.O.S.S.

One. The reader will be interested to know that **The Order we are about to investigate had great foresight, back in the 1880s, to create both the American Historical Association and the American Economic Association (most economists were then more historians than analysts) under their terms, with their people and their objectives.** Andrew Dickerson White was a member of The Order **(S&B 1853)** and **the first President of the American Historical Association.**

And don't think it is only Yale that has been corrupted. Every school in the Ivy league has been infiltrated by The Order (and their bogus dogmatic teachings), and all of their trickle down schools look to them as leaders in education.

Bohemian Grove is littered with these creeps, and it has been said that there is not a college in California whose administration doesn't harbor those who are affiliated with Bohemian Grove *and or* Skull and Bones.

The Morrill Land Bill Act of 1862 was the piece of legislation which The Order used to swipe much of the property in New Haven, right out from under the nose of its unsuspecting citizens. Daniel Coit Gilman **(S&B 1852)** encouraged The Order's old patsy Abraham Lincoln to sign the Bill after it had been previously shot down by Buchanan in 1857.

Here is what the New Haven Register had to say about the consequences of the infamous Skull and Bones land grab **(headline: Yale's tax exempt New Haven property worth $2.5 billion)**:

s.s.O.s.s.

If you're in downtown New Haven, whether on Chapel, York Street, Broadway or at Whitney Avenue and Audubon Street, it's a good bet you're near a Yale-owned building.

It's not true, though it may seem so, that "the city *is* the university," as a visitor from Brazil, Susana Moreira, said recently on Broadway during a tour of the Northeast with her daughter.

What is true is that Yale University, a premier, world-renowned research institution, takes up large portions of downtown, and **doesn't pay taxes on its dorms, classrooms, libraries, research labs or the grassy oases inside the residential quads.**

Those properties, spread over the Hill, East Rock and other neighborhoods, are worth $2.5 billion in assessed value, according to the 2013 grand list, **but are all tax-exempt by state law.** (Yale and other colleges are specifically exempted by state law.) **They include Sterling Memorial Library on Cross Campus, the Yale Center for British Art on Chapel Street and the Yale Health Center on Lock Street.**

Yale recently bought *Bayer Medical Complex (Bayer being another great empire of The Order)*, and why wouldn't they?

S.S.O.S.S.

The School continues to monopolize the real estate of the area, despite the fact that they don't pay a penny in property tax, which is simply lost to the state with every profitable acquisition.

Student loans and taxes remain the only forms of debt which cannot be discharged in a bankruptcy, but Yale and other universities continue to pay nothing for property and other taxes, regardless of their reported 25.6 billion dollar endowment, and the fact that, *much of their land was donated to them, for free, by the common citizen of Connecticut.*

The amount of impish influence wielded by Yale is beyond measure. To understand it completely, you really should go back and read Sutton's whole work—it will fill in a lot of the empty spaces. Inside Sutton's work you will see for yourself that, The Order is behind the foundation of the UN, the Historical Society, and nearly every other regulatory society and agency in America.

s.s.O.s.s.

50. Yale's Bible Reveals the Antichrist

It must now be quite obvious to you (as it is to me) that, if Yale makes an announcement which reveals the identity of the antichrist, we *should* all listen. Well, apparently, that is exactly what they did hundreds of years ago. The passage below was taken from the Yale website:

> Clarification of the Hebrew words (on Yale's New School Seal) may reside in Yale's primary divinity text, Johannes Wollebius's *The Abridgement of Christian Divinitie, which was then studied all afternoon every Friday by Yale students as part of the long preparation for the Christian Sabbath.* Wollebius's book was of such importance, Samuel Johnson (Class of 1714) noted sarcastically, that it was: *"considered with equal or greater veneration than The Bible itself."*

> The "New Lights" attacked the established order by questioning the value of education outside of understanding Jesus. Many "Old Lights" thought religious knowledge was central to an education, but hardly sufficient for one. The latter opinion prevailed at Yale.

Here is what Yale's "Bible" was nice enough to elaborate for us about the "Antichrist":

s.s.O.s.s.

—1 Joh. 2.18. **Little Children, now is the last time; and as ye have heard that Antichrists would come, even now many Antichrists are begun.** Epist. c. 4. v. 3. Whatsoever spirit doth not confess that Jesus Christ is come in the flesh, **he is not of God**▪ but this is that spirit of antichrist, of whom you have heard, that he was to come, and that he is now in the World.

—"THE RULES"—

I. The name Antichrist belongs not to one person alone, but to a whole state or *order of men*, as it were in the same Kingdom succeeding each other.

II. Even as the word of High-Priest. He is not then opposite to Christ, as one person is to another, in respect of substance; but he is opposite to him in respect of quality or office.

III.I. The Papists will have Antichrist to be one particular

s.s.O.s.s.

man; a Jew of the Tribe of Dan, the Jews Messiah, and the restorer of their Religion, who shall reign at Jerusalem three years and a half, shall fight with Henoch and Eliah, shall offer to ascend to heaven from Mount Olivet, but shall be destroyed by Christ.

IV. But we out of Scripture describe Antichrist thus. 1. **That he is a man at one time, one; but in succession of time,** *an Order of men*; **in the same state** *succeeding each other* **[Skull and Bones]**. 2. *Raised by satan.* 3. **A** *Christian in name only.* 4. **In very deed** *Christ's Enemy.* 5. **Sitting in the Temple of God as God.** 6. **Reigning in that great City, which ruleth over the Kings of the Earth.** [I think that we all know the City to which the Author is referring.

326

s.S.O.S.s.

51. Why The Order Hates The Bible

The Bible has become a subject of ridicule in today's times. If you believe literally in its content you are scoffed at, as if you…Well, as if you believe that a jolly, old, fat and indulgent man climbs down your chimney in the middle of the night, wielding a bag of goodies and gifts for your children. Or, you are treated as if you believe that a giant rabbit who speaks fluent English hopped around your backyard, scattering colorful eggs with material prizes and candy within them. Or, you are treated as if you believe that, if you lose a tooth you can place it underneath your pillow and a magical, flying fairy will have such great adoration for the organic reject that she will pay you handsomely for the relic.

    The 'satan' must be grinning from ear to ear that a fellow nymph, dressed in red, has stolen the wonder of our children's minds—a fellow who nearly shares the same name….*How did that ever work?*

    The Bible is a series of historic warnings from civilizations which have risen and fallen, due to the same harmful dialectic of good verses evil as I am currently describing. If you study the rise and fall of civilizations it will become quite clear to you that a war, a controlled conflict which satisfies financial and eugenic demands on both sides of an event, many times will implode the very fabric of that civilization. In fact, the very philosophy, on which societies today are built, relies on this destruction and rebirth as part of its synthesis.

s.S.O.S.s.

Complete societal demise is an event which is planned for by the elite citizens of its inhabitants. Hence your tax dollars having paid for an entire underground city in which your president, and congress, *will* live, upon the inevitable implosion of our society. This is also why we see crumbled remains of great cities throughout the landscape of this planet, and, meanwhile, The Order's media scoffs at we so-called *'preppers.'*

A new civilization will birth from the remains of the past, of which its evil leaders had hoarded the wealth of its citizens (you're relatives) in exchange for worthless paper fiat currency. Remnants of past technology is destroyed, then doled out slowly over time in their new settlement, in order to have a handy advantage over its new citizens. The new society which rises from the ashes of the one fallen, having seen the evils of war and destruction, gravitates back toward Christian (moral and ethical) values, and fills the plates of the false prophets of the world, which were also a creation of The Order.

I happen to live within the city of Phoenix—a city which has indeed 'risen from the ashes'—literally. *Phoenix derives its name from Ancient Phoenicia.*

With time, the evil of the luciferian, overindulgent and self-serving humanistic philosophies are injected back into a society by the evil ones, imposing inevitable societal destruction, and the dialectic cycle is repeated. At the twilight of this evil cycle, a society usually will resort to the worship of idols, to which human sacrifice is offered. Again, we see proof of human sacrifice in nearly every, if not *every,* fallen civilization, including Nazi Germany.

We are now at that point in American society.

s.S.O.S.s.

Modern technology has simply allowed The Order to make these human sacrifices in the covert form of our soldiers and their 'enemies' killed at war (illicit drugs have even been smuggled back into the US in their desecrated bodies); cancers caused by party favors such as cigarettes and alcohol; prescription or illicit drugs which are also dealt by the elite of our government; the mountains of carbohydrates prescribed by our government in the form of the **'food *pyramid*,'** or the killing of innocent civilians by long-range missiles and drones. Here is some more of The Order's handiwork: If you have the stomach for it, a google search will turn up 'modern day crucifixion,' or, 'beheadings' of children and men and women of all ages.

In response, we so-called 'Americans' make ignorant and naive comments such as, 'I *really* hope those terrorists all kill each other,' or, 'we should turn the entire Middle East into a glass parking lot.' Shame on us.

These modern offerings to molech are being bundled, and celebrated in the way of 'mock' human sacrifice at places such as Bohemian Grove California and Burning Man, where pagans worship satan (whether they realize it *or not*) and burn 'effigies' of children before the individuals who lead our country, and the world. It's crazy! *I am not judging....Six months ago I wanted to go to Burning Man!*

These are not the acts of Muslims *or* terrorists. They are the acts of secret societies of satanists who have been corrupted by The Order with money, *and power.* Just as The Order had historically protected themselves by creating racism, and making the supposed *'Jews'* the 'victims' in history, so they are now doing the same for Islam. SATANISTS ARE RUNNING AROUND

S.S.O.S.s.
KILLING IN THE NAME OF NIMROD, UNDER THE RUSE OF BEING MUSLIM!

The **Jews** *are* the **victims**, but we are *all Jews*, and are *all 'The Victims!'* Under this race ruse, The Order is offered a safe haven in which to freely behead Christians *and Muslims*, and offer uploads of the Modern Crusades to the internet for the viewing pleasure of a bloodthirsty counterculture of demonic jackals who now run *EVERYTHING!*

The terrorists are now free to run, and revile, rampantly, to terrorize many states of loving, God-fearing people. Still parading around under the ruse of being Muslim, the Egyptian God Isis (who also dons black garments), now makes daily Christian sacrifice, indiscriminately, in all of our homeland, *The Middle East.*

As the ground-forces of this legion of demons beheads Christian *and Muslim* men, women and children, in the Middle East, The head of the Jesuit Military, America, and her allies, kills even more innocents by throwing some of the starry host down to the earth and trampling upon them.

If you truly believe that these evildoers are Muslim, I have a nice beach house in Syria in which you may be quite interested.

On February 1, 2013, John **Forbes** Kerry (Skull & Bones 1966) was sworn in as the 68th Secretary of State of the United States. The **Secretary of State**, appointed by the President with the advice and consent of the Senate, is the President's **chief foreign affairs adviser**. The **Secretary carries out the President's foreign policies through the State Department and the Foreign Service of the United States.**

The date (above) marking John Kerry's presidential appointment, marks the beginning of high resolution, professional

s.S.O.S.s.

level production of ISIS videos showing live burnings and beheadings. All of which, are no doubt the result of the same creeps at the Bohemian Club, who would all love to view the evil deeds done to Christians; and Muslims; and *'The Jews.'* Which, of course, are all celebrated in *'effigy.'*

Most of the major atrocities, and acts of war perpetrated against these poor and oppressed people in the Middle East, are carried out on dates which correspond to major satanic, and pagan holidays, at the same exact time in which our elite our carrying out the cremation of Care Ceremony at Bohemian Grove. We have surpassed the atrocities committed by the ancient Romans, in the coliseum.

The atrocities are now just witnessed by the evildoers remotely, at their leisure—not in plain site, but, right under our very noses. (Thor's dreaded, 'mythical' 'bolt of lighting' has indeed been given life.)

A google image search will reveal a photo of John Kerry chumming it up with Anton Szandor Lavey (Author of the satanic bible). We must open our eyes. From one cover to the other The Bible warns of the corruption of evildoers, and bastardization of society in exchange for temporary comfort for the privileged few. Personal gain and power in this world, for our few governing parties, is traded for our inevitable societal destruction.

Even in the event that one still denies the possibility of a higher power, it seems the common concerned citizen would adopt The Bible, and its teachings of good, by the same premise under which satanists *claim to* worship the devil—"he doesn't exist"—in order to perpetuate and promote good within a society.

S.S.O.S.s.

Nearly every prophecy written in the Holy Bible has come to pass with precise historic accuracy, which in itself should be miracle enough to believe in God without the need for faith. However, the so-called 'Discovery' channel glorifies the vague predictions of the supposed prophecy of Nostradamus as if he slipped a sliver of paper, having tomorrow's winning lottery numbers, into your pocket.

Though to ourselves we always appear to be highly evolved, and believe that our society is somehow impervious to these forces because of our 'evolution,' no society ever sees the inevitability of the destructive forces which follow, since we are always in some phase of this dialectic—therefore, we never see the demise of our society until it is far too late.

There is one reason the people who have enslaved our society wish to destroy the credibility of the historically accurate Holy Bible, and that is the fact that, it itself is a warning from our ancestors of the same corruption we see today, and which destroyed their societies.

The satanic bible encourages one to serve one's flesh by committing the seven deadly sins which are: *pride, envy, wrath, gluttony, lust, sloth and greed.* The satanist loves one's self above all else. The satanist is a magician who strives to live lavishly at the expense of the good at heart, whose underpaid works fund and furnish the excess in which the satanists relish.

Look:

The Satanic Bible

The signs are everywhere that humanity is striving to burst the restrictive bonds of religion. **It was**

S.S.O.S.S.

predicted in the Bible, for that matter, in symbolic passages that dealt with satan chained for a thousand years, after which he would break free and foment deviltry on the earth. Now it is happening. Sex is exploding in movies and literature, on the streets, and in the home. People are dancing topless and bottomless. Youths are throwing off restrictions that deny pleasure in mind and body. There is a ceaseless quest for entertainment, gourmet foods and wines, adventure, enjoyment of the here and now. Man is no longer willing to wait for any afterlife that promises to reward the clean, pure—translate: ascetic, drab—spirit. There is a mood of neopaganism and hedonism, and from it have emerged a wide variety of intelligent individuals—doctors, lawyers, engineers, writers, actors, stockbrokers, clerks, printers, nurses (to cite just a few categories of satanic church members)—who are interested in carrying the liberation of the flesh all the way to a formal religion.

s.S.O.S.s.

52. All Fired up

Around the time of the founding of our country, a rash of 'witch-burnings' grew rampant in Europe. There was intense paranoia surrounding the events, and for the most part the art of confusion created a sort of who-made-who atmosphere. In other words, were the accused and burnt witches—people who were known to be a danger to mankind because of his *or her* practices which lead to human sacrifice—or were their accusers simply rationalizing their own offering of human sacrifice to the devil, consequently, deeming their victim a 'witch' as a smokescreen with which to condone the activity of human sacrifice to the general public?

Below is a myriad of outtakes from: Extraordinary Popular Delusions, by, Charles Mackay:

> For fear the zeal of the enemies of satan should cool, successive Popes appointed new commissions. One was appointed by Alexander VI, in 1494; another by Leo X, in 1521, and a third by Adrian VI, in 1522. They were all armed with the same powers to hunt out and destroy, and executed their fearful functions but too rigidly. In Geneva alone five hundred persons were burned in the years 1515 and 1516, under the title of Protestant witches. It would appear that their chief crime was heresy, and their witchcraft merely an aggravation. Bartolomeo de Spina has a list still more fearful. He informs us

that, in the year 1524, no less than a thousand persons suffered death for witchcraft in the district of Como, and that for several years afterwards the average number of victims exceeded a hundred annually. One inquisitor, Remigius, took great credit to himself for having, during fifteen years, convicted and burned nine hundred. In France, about the year 1520, fires for the execution of witches blazed in almost every town. Danaeus, in his "Dialogues of Witches," says they were so numerous that it would be next to impossible to tell the number of them. **So deep was the thraldom of the human mind, that the friends and relatives of the accused parties looked on and approved.**

I am sure that you weren't surprised to see that **France** *seemed to have the most 'witches' in her regions.*

The practice of witch burning was deemed socially acceptable in Europe for several centuries. There were known to have been 40,000-50,000 deaths over that period of time—many sources recount numbers ranging in the millions. These are the reported figures, and, as we now know, these evildoers most likely only reported the events, of which, they had no choice but to do so. If you will remember, there were flare-ups of the same 'witch-burning' activities in early America, in Salem Massachusetts, with the events of the *Salem Witch Trials*. This is the type of diabolical behavior to which the moral degradation of society will lead.

The satanist wishes for you to have the understanding that eating good food and drinking good wine are sins; they are not! In

s.S.O.S.s.

fact, even the use of recreational drugs, in itself, is not a sin. Though, the satanist would like for you to believe this in order to implode your belief in God, out of mere frustration.

The satanist is a worshiper of self. The satanist teaches that there is no heaven, so to underscore and promote these vices with which bodies and minds of people are destroyed. The Holy Bible is a historic account, and a powerful warning from our ancestors, as to the evils which had destroyed their ancient societies. These are the vices which, without good, crumble all societies as well as causing the individual's body to succumb to death, with no hope for everlasting life.

The satanist believes he or she is an animal, no different from the beasts of the earth, in contradiction with the teachings of God.

Genesis 1:26 King James Version
26 And God said, Let us make man in our image, after our likeness: and let them have dominion over the fish of the sea, and over the fowl of the air, and over the cattle, and over all the earth, and over every creeping thing that creepeth upon the earth.

This is why Fred Flintstone and Barney Rubble wear horns on their heads at the *'Water Buffalo Lodge,'* the Vikings wore horns on their helmets, and why satanists of all sorts, from all around the world, attach antlers and horns to their heads—it is *rebellion*. Humans acting as animals brings us to our next section, *The Greatest Lie Ever Told—Darwinism...*

s.s.O.s.s.

Fun fact: The word *infidel*, which is an unusual word in our culture even by military, is used six times in the Encyclopedia of Freemasonry, in the second volume alone.

53. The Greatest Lie Ever Told

The premise by which the satanist begins the recruitment of new devil-worshippers, is, the idea that, if one is already an atheist (doesn't believe in God, which kids are now taught in school), they are simply satanists without the benefits. So, why not join the satanic Order and indulge in the social and self-serving benefits of evil?

When The Order again killed Christ (at schools), they also had to kill their precious satan—well, until you really figure out that that too is a lie. Here is an outtake from the Q&A section of the website for the church of satan:

Q—WHY DO SATANISTS WORSHIP THE DEVIL?

A—**We don't. Satanists are atheists.** We see the universe as being indifferent to us, and so all morals and values are subjective human constructions. Our position is to be self-centered, with ourselves being the most important person (the "God") of our subjective universe, so we are sometimes said to worship ourselves. **Our current High Priest Gilmore calls this the step moving from being an atheist to being an "I-Theist."**

Satan to us is a symbol of pride, liberty and individualism, and it serves as an external metaphorical

s.S.O.S.s.

projection of our highest personal potential. **We do not believe in satan as a being or person.**

The, 'satan is not a being or a person,' premise, is an oxymoron, since, if those individuals deem *themselves* to be 'god,' and he *or she* adopts the *creed* of satan, wouldn't they, themselves, become...*satan*—not God? Despite that premise, devil worshippers describe rituals in which the devil himself appears to the practitioner of their 'magic.' Sometimes a practitioner even draws their sacred pentagram on the floor, in which to stand, to 'protect' the practitioner of magic from the evil one who appears within it.

The very next Q&A question on the church of satan website, after, *'Do satanists worship the devil,'* is....

Q—DO SATANISTS PERFORM SACRIFICES?

A—No. We are atheists. The only people who perform sacrifices are those who believe in supernatural beings who would consider a sacrifice to be some form of payment for a request or form of worship. Since we do not believe in supernatural beings there is no reason for a Satanist to make a sacrifice of any sort.

The satanic so-called 'bible' also scoffs at a 'white witch' who would dare harm an animal, when the *'choice of a human sacrifice* would be far more suitable.' This is *particularly* funny since PETA's (People for the Ethical Treatment of Animals) new activist,

s.s.O.s.s.

is Dave Navarro. Dave has a tattoo on his *throat* which is frequently used in the satanic bible—Navarro *is quite obviously a satanist...Apparently, satanists save animals but condone killing people* (google image search Dave Navarro PETA ad). The same 'Leviathan' cross was initially used by *the Knight's Templar.*

The balance of the satanic bible holds the evil one in high reverence. The, 'we don't believe in satan,' premise, like everything else in their so-called 'religion,' is an out-and-out lie.

Here Anton Lavey admits to his identification with 'the father of lies':

"I'm one helluva liar. Most of my adult life, I've been accused of being a charlatan, a phony, an impostor. I guess that makes me about as close to what the Devil's supposed to be, as anyone. It's true. I lie constantly, incessantly. Because I lie so often, I'd really be full of shit if I didn't keep my mouth shut and my bowels open." [Anton LaVey, Satan Speaks, page 101]

In light of the many millenniums of attacks upon the truth within the Holy Bible, I will point out the most blatant 'lie' between the covers of the satanic pile of ordure, which Lavey refers to as the *satanic bible.*

Outtake from their own *Satanic Bible*—Whole Section:

ON THE CHOICE OF A HUMAN SACRIFICE

The supposed purpose in performing the ritual of sacrifice is to throw the energy provided by

S.S.O.S.S.

the blood of the freshly slaughtered victim into the atmosphere of the magical working, thereby intensifying the magician's chances of success.

The "white" magician assumes that since blood represents the life force, there is no better way to appease the gods or demons than to present them with suitable quantities of it. **Combine this rationale with the fact that a dying creature is expending an overabundance of adrenal and other biochemical energies, and you have what appears to be an unbeatable combination**

The "white" magician, wary of the consequences involved in the killing of a human being, naturally utilizes birds, or other "lower" creatures in his ceremonies. It seems these sanctimonious wretches feel no guilt in the taking of a non-human life, as opposed to a human's.

The fact of the matter is that if the **"magician"** is worthy of his name, he will be uninhibited enough to release the necessary force *from his own body*, instead of from an unwilling and undeserving victim!

Contrary to all established magical theory, the release of this force is NOT effected in the actual spilling of blood, *but in the death throes of the liv-*

S.S.O.S.S.

ing creature! This discharge of bioelectrical energy is the very same phenomenon which occurs during any profound heightening of the emotions, such as: sexual orgasm, blind anger, mortal terror, consuming grief, etc. Of these emotions, the easiest entered into of one's own violation are sexual orgasm and anger, with grief running a close third. Remembering that the two most readily available of these three (sexual orgasm and anger) have been burned into man's unconscious as "sinful" by religionists, it is small wonder they are shunned by the "white" magician, who plods along carrying the greatest of all millstones of guilt!

The inhibitive and asinine absurdity in the need to kill an innocent living creature at the high-point of a ritual, as practiced by erstwhile "wizards," is obviously their "lesser of the evils" when a discharge of energy is called for. These poor conscience-stricken fools, who have been calling themselves witches and warlocks, would sooner chop the head off a goat or chicken in an attempt to harness its death agony, than have the "blasphemous" bravery to masturbate in full view of the Jehovah whom they claim to deny! **The only way these mystical cowards can ritualistically release themselves is through the agony of another's death (actually their own, by proxy) rather than the indulgent force which *produces* life!** The treaders of the path

s.s.O.s.s.

of white light are truly the cold and the dead! **No wonder these tittering pustules of "mystical wisdom" must stand within protective circles to bind the "evil" forces in order to keep themselves "safe" from attack**—ONE GOOD ORGASM WOULD PROBABLY KILL THEM!

Even *if* the devil *worshipper* is simply 'worshipping one's self,' as their heretical chronicles proclaim, it does nothing to quail my disdain for their kind. The fact that a single evil one whom most of us cannot see or hear in this world, is replaced by an entire army of greedy, heartless and soulless human beings stripped of their conscience and performing human sacrifice, in effigy *or otherwise*, is indeed far more sinister than the existence of one actual 'devil.'

Since the first step to satanism is atheism, it is fitting that The Order invented Darwinism, or, the *theory of evolution*, in order to coax humanity into this damning first step to the real *dark side*, in grade school. Darwinism was necessary for bringing the *age of enlightenment* to the forefront of the human collective conscious—out of the proverbial dark—and, indeed, it has replaced the Christian faith, in schools.

Charles Darwin *crooked* the idea of evolution from another colleague who was compensated for his textual collection of ignorance, **in the form of East India Railroad Company stock.** Darwin was sent to India to learn the evil ways of The Order, under the tutelage of East India Co. (In India there is still a festival named in Darwin's honor.)

s.s.O.s.s.

Darwin returned from India with 'his' fictionalized book, *On the Origin of Species*. The full name of Darwin's book which has been truncated for obvious reasons, was, *'On the Origin of Species **by Means of Natural Selection, or the Preservation of Favoured Races** in the Struggle for Life.'* In other words, Darwin's pirated book was created by The Order, also to persuade the masses that eugenics was an acceptable practice, and, it worked.

The article below confirms much of what you've read, in addition to, identifying the evil mechanism behind the greatest lie ever told—*Darwinism.*

On the term *BEIC* (frequently used in the following outtake), I used EIC, or simply, East India Company (throughout this paper), in order to prevent The Order's intended purpose of creating confusion, and to give the paper continuity. EIC changed their name several times during the course of the operation but it was the same company. *BEIC* stands for, *British East India Company.*

Enjoy:

> by Ann Lawler
> *Presented at the July 23-24 National Conference of the Citizens Electoral Council by CEC Chairman Ann Lawler. This and other presentations from the conference, which was titled "Educating the Mass Strike: Cosmic Radiation Beats Green Fascism," together with a feature report, "The British Crown Created Green Fascism," were published in the October/November 2011 issue of the CECs **New Citizen** newspaper.*

S.S.O.S.S.

Charles Darwin is the acclaimed granddaddy of the entire environmentalist movement, that is, of today's plague of Green Fascism. Who can tell me what he is famous for?

[Answers from the audience: "the theory of evolution"; "the 'survival of the fittest' and 'natural selection' as the method of evolution"; "the 'Tree of Life': that all existing species arose from one primitive life form, via 'transmutation of species'," "that man descended from apes, so man is just another animal, and therefore just another part of Nature, not its master."]

Yes, all that is true, but Darwin himself credited his so-called discovery of evolution to Parson Thomas Malthus (1766-1834), who claimed that mankind faces "scarce, limited resources," and that human population growth will sooner or later outgrow those fixed resources. Darwin emphasized his dependence on Malthus right in the introduction to his 1859 book *The Origin of Species*, whose full title is *On the Origin of Species by Means of Natural Selection, or the Preservation of Favoured Races in the Struggle for Life*:

"[T]he Struggle for Existence amongst all organic beings throughout the world ... inevitably follows from their high geometrical powers of increase.... This is the doctrine of Malthus, applied to the whole animal and vegetable kingdoms. As many more individuals of each species are born than can possibly survive; and as, consequently, there is a frequently recurring struggle for existence, it follows that any being, if it vary however slightly in any manner profitable to itself ... will have a better chance of surviving, and thus be *naturally selected*." This Malthusian process, Darwin claimed, is the "origin of species."

Darwin proclaimed repeatedly that Malthusianism held true for mankind, as well as animals. The British oligarchy had made Malthus a great hero already by the mid-19th Century, so Darwin well knew that Malthus had proposed *mass murder* as a "solution" to mankind's "overpopulation." Malthus wrote, in his 1798 "An Essay on the Principle of Population":

"All the children born beyond what would be required to keep up the population to this level, must necessarily perish, unless room be made for them by the deaths of grown persons.... [T]herefore, we should facilitate, instead of foolishly and vainly endeavouring to impede, the operations of nature in producing this mortality; and if we dread the too frequent visitation of the horrid form of famine, we should sedulously encourage the other forms of destruction, which we compel nature to use.... But above all, we should reprobate specific remedies for ravaging diseases; and those benevolent, but much mistaken men, who have thought they were doing a service to mankind by projecting schemes for the total extirpation of particular disorders."

Malthus and the British East India Company

Malthus was not just any old country parson, but the official chief economist for the British East India Company, the largest monopoly the world had ever seen, with an army in the late 18th and early 19th centuries that was larger than that of the British government itself. In fact, the slave-trading and dope-pushing BEIC *was* the British Empire. And when the BEIC set up its Haileybury College in 1805 to train its officials, they appointed Malthus as the very first professor of political economy in Britain, actually in the world. Malthus's students over the next several decades became the BEIC's administrators, and systematically applied his policies of genocide to keep the native populations under control. They killed tens of millions in India alone, including by forcing them to grow opium

S.S.O.S.S.

instead of food, which opium the BEIC then used to poison the Chinese.

It is likely that the BEIC promoted Malthus precisely *because* he was a reverend, to justify the kind of mass murder which most even nominal Christians would find objectionable. **Darwin and his gang attacked Christianity because its fundamental tenets were a stumbling block to British imperial rule. In particular, the notions of *imago Dei*, as expressed in the Book of Genesis: that man was created in the "image of God"** to be fruitful, multiply, and have dominion over the Earth; and of *capax Dei*, as expressed in the opening verses of the Book of St. John: that man "is capable of God," capable of participating in the Creator of the universe (the Word, the Logos), and can thereby become a willful co-creator in God's continuing process of creation.

There is nothing mystical about this.... It is all fully accessible to man's creative reason, whether you happen to be a professing Christian, or not. **But this reality can never be understood through mere sense certainty, nor through the impotent formal logic of induction/deduction, so beloved of the British oligarchy and its stooge Charles Darwin.** On the very first page of his *Origin of Species*, Darwin approvingly quoted *****Sir Francis Bacon,**

s.s.O.s.s.

the so-called founder of the "modern scientific method" of induction, which is no method at all, but just sense-certainty-based brainwashing. **Throughout his life, Darwin maintained, correctly, that his** *Origin* **was based upon Bacon's method.** The perpetuation of the British Empire depends on controlling how people think, that is, to make sure that they *don't* think. **That was the whole point of the Darwin project—to convince human beings that they are mere animals, without a divine spark of creativity.**

Note*: The historic book, *Memoirs of the House of Russell; From the Time of the Norman Conquest,* begins with a quote from this animal, **Sir Francis Bacon**, who is also revered in our schools. Let us look:

"It is a reverend thing to see an ancient castle or building not in decay, or to see a fair timber tree sound and perfect: how much more to behold an ancient noble family, which hath stood against the waves and weathers of time!"

Well, well, well, if it isn't more recycled feculence from the past....With all of those points being made, the job of The Order (if they were to commit the ultimate act of piracy—stealing *YOUR SOUL*), was simple: There was only one huge shred of evidence pointing toward the existence of God, and his miraculous creation of the universe—*YOU!*

Since you and I standing here, contemplating our very existence as created by a higher power is equally as perplexing to the question of the existence of God himself, The Order would need to devise a lie bigger than any ever told. This stumbling block is what had held satanism in the dark for millenia, and with the thesis for this problem formed—in the way of the theory of evolution—their job was complete.

Below are a series of quotes from Anton Lavey, which are exemplary of the mechanism of hate with which prepares great hoards of a society for things like witch-burnings, financially inspired famines, genocides, and Christians being torn to shreds by a hungry wild beast at a public venue. Today however, they are satellite guided missiles which are striking civilians and children down remotely, and all of The Order's remedies, party favors and dietary suggestions.

Darwinism=Atheism=Satanism=Outward Domestic Human Sacrifice=social and financial collapse of a society.

Here are some whispers which describe the mechanism of hate.

Quote 1:

—The Satanic Bible
"The person who takes every opportunity to "pick on" others is often mistakenly called "sadistic." In reality, this person is a misdirected masochist who is working towards his own destruction. The reason

s.s.O.s.s.

a person viciously strikes out against you is because they are afraid of you or what you represent, or are resentful of your happiness. They are weak, insecure, and on extremely shaky ground when you throw your curse, and they make ideal human sacrifices."

Anton Szandor LaVey—

Quote 2:

—**satanic bible Introduction**
"It is not an easy religion to adopt in a society ruled so long by Puritan ethics. There is no false altruism or mandatory love-thy-neighbor concept in this religion. Satanism is a blatantly selfish, brutal philosophy. It is based on the belief that human beings are inherently selfish, violent creatures, that **life is a Darwinian struggle for survival of the fittest, that only the strong survive and the earth will be ruled by those who fight to win the ceaseless competition that exists in all jungles—including those of urbanized society.**"
Burton H Wolfe—

54. Sex-Ed

I suppose you thought we were gonna talk yards-and-yards of pseudoscientific nonsense, nope....We won't be doing any of that....We will be talking about *liars* again.

Alfred Kinsey, was Author of the two-part book, *The Kinsey Reports*, which spawned a sexual revolution. The man who brought homosexuality, transsexuality, bisexuality, and pedophilia, back out into the public light, was also a satanist. (For the record, I do not judge those who live alternative lifestyles. I am a reporter.)

Before there was Anton Lavey (writer of the satanic bible and founder of the church of satan), there was a gentleman named Aleister Crowley, who fueled the satanic orgy of the masses. You may remember this pudgy satanist who strongly favored *Uncle Fester* on *The Munsters*, from the hit *Ozzy Osbourne* song, *Mr. Crowley*.

According to Kinsey Report contributor, Wardell Pomeroy, Kinsey not only loved Crowley's perverse homosexual writings, but Kinsey had also attended Crowley's former sex temple in Italy, called the *Abbey of Thelema*, to obtain Crowley's creepy sex diaries.

Crowley had been grooming a number of satanic sexual deviants, whom he had instructed to keep sex diaries, to document the details of their lust. (The creepy accounts would be the basis for Kinsey's work.) Crowley was known during his time as, 'The Wickedest Man on Earth,' and soon, as this brief account continues, you too will see why.

s.S.O.S.s.

Well, as the story goes, Mr. Kinsey and Mr. Crowley were tight pals. Free sex, masturbation (public and private), and all sorts of sexual deviance in between, are all common themes of the satanist. With that in mind, what better way to create cultural deviance than to write a couple of books which outline a whole host of sexually deviant activities and make them all seem perfectly normal.

By creating a foundation which put the evil creed in trust, and then injecting these vile behaviors into the populace, the well-placed propaganda created the appearance to onlookers that they were just, 'born that way.' You guessed it—enter, *the Kinsey Reports*—the two volumes which were written as Kinsey reportedly put all of the different acts of sexual deviance to the test. Act by act, experimentation through the all-new *scientific method* was underway (in the presence of Kinsey and a select group of his horny satanic pals).

Kinsey's pair of books was a great hit. The country of America was glad to have this dual-volume of hogwash, for they were all now '*free.*' Free from what, though? They still did not rightly know, but you and I will discuss here further, that it was satan who actually became free within our culture. Even the famous songwriter, *Cole Porter,* wrote a hit song which praises what Kinsey's perverted teachings did for those times. The catchy tune was aptly titled, *Anything Goes.*

The pair of books which surveyed groups of men for one volume *and women for the other,* supposedly surveyed six thousand individuals. The individuals were posed with many perverted questions regarding one's sexual disposition and habits. After the data was collected, the large group would be sexually experiment-

s.S.O.S.s.

ed upon, *using little 'method' whatsoever.* And this new data was recorded and processed with Kinsey's newly formulated Kinsey Scale, which ultimately tells an individual how gay they are. His experiments turned up striking levels of homosexual tendencies within the entirety of the population.

Kinsey's human lab rats were exposed to a set of gay, and straight, stimuli (use your imagination), both visual and physical. While observing the individuals the group gauged the individual's physical reactions to the sexual prodding and probing, which was then recorded and rated by the onlookers (again, using your imagination).

The Kinsey Scale is as follows....

Rating Description

0—Exclusively gay

1—Predominantly straight, only incidentally gay

2—Predominantly gay, but more than incidentally gay

3—Equally heterosexual (and, uh....*gay)*

4—Predominantly gay, but more than incidentally heterosexual

5—Predominantly gay, only incidentally heterosexual

s.s.O.s.s.

6—(SUPER) GAY

X—No socio-sexual contacts or reactions—Asexual

Note: According to the chart, everyone is at least somewhat gay, with the exception of those who are at the extreme end of the so-called Kinsey Scale— those who *have no* sexual desire or function—or, 'asexual.' And, while the zero-end of the scale indicates the individual to be 'exclusively gay,' there is no option, *on the Kinsey Scale*, for an individual to be exclusively *heterosexual*. So in other words, *no one is 'straight.'*

Again, the public raved about the nonsense, so much so, that, the Kinsey reports supposedly got the attention of that new-ager, and seeker of world dominion for satan, *Rockefeller*.

Rockefeller was so impressed with the smut that he further funded Kinsey's porn to the highest level, calling it, *The Kinsey Institute for Research in Sex Gender and Reproduction* (more widely known as *the Kinsey Institute)*. The foundation was funded by the Rockefeller Foundation, through the National Research Council's [NRC] Committee for Research in the *Problems of Sex,* Established in 1921. On short order the textual puke had the steam it needed with which to teach Kinsey's garbage in your kids' schools. *(Our current Sex Ed programs are based mostly on The Kinsey Reports.)*

This all makes perfect sense, right? Wrong!

s.s.O.s.s.

It was all fun and games, and 'people were just born that way,' until one crazy thing happened…**Many of Kinsey's test subjects to which the *scientific methods* were applied in his sex reports, were children, and babies as young as *a few months old.***

The infamous 'Chart 34,' which to Judith A. Reisman, Ph.D., raised concerns as to the 'scientific method' Kinsey had been using during the *research* performed by Kinsey and his satanic counsel of creeps.

Dr. Reisman noticed that the unfortunate victim three-down on the left-hand column was only eleven months old! The child had been sexually manipulated, and produced a reported fourteen orgasms within a thirty-two minute study.

Despite these, and many other, disgusting facts which were also brought to light upon the doctor's disturbing discovery, the Kinsey Reports remain the scientific standard for sexual development, and sex education communities countrywide. Let there be no doubt that Kinsey has been publicly exposed as a total fraud, and, moreover, a creep of the creepiest sort, yet the story barely cracked the news feeds.

In Dr. Resiman's writings she discusses her frustration with the stonewalling of her ideas, by her peers, and the authorities governing this issue. This was another great victory for the Russell Trust of Evil, and a giant step for satan.

Anton Lavey, the writer of the satanic bible, takes credit for, not only the sexual revolution, but also for women's lib—taking the mother out of the home. But, to most, Alfred Kinsey is known as the *'Father of the Sexual Revolution.'*

s.S.O.S.s.

55. The Yale Spooks (CIA)

The CIA is another Great Bones achievement—*it may be the greatest achievement of The Order, to date.* A history professor at Yale, Gaddis Smith, had this to say about the CIA—America's secret branch of The Order:

"Yale has influenced the Central Intelligence Agency more than any other university, giving the CIA the atmosphere of a class reunion."

"Bonesmen" have been foremost among the "spooks" building the CIA's "haunted house."F. Trubee Davison ('18) was Director of Personnel at the CIA in the early years. Among the Bonesmen connected with the intelligence community are:

Sloane Coffin, Jr. ('49)
V. Van Dine ('49)
James Buckley ('44)
Bill Buckley ('50)
Hugh Cunnigham ('34)
Hugh Wilson ('09)
Reuben Holden ('40)
Charles R. Walker ('16)
Yale's 'unofficial' Secretary of War, Robert D. French ('10)
Archibald MacLiesh ('15)

s.s.O.s.s.
Dino Pionzio ('50), CIA Deputy Chief of Station during Allende overthrow
William and McGeorge Bundy
Richard A. Moore ('3?)
Senator David Boren ('63)
Senator John Kerry ('66) ...and, of course, George Herbert Walker Bush. Bush tapped Coffin, who tapped Buckley.

Below is an outtake from *George Bush: The Unauthorized Biography,* concerning the rights Americans' lost after the fear-mongering which followed The droppings of the A-bombs:

"On October 22, 1945, Secretary of War Robert Patterson created the Lovett Committee, chaired by Robert A. Lovett, to advise the government on the post-World War II organization of US intelligence activities.... The new agency would 'consult' with the armed forces, but **it must be the sole collecting agency in the field of foreign espionage and counterespionage. The new agency should have an independent budget, and its appropriations should be granted by Congress *without public hearings.*** Lovett appeared before the Secretaries of State, War, and Navy on November 14, 1945....Lovett pressed for a virtual resumption of the wartime **Office of Strategic Services (OSS)**.... The CIA was established in **1947** according to the prescription of **Robert Lovett**, of **Jupiter Island**.

s.S.O.S.s.

In a very similar loss of life, liberty, happiness and privacy, the Patriot Act followed 9/11.

The vote in favor of the so-called 'Patriot Act' was overwhelming and bi-partisan—98 to 1 in the US Senate and 357 to 66 in the US House of Representatives. The bill skated past the Senate and House, despite the fact that, the bill was 342 pages in length and many members of Congress now admit that they didn't even read it before voting in its favor.

The A-bombs were dropped on Hiroshima (and Nagasaki) on, 6 August 1945—Congress approved Yale's Federal International Branch of Skull and Bones (The CIA) 3 months later—the Twin Towers were knocked down on, 11 September 2001, and the 'Patriot' Act was approved only 1.5 months after that.

Below is another outtake from the book, *Fleshing out Skull and Bones,* which quite adequately describes The Order's cavalier attitude toward the dark business handled by the international 'Merchants of Death'—*the 'black sheep' who have 'gone astray':*

Name Roster of the Secret Establishment
There were so many "Yalies" in the OSS that Yale's drinking tune, the "Whiffenpoof Song," became an "unofficial" song of the OSS. Many in the OSS were "Bonesmen" or belonged to the other Yale senior societies. Robert Lovett ('18), Harriman's childhood friend, had been tapped into Skull & Bones by Prescott Bush's cell of '17 and was a director at Brown Brothers, Harriman.

s.s.O.s.s.

Below, I took it upon myself to document the lyrics of this "Yale drinking song."

Lyrics
Yale's Whiffenpoof 'Drinking' Song

Yes, the magic of their singing of the songs we love so well
Shall I wasting and Mavourneen (term of endearment) and the rest
We will serenade our Louie while life and voice shall last
Then we'll pass and be forgotten with the rest
We're poor little lambs who have lost our way
Baa, baa, baa
We're little black sheep who have gone astray
Baa, baa, baa
Gentleman songsters off on a spree
Doomed from here to eternity
Lord have mercy on such as we
Baa, baa, baa, baa!

Bible Verse from which The Order derived their lyrics:

Isaiah 53:6 King James Version
6 All we like sheep have gone astray; we have turned every one to his own way; and the Lord hath laid on him the iniquity of us all.

s.s.O.s.s.

The *'Black Sheep'* now carry out clandestine missions and acts of war; acts of espionage, upon me, and on you, and on poor souls in third world countries around the world, without any Congressional supervision whatsoever.

The 'Black Sheep' have also, by legislation, hacked into every iPhone on the planet, at the behest of CEO Tim Cook, who refused to cooperate with the spooks. (This gives new meaning to the all-seeing eye of Horus.)

Fun fact: Brandon Hale, supposed Revolutionary spy (who was also a Yale graduate), is *haled* as the *first* intelligence agent in America. Hale, whose famous last regrets were, 'I only regret that I have but one life to lose for my country,' has had at least three statues erected in his honor.

One Hale statue is located at the FBI headquarters; another proudly stands upon the Yale Campus; the third stands in New York.

S.S.O.S.s.

56. How The Order Killed Christ

Following the scattering of the inhabitants of Babel, The Order went on to shape-shift their bloodline into the leaders of each civilization around the globe. This tactic allowed The Order to disguise themselves as the leaders of people of all races, even those of us who are said to be 'Gentile' *(though we are all from the 12 tribes).*

There remains no doubt that the religious leaders of Israel played their part in the death of Jesus Christ. Matthew 26:3-4 says, '**the chief priests**, the scribes, and the elders of the people, assembled together to the palace of the **high priest' (Aaron's tribe's post)**, who was called **Caiaphas**.

There is much confusion about the intentions of Jesus's accusers, but it is now clear that Jesus and his message threatened The Order and their luxurious way of life, which the molested office of the High Priest had afforded these charlatans. Jesus warned the usurious money lenders of his time of the sinful practice of placing a financial yoke on the People of God. Taxes had grown out of hand too *(just as they have today)*. The message today is the exact message which Jesus had been preaching to the exact same churches and oppressors in those times.

Jesus was *officially* charged with three things....

1. Encouraging non-payment of taxes
2. Threatening to destroy the Temple of Solomon
3. Proclaiming to be King

s.s.O.s.s.

The Bible says, 'And the oppressors consulted so that they might take Jesus by guile and kill Him.' The Jewish leaders demanded of the Romans that Jesus be put to death (Matthew 27:22-25). They couldn't continue to allow Jesus to work signs and wonders because it threatened their position and place in the religious society they dominated (John 11:47-50), so 'they plotted to put Him to death' (John 11:53). Jesus was attempting to take back Aaron's blood right to the priesthood, even back then.

The Romans were the ones who actually crucified Jesus (This proves that the 'Romans' were also in cahoots with The Order), Matthew 27:27-37. Crucifixion was a Roman method of execution, authorized and carried out by the Romans under the authority of Pontius Pilate, the Roman governor who sentenced Jesus to death. Roman soldiers drove the nails into His hands and feet; Roman troops erected the cross, and a Roman solider pierced His side (Matthew 27:27-35).

The common people of Israel were also complicit in the death of Jesus Christ. They were the ones who shouted, 'Crucify Him! Crucify Him!'…as Jesus stood on trial before Pilate (Luke 23:21). They also cried for the thief Barabbas to be released instead of Jesus (Matthew 27:21). Peter confirmed this in Acts 2:22-23 when he told the men of Israel 'you have taken by lawless hands, have crucified and put to death,' Jesus of Nazareth.

In fact, the murder of Jesus was a conspiracy involving Rome, Herod, the Jewish leaders, and the people of Israel. This was a diverse group of people who had never before worked together on anything, before or since, but who came together this one time to plot and carry out the unthinkable—the murder of the son

s.s.O.s.s.

of God. Here is a great passage which describes the 'Jews' who were responsible for the Crucifixion of Christ:

Revelation 2:9 King James Version
9 I know thy works, and tribulation, and poverty, (but thou art rich) and I know the blasphemy of them which say they are Jews, and are not, but are the synagogue of Satan.

At that time, Christ's living flesh was terminated and the scribes recorded the series of miracles of Christ—God's Word—which, along with the many Biblical wonders hoarded by the Crusaders of the Pope, had migrated into the temple of the false prophet. Powerful imagery, and mindless rituals and chants have allowed the false prophet to flourish. The following governments which have risen and fallen by the mechanism of the evil dialectic, over time, have grown and shrunk the nation of God's people as the great breaths of an ugly beast.

The known and reachable world was terrorized by the actions of the Pope. Countless cities have been plundered for their technology, wealth, and land. The Pope uses Christ's holy name, which was spread by the sword, in vein, to *loot cities throughout the ancient and contemporary world,* and the priceless hoarded treasures of the Vatican remain.

The temple of the false prophet remains intact, guarded by only 150 so-called 'Swiss Guards' dressed like clowns. We are on the precipice of the one they call the 'false prophet,' again, demanding his due. For in our times the side of the dialectic machine, the governing esoteric cabalists, have had their day long

s.S.O.s.s.

enough. And the imminent death and destruction caused by the evil which grows over time under this system will soon push the masses back into the Pope's counterfeit temples; filling his dusty pews, and forcing weight back upon his passed-plates.

Aaron's Priesthood, and as it was passed down, was prohibited by God from even owning land. Imagery was also highly forbidden to all, and the Catholic Church has its own country and the greatest collection of art, wealth, and holy antiquities in the world, at the cost of hundreds of millions, if not billions of God's Peoples' lives.

The evil charlatan has idly sat upon his throne for many centuries, whilst God's children have been enslaved; starved to death; cursed with manmade plagues; poisoned; burned alive; ridiculed, and deceived as to their origin. Our origin was born through the work of The Almighty, not through fire as the world has been taught, and you sit upon your wealth, wearing your stinking, evil tongue in a knot. One great event which would Bang 'Big' would burn, at sterilizing degrees, and as your so-called 'scientists' know….Sterilization would find no insulation in that environment. However, it would find insular amongst your followers, and in the fecal matter of your BIG LIE! Numbers 18:20:

> The LORD said to Aaron, "You will have no inheritance in their land, nor will you have any share among them; I am your share and your inheritance among the Israelites."

Instead, they took it all! In direct violation to God's word, the High Priesthood was stolen and God's strict orders were directly violated. For not only did the High Priesthood own property, The Order took that of the entire world, through conquest, by creating one little magic trick—a raging beast of war and the false prophet, who, back-and-forth, repeatedly wash God's people with muddy water.

Anton Szandor Lavey (writer of the modern satanic bible and founder of the so-called 'church' of satan) was called 'The Black Pope' by many of his followers—Anton LaVey began the road to *High Priesthood* of the church of satan when he was only 16 years old—an organ player in a carnival:

> *"On Saturday night I would see men lusting after half-naked girls dancing at the carnival, and on Sunday morning when I was playing the organ for tent-show evangelists at the other end of the carnival lot, I would see these same men sitting in the pews with their wives and children, asking God to forgive them and purge them of carnal desires. And the next Saturday night they'd be back at the carnival or some other place of indulgence. I knew then that the Christian Church thrives on hypocrisy, and that man's carnal nature will out!"*

From that time early in his life his path was clear. Finally, on the last night of April, 1966– *Walpurgisnacht*, the most important festival of the believers in witchcraft–LaVey shaved his head in the tradition of ancient executioners (but really of the nazirites) and announced the formation of The

s.S.O.S.s.

Church Of satan. He had seen the need for a church that would recapture man's body and his carnal desires as objects of celebration. "Since worship of fleshly things produces pleasure," he said, "there would then be a temple of glorious indulgence..."

It appears that Anton was himself tricked from his soul by the elaborate fiasco set in place by the seated, blood-shifted-form of the Ancient Pharaohs of Egypt. In this passage Anton takes credit for capitalizing on the dark side of an age old grift, which sends God's Children into a never ending washing machine of lies, back and forth, between evil, false teachings, more evil, and money for sins.

Another outtake from the book of fecal matter:

> In a Satanic magical ceremony, the participants do NOT: join hands and dance "ring around the rosy" in a circle; burn candles of various colors for various wishes; call out the names of "Father, Son and Holy Ghost" while supposedly practicing Black Arts; pick a "Saint" for their personal guide in obtaining help for their problems; dunk themselves in smelly oils and hope the money comes in; meditate so they can arrive at a "great spiritual awakening"; recite long incantations with the name of Jesus thrown in for good measure, between every few words, etc., etc., etc., *ad nauseam!*

s.S.O.S.

BECAUSE—This is NOT the way to practice Satanic magic. If you cannot divorce yourself from hypocritical self-deceit, you will never be successful as a magician, much less a Satanist.

The Satanic religion has not merely lifted the coin —it has flipped it completely over. Therefore, why should it support the very principles to which it is completely opposed by calling itself anything other than a name which is totally in keeping with the *reversed* doctrines which make up the Satanic philosophy? Satanism is not a white light religion; it is a religion of the flesh, the mundane, the carnal—all of which are ruled by satan, the personification of the Left Hand Path.

Another Quote By Anton Lavey:

"satan has certainly been the best friend the church has ever had as he has kept it in business all these years. **The false doctrine of hell and the devil has allowed the protestant and Catholic Churches to flourish far too long.**"

The Book of the Good News:

Matthew 23:2-12 King James Version
2 Saying *The scribes and the Pharisees sit in Moses' seat*:

s.s.O.s.s.

3 All therefore whatsoever they bid you observe, that **observe and do; but do not ye after their works: for they say, and do not.**
4 *For they bind heavy burdens and grievous to be borne, and lay them on men's shoulders; but they themselves will not move them with one of their fingers.*
5 But all their works they do for to be seen of men: they make broad their phylacteries, and enlarge the borders of their garments,
6 And love the uppermost rooms at feasts, and the chief seats in the synagogues,
7 And greetings in the markets, and to be called of men, Rabbi, Rabbi.
8 But be not ye called Rabbi: for one is your Master, even Christ; and all ye are brethren.
9 And call no man your father upon the earth: for one is your Father, which is in heaven.
10 Neither be ye called masters: **for one is your Master, even Christ.**
11 But he that is greatest among you shall be your servant.
12 And whosoever shall exalt himself shall be abased; and he that shall humble himself shall be exalted.

I think this passage says it all.

The Holy Bible has been around for thousands of years, within which thousands of prophecies have come to pass—letter-

s.S.O.S.s.

for-letter. The Holy Bible gives us a look into the true history of mankind.

The United States Government has been lying about our history for going-on 300 years, and they cannot be honest with us about what may *or may not have* occurred just yesterday.

For example: *Just yesterday*....**1.3 billion dollars in the form of unmarked euros were discovered to be destined for Iran (a** *"hostile terrorist state" having nuclear arms)*, *in an unmarked American plane.* You try this one and see what happens! The man responsible for the giant, underhanded payoff (using *our* money) by The Order, was none other than Bonesman John Kerry **(S&B 1966)**. The excuses surrounding the event, as you might have guessed, are swarming. The art of confusion has been fully deployed.

> Hebrews 10:12-13 (NIV)
> **12 But when this priest had offered for all time one sacrifice for sins (crucifixion of Jesus Christ)**, he sat down at the right hand of God,
> **13** and since that time **he waits for his enemies to be made his footstool.**

57. King Solomon's Temples

Though Freemasonry is a highly related topic, my intentions for this body of work was to uncover the bloodline trail of one family's uncanny ability to kill for power and money—*the Russells*. And, though this book is not necessarily about Freemasonry, there are a few points which are worthy of mention here.

King Nimrod, King of Ancient Babylonia, a metropolis of ancient cities, is also held in extremely high reverence by the Freemasons. I will again refer you to the Encyclopedia of Freemasonry 1916 Vol 2—A G Mackey, version:

> **Nimrod**—The "Legend of the Craft" (beginning of Freemasonry) in the *Old Constitutions* refers to Nimrod as one of the founders of Masonry. Thus in the York MS., No. 1, we read: "At ye making of ye Tower of Babel there was Masonry first much esteemed of, and the King of Babylon was called Nimrod, a Mason himself, and loved Masons well." And the Cooke M S thus repeats the story: "And this same Nembroth began tower de Babylon and he taught to his workman the craft of Masonry, and he had with him many Masons more than forty-thousand. And he loved and cherished them well." (line 343.) The idea no doubt sprang out of the Scriptural teaching that Nimrod was the architect of many cities; a statement not so well expressed in the authorized version, as it is in the improved one of

s.s.O.s.s.

Bochart, which says: "From that land Nimrod went forth to Asshur, and builded Nineveh, and Rehoboth City, and Calah, that is the Great City."

Note: What great care in detail The Order's customary dark side of the Bible has not been spared (though, again, they proclaim their stories to be *allegorical),* as the light side has been edited to cryptic parables, and deemed complete *Myth.*

Nimrod, again, was the Great-Grandson of Noah. Nimrod, the King who oversaw the building of the Tower of Babel, was the very first post-deluge Mason—the reviver of 'The Craft' as they call it. (Wicca, and many other practicing witches, also refer to *witchcraft*, as, '*The Craft!*')

From the last quote of the passage it becomes clear exactly how their grift works—dissecting peoples' native lands for the purpose of manipulation of markets, and to create wars between the peoples for financial gain—the most basic ingredient to warmongering and usury is racial segregation and strife.

In Freemasonry they tell *a lot* of Bible Stories, but they are all of the creepy ones which discuss human sacrifice, betrayals of God, Jacob's ladder, idol worship, Babel, and King Solomon.

The throne located in the Mason's lodge is referred to as the Throne of Solomon—it is also acknowledged in some masonic literature that this *was* the throne of *Aaron (who was the original owner of the 'Breastplate of Judgment').*

The Freemasons hold the *Temple of Solomon* (The building for which the Knights '*Templar*' were originally named) in high regard, which is made quite obvious since all of their Masonic temples have architectural elusion to the structure. So, it is not entirely surprising that the Mason's also worship Hiram Abiff.

Hiram Abiff was only mentioned once in The Bible, as the chief architect of King Solomon's Temple. Hiram is revered by the Masons, as one of the forefathers of their 'craft.' Though, it is now obvious that, **Freemasonry goes back to the Tower of Babel, which was the first pyramid ever built.**

Remember?:

"'Come, let us make bricks and bake them thoroughly.' They had brick for stone, and they had asphalt for mortar."

Towers of Babel (pyramids) are now found in every culture, on every continent around the globe.

Hiram was murdered in the Temple he had designed by three Ruffians during an unsuccessful attempt to force him to divulge 'the Master Mason's secret passwords.'

For the third Rite of the Freemasons, the initiate acts out a creepy play which is the reenactment of the murder of Hiram Abiff. The initiate, who portrays the famous Mason, is murdered in effigy to show what would happen were the initiate to violate 'the secret oaths of the Freemasons.' This is where the saying, *"He gave me the third-degree,"* originates.

s.s.O.s.s.

Daily Sacrifice is reopened at the Temple of Solomon

At a Freemasonic Temple ('lodge') in Turkey, a hidden camera was placed within the *'Holy of Holies,'* which amounts to a room with a large round altar baring a pentagram in its center. A video was recently obtained, and made public, of a blood sacrifice of a live goat being offered to satan (google video 'Freemason sacrifice video, Turkey').

As discussed, the Freemason's hold the Temple of Solomon in very high reverence, and even design their temples with much symbology dating back to the original ancient structure. Again, it could be said that the Freemasons *have* rebuilt the Temple of Solomon. And, if so, the aforesaid video is proof that the altars are again open for daily sacrifice, which is one of the *only* prophecies left to be fulfilled before the second-coming of The Messiah.

Below are the supporting scriptures:

2 Thessalonians 2:3-4 (NIV)
[3] Don't let anyone deceive you in any way, for that day will not come until the rebellion occurs and the man of lawlessness is revealed, the man doomed to destruction. [4] He will oppose and will exalt himself over everything that is called God or is worshiped, so that he sets himself up in God's temple, proclaiming himself to be God.

Daniel 9:27 (NIV)
[27] He will confirm a covenant with many for one 'seven.' In the middle of the 'seven' he will put an

S.S.O.S.S.

end to sacrifice and offering. And on a wing [of the temple] he will set up an abomination that causes desolation, until the end that is decreed is poured out on him."

Fun fact: The image of the *'Skull and bones'* is one of the most important symbols to the Freemasons.

58. Flat Crazy

It is only a matter of time before a major contrived event causes the curtains below the stage of the puppet show to fall, revealing the long red arms which control the candidates on both sides of the aisle. Many believe that 9/11 accomplished just that. With the S&B leadership that was in charge at the time, I think it deserves another look, if you're still not convinced. But, I *don't* have the stomach for that one.

The *information age,* as they call our particular scene of the puppet show, is yet to reveal many inconsistencies in The Order's practice in which they giveth and taketh away technology. The curtains have fallen from the teachings of academia many times over the years.

The best example for which to explain what I mean is, *round earth* theory...Round *versus flat* earth theory is nothing new. In fact, in ancient Greece, spherical earth wasn't a theory at all, but, accepted fact! (That was in the 6th century BC!)

Over time, time-and-time-again, The Order began their people farms (societies) with a minimal amount of information and technology. And, as the dialectic turned, we were again wowed with what the elite could do technology-*wise.*

Just to name a few...Here are the most-documented 'discoverers' of *'round earth theory'—these accounts begin in the 8th century BC:*

Example 1— 8th Century BC—The Holy Bible:

s.s.O.s.s.

Isaiah 40:22 King James Version
22 It is he that sitteth upon the **circle of the earth**, and the inhabitants thereof are as grasshoppers; that stretcheth out the heavens as a curtain, and spreadeth them out as a tent to dwell in:

Somehow the earth became flat again!

Example 2—In around **600 BC** Pythagoras proposed the earth to be round.

Flat earth theory again!

Example 3—**The Greek philosopher Aristotle (384-322 BC)** argued in his writings that the Earth was spherical, because of the circular shadow it cast on the Moon during a lunar eclipse.

The Alexandria philosopher **Eratosthenes** went one step further and actually estimated how large the *"round"* Earth was.

The Arab Khalif El Ma'mun, who ruled in Baghdad from 813 to 833 AD, sent out two teams of surveyors to measure a north-south baseline, and from it, also obtained the radius of the Earth. Compared with today's known earthly dimensions, those estimates were pretty close to the mark.

Back to flat earth theory again!

S.S.O.S.S.

Example 4—Copernicus (Poland) published a *round earth* theory in the year 1543. He was said to have made the discovery in 1514, but he did not '*decide*' to publish it until he was urged to do so, late in his life by his pupil Rheticus. It looks like The Order held back this '*discovery*' for nearly 40 years for some reason?

Back to flat earth theory again!

Example 5—Galileo (Italy) was imprisoned for proposing that the earth was round, in 1633, **by the Catholic Church, whose Holy Book recorded the very first record of round earth in history!** Bear in mind, this was after Columbus supposedly discovered America, upon which a continental civilization existed prior to an arrival to America that many argue *never even happened!*

And, notice that, Poland, and Italy, both, taught conflicting science at the same exact time! The two countries are only 800 miles apart, and aren't even separated by water! (The original band of satanist Russells - the 'Knights Templar') travelled 2800 miles to kick-off the first 'Crusade' in 1095!...five centuries prior.)

Propoganda—printed by The Order in America in *1919!*:

"When Columbus lived, people thought that the earth was flat. They believed the Atlantic Ocean to be filled with monsters large enough to devour their ships, and with fearful waterfalls over which their frail vessels would plunge to destruction. Columbus had to fight these foolish beliefs in order to get men to sail with him. He felt sure the earth was round."

s.s.O.s.s.
–Emma Miler Bolenius, **American Schoolbook Author, *1919—***

And now, again, many are back to flat earth theory....Have we really 'evolved,' or do you now see that we only *re*-volve? Don't think this is the only example for The Order's arrogance—I am only making a point. The entire academic force could write volumes, indefinitely, concerning the lies which have been taught to our people, by The Order.

s.S.O.S.s.

59. The Idol and the Ephod

In another book of The Bible we can view the evilness that the ephod took-on, by the perverts of faith who stole it, look:

Judges 17:7-13 King James Version
7 And there was a young man out of Bethlehemjudah of the family of Judah, who was a Levite, and he sojourned there.
8 And the man departed out of the city from Bethlehemjudah to sojourn where he could find a place: and he came to mount Ephraim to the house of Micah, as he journeyed.
9 And Micah said unto him, Whence comest thou? And he said unto him, I am a Levite of Bethlehemjudah, and I go to sojourn where I may find a place.
10 And Micah said unto him, **Dwell with me, and be unto me a *father and a priest**, and I will give thee ten shekels of silver by the year, and a suit of apparel, and thy victuals. So the Levite went in.
11 And the Levite was content to dwell with the man; and the young man was unto him as one of his sons.

S.S.O.S.S.

12 And Micah consecrated the Levite; and the young man became his priest, and was in the house of Micah.

The story picks back up with a group of 600 well-armed *Danites*, who broke in and swiped the several objects *(idols)* which were used for the dark arts, including the priest's ephod *(breastplate of judgment)*.

Judges 18:18-21 King James Version
18 And these went into Micah's house, and **fetched the carved image, the ephod, and the teraphim, and the molten image. (idols and objects of divinity)** Then said the priest unto them, What do ye?

Note*: Matthew 23:9 (KJV) says…
9 And call no man your father upon the earth: for one is your Father, which is in heaven.

This is likely when and where the Catholics got their start.

The surprised Levite priest who reluctantly forfeited his magic plate (another Breastplate of Judgement) and idols, would, I am sure, be surprised to know that the swipers of the jeweled wonder took over the entire world. And though this passage speaks of another breastplate of judgement, which the mentioned 'priest' had 'made himself,' this passage gives credence to the fact that, these *ephods* were coveted by those

s.S.O.S.s.

who practiced the dark arts. *The owner having had idols in his possession (along with the ephod) is evidence enough for that.*

And, again, I don't think that the definite whereabouts of the object in question is important, anyway. After all, it is *just an old plate of metal*—the intentions of the individual, who has stolen its meaning and perverted its purpose for evil, is what gives the 'grail' (or any physical object, skull, or idol) its power.

Just as the baphomet replaced the human head in the rites of 'knighthood,' so does any old square having 12 colored boxes, on its face, replace the Breastplate of Judgment.

Fun fact: The men in the above Bible passage, concerning the idol and the ephod, were from the Tribe of Dan. When these 'Danites' stole the ephod, they were on their way to conquer the land of Laish, just like they have the rest of the world, since. *The Tribe of Dan were descendants of Ham, son of the Great Sailor, Noah.*

s.s.O.s.s.

60. Dirty Dan

The Antichrist *will* descend from the 'Lost Tribe of Dan.'

Look:

Jeremiah 8:15-17 King James Version
15 We looked for peace, but no good came; and for a time of health, and behold trouble!
**16 The snorting of his horses was heard from Dan: the whole land trembled at the sound of the neighing of his strong ones; for they are come, and have devoured the land, and all that is in it; the city, and those that dwell therein.
17 For, behold, I will send serpents, cockatrices, among you, which will not be charmed, and they shall bite you, saith the Lord.**

Dan would be used to judge God's people. The very name, Dan, means Judge, which explains why our founding 'fathers' were mostly judges and attorneys. And it's another reason that The Order would have such great adoration for the **Breastplate of '*Judgment.*'** Please, read this passage:

Genesis 49:16-18 King James Version
16 Dan shall judge his people, as one of the tribes of Israel.

s.s.O.s.s.

17 Dan shall be a serpent by the way, an adder in the path, that biteth the horse heels, so that his rider shall fall backward.
18 I have waited for thy salvation, O Lord.

Ever since the Garden of Eden in the Book Genesis, the evil one has been said to take the form of a snake. Many ancient Hebrew texts identify the snake in Genesis, as, Lilith. If you look at their many works of art in the Egyptian times, you will quickly find that the cobra was especially sacred to them as well. King Tut's golden sarcophagus donned the image of the snake. A scoundrel too, is known to be a snake—this is by no accident, my *Friend*.

Serpents slither upon their bellies, and like a serpent whose slimy scales scar the sand, so does the Tribe of Dan's stinking trail of sorrows scar the world. So too, as sure as God cursed the evil one to crawl upon his belly and eat dust for all his days, we will track down the lost Israelite Tribe which produced the antichrist.

Now, what else does The Bible tell us about the evil one? The passage below was eloquently written by a man named Keith Krell. We will listen to his truncated version of The Bible's first villainous account of the initial conquest of the Tribe of Dan:

> The Tribe of Dan was offered an inheritance of land by the Lord. In 18:1–31, the author of Judges focuses on the Danites—a small tribe in Israel 21 who begin "seeking an inheritance for themselves to live in" (18:1b). The Lord had assigned the tribal allotments under the direction of Joshua, with the help

s.S.O.s.s.

of Eleazar, the high priest, and the elders from the tribes (Josh 19:51). God put each tribe just where He wanted it. For the tribe of Dan to reject God's assigned territory and covet another place is to oppose His divine will. Dan eventually discovers Laish—a place of security and comfort. Dan ends up conquering this land and claiming it for themselves in the name of ease and prosperity.

Note: Remember King John Lackland? He was the evil King whom Paul Giamatti portrayed in his movie, King John? He is also the guy to whom nearly every one of the creeps in this volume are related. His last name literally translates to....'*Lacks Land,*' or *no land*...

Remember the very last section, *The Idol and the Ephod?* Which described the scoundrels who stole another Ephod from the priest? Well, the, *'they'* in these scriptures, were *of the Tribe of Dan, and were on their way to conquer the land of Laish (described in the grouping of verses above)!*

Dan is missing from the chosen 144,000 who will reside in the 'New Jerusalem,' spoken of in Revelation:

Revelation 7:4-8 King James Version
4 And I heard the number of them which were sealed: and there were sealed an hundred and forty and four thousand of all the tribes of the children of Israel.

S.S.O.S.S.

5 Of the tribe of Juda were sealed twelve thousand. Of the tribe of Reuben were sealed twelve thousand. Of the tribe of Gad were sealed twelve thousand.
6 Of the tribe of Aser were sealed twelve thousand. Of the tribe of Nephthalim were sealed twelve thousand. Of the tribe of Manasses were sealed twelve thousand.
7 Of the tribe of Simeon were sealed twelve thousand. Of the tribe of Levi were sealed twelve thousand. Of the tribe of Issachar were sealed twelve thousand.
8 Of the tribe of Zabulon were sealed twelve thousand. Of the tribe of Joseph were sealed twelve thousand. Of the tribe of Benjamin were sealed twelve thousand.

If you noticed, the tribe of Dan was given no inheritance here, either.

Fun fact: Yale University's football team has an ugly little mascot with a wicked underbite—*a bulldog*. As with all of The Order's pals, his remains have been preserved, and are now on display at Yale; his name is 'Handsome **Dan**.'

s.s.O.s.s.

61. The Reptilian Drain

Now that we have established the exact tribe from which the antichrist will come, now let us gaze upon the slithering serpent's trail, so that we may identify the connection between the House of Russell and this lost tribe of evil ones.

Special thanks to *Hope of Israel Ministries'* marvelous work for this one....Let us look:

> **Outtake from http://www.hope-of-israel.org:** Denmark, the name of the modern country in Europe north of Germany, means, literally, "Dan's mark." Its people are called "Danes." At one time in history Denmark ruled all the surrounding region—the whole region took its name from them—the ScanDINavian peninsula! Clearly, there are remnants of the people of DAN, who migrated westward overland from the Caucasus to their present location in northern Europe!
>
> **Other Danites, lived on ships, and became sailors of Tyre** *(the monks who followed the Russell Templar around, and documented their deeds, were from Tyre)* **and Sidon, fleeing westward through the Mediterranean when northern Israel fell. Early Danites fled Egypt at the time of the Exodus, and migrated through SarDINia, and left their trail along the sea-coasts of the Mediter-**

ranean. Thus Dan, who was a "lion's whelp" who would "leap from Bashan," leaped all the way to Ireland, where historians explain that **the early settlers were known as the "Tuatha de Danaan"—literally, the "tribe of Dan."** The Greeks called them the Danoi, the Romans called them Danaus.

In Ireland, today, we find their customary evidence—their place names—in abundance. Such names as Dans-Lough, Dan-Sower, Dan-Monism, Dun-dalke, Dun-drum, Don-egal Bay, Don-egal City, Dun-glow and Lon-don-derry, as well as Dingle, Dun-garven and Duns-more, which means "MORE DANS." Of course, **the most famous Irish ballad of all time is the song, "Danny Boy."** It should be plain that the country of Ireland is replete, filled with names which derive from the ancient patriarch of the Hebrews—DAN, the son of Jacob! **It is also quite clear that the ancient Danites settled in Ireland, and most of them dwell in that land, today.**

There is a River Don in Scotland, and another in England. These countries also show the evidence of the presence or passing of the tribe of Dan, **who migrated with the other tribes of the northern kingdom of Israel**, especially the tribe of Joseph (Ephraim and Manasseh). Here we find such names markers, or "guide posts" as YEHO-

s.s.O.s.s.
VAH God called them in Jeremiah—as Dun-dee, Dun-kirk, Dunbar, Dunraven, **E-din-burgh, and Lon-don**.

Enough said.

Fun fact: Viking ships were notorious for having giant serpents carved into their hulls **(google image 'Viking Ship')**. If you did indeed google image 'Viking ships,' you will see that the red-and-white-striped flag is an ancient tradition of The Order, which dates back thousands of years, long before becoming our modern version of 'Old Glory.'

s.s.O.s.s.

62. Ancient Satanists

On the topic of Dan's Mark, Swiss Author, Erich Von **Dän**iken, penned the Best selling book *Chariots of the Gods* (the work which spawned the History Channel's hit show *Ancient Aliens)*. Believe it or not, Von Däniken himself is, admittedly, in on this unbelievable conspiracy.

Von Däniken, who famously proclaimed that, 'Much of the History We Have Been Taught is Wrong,' substitutes our true God for the theory that ancient aliens visiting earth are responsible for our technology, DNA alterations within our species, and even the idea of Panspermia—*aliens being responsible for our very existence upon this earth.* An idea which, quite clearly, is a replacement for the God of Creation *truth*. *('Panspermia' translates literally, to, 'Devil's Spawn.')*

I personally find it farfetched that someone would explain God away with such a bizarre theory that only compounds the mystery, rather than offering a solution to the conundrum. After all, wouldn't someone, or some *thing*, have had to create the aliens —which would in theory be more advanced than us to begin with? God 'theory' even came with an instruction manual. *The Bible* is a comprehensive history book which is a collaboration of many men over vast expanses of time, of which tens of thousands of handwritten copies have been found. Over thousands of years of history, The Word has been spread over many untold kingdoms, and nearly every copy matches up flawlessly.

In a wonderful exposé essay concerning Von Däniken's sketchy past, Author Jason Colavito wrote this tell-all blurb:

s.S.O.s.s.

Erich Anton Paul von Däniken was born in Switzerland in 1935, raised a strict Catholic, and in Catholic school developed an interest in UFOs, like many youths in the early 1950s. He had a criminal record. He was convicted of theft when he was 19, and he left school to become a hotelier. He was convicted of embezzlement after leaving that job. He took another hotel position, and he stole money there, too, by falsifying records in order to obtain tens of thousands in fraudulent loans to finance his interest in space aliens and what the court later called his "playboy lifestyle." The court psychiatrist declared him a pathological liar. Eventually, he would be convicted of embezzlement and fraud yet again, serving a year in prison.

In 1960, two French authors who were interested in the occult, Nazis, UFOs, and *H. P. Lovecraft put out a book called Morning of the Magicians in which they tried to show that Lovecraft's vision of ancient astronauts could be correlated to the "occult" truths of Theosophy and the UFO movement.

Jacques Bergier and Louis Pauwels put together the entire case for ancient astronauts as we currently know it—from the claims about ancient atom bombs to the claims about "impossibly" precise and heavy stone architecture. Their book inspired sev-

s.S.O.S.s.

eral by Robert Charroux, who presented Bergier's and Pauwel's discursive, disorganized ideas in a more popular and readable format.

In 1964, von Däniken simply appropriated this material wholesale for a magazine article, and on the strength of the magazine article, he received a book deal for what became Chariots of the Gods...

Note*: If you will recall, H.P. Lovecraft was one of the fellows to whom the Author of the satanic bible gives a shout out. Also, Stephen King, *a horror novelist,* drivels madly about the creep in his work, *On Writing.*

Now that we have had a good look at Von Däniken's work, let us now take a closer look at his felonious resumé. Von Däniken, in all of his intergalactic and terrestrial knowledge of ancient history, was actually involved in hotel management as a career (as aforementioned).

You may not have been too surprised to also learn that Von Däniken's gift for the manipulation of truthfulness had, at times, brought him into conflict with the law (again, as mentioned above). Erich's native Switzerland found Von Däniken guilty of embezzlement, forgery, and fraud, and sentenced the convicted liar to three and a half years in prison. The exact charges for Von Däniken were, fraudulently obtained loans by misrepresenting his financial assets.

S.S.O.S.S.

While a guest of a Swiss Prison, Von Däniken would have had ample time to pen his second fantastic, heretical work, *Gods from Outer Space,* which also went on to be a best seller.

Now we will take a quick look at Von Däniken's self-admitted inspiration for his work *Chariots of the God's*....It is an outtake from an online Q&A session with Von Däniken.

Below is a question posed to Erich during one of those Q&A sittings:

Q—What led you to reject your Catholic school teachings on God and The Bible and instead take an interest in astronomy and flying saucers?

A—I was, and I still am, a deep believer in God. But God has to have some fundamental qualities: He is timeless–He knows the present, the past and the future and He is omnipotent, which means He would never use some vehicle to move from one place to the other (?). **In my boarding school in Switzerland, led by *Jesuits,** we had to translate some parts of the Old Testament from one language to the other and by doing this **I realized that the God of The Bible had none of these fundamental qualities. So I had doubts in my own religion, and I simply wanted to know what the communities in antiquity said about their God.**

Note*: The Jesuits strike again!

s.s.O.s.s.

The basis of all of Von Däniken's claims is that, geographically separated historical cultures share artistic themes, which to Von Däniken, *'implies a common origin.'*

One such example is the aforementioned image of the swastika which can be found on nearly every continent, in nearly every culture, and dates back to the beginning of recorded history; or else the practice of building pyramids; or the mummification and worship of the dead; or the creation of idols and human sacrifice to those deities (remember, the swastika was used in Nazi Germany, by the Native Americans, *and* was found on the children-burning temples of Baal).

Another worldwide phenomenon is the Templar Cross. This, not so holy, version of the *Holy Cross* can be found literally everywhere. It can be seen on ship sails from every country throughout time; on flags (everywhere); on currency; on Viking sundries; on Bayer Aspirin tablets; in every military including American; the Templar Cross can even be seen on the lapels of people ranging from Adolf Hitler to the Pope. In fact, the oldest imagery of the Templar Cross was found on an ancient stone relief of King Nimrod of Babylon—google it!

Unfortunately for The Order, the stink of their ugly rituals of oppression are found *everywhere.* Jesuit trained Von Däniken was right, the evidence *is 'profound,'* but the mechanism is hardly believable, and the source, as you now know, is completely bunk. The Order knew that the interconnectedness of our modern cultures would cause serious rifts in their contrived version of human history, and we now subscribe to such fairy tales with volume.

Please, once again, review with me some of the vows made during the Jesuit oath:

s.s.O.s.s.

—**The Superior speaks**—

My son, heretofore you have been taught to act the dissembler: among Roman Catholics to be a Roman Catholic, and to be a spy even among your own brethren; to believe no man, to trust no man.

Among the Reformers, to be a Reformer; among the Huguenots, to be a Huguenot; among the Calvinists, to be a Calvinist; among other Protestants, generally to be a Protestant; and obtaining their confidence, to seek even to preach from their pulpits, and to denounce with all the vehemence in your nature our Holy Religion and the Pope; and even to descend so low as to become a Jew among Jews, that you might be enabled to gather together all information for the benefit of your Order as a faithful soldier of the Pope.

Remember, this?

63. Russell Family Viking Kings

The Order came to Europe, and the rest of the world, as *Viking Raiders*. In this section we will give those ideas a closer look. In the Russell Memoirs book, the Writer makes mention of a lineage leading back to *Rollo, Ragnar Lothbrock, and even Odin and Thor*—two *angry* fellows, who we have always been taught don't even exist. But, again, Wiffen, the Writer of the Memoirs book in question, has given us many clues, which we have followed in order to decode the apocalyptic message from the past.

Rollo was a big, feared man, and a great sailor. After breaking off ties from *King Harald *Fairhair* of Norway (mentioned in 'Fun fact' below), Rollo became well known as a roving Pirate, plundering his way through Ireland, Scotland, and Flanders—the exact same route taken by the 'Lost' Tribe of Dan.

As stated, the Russells also claim to be related to both **Thor,** and **Odin,** in the opening of their book *Memoirs of the House of Russell,* in which they describe their many conquests. Admittedly the fact is downplayed as myth since these men '*didn't really exist*'—however, what if we could prove that these men *did* '*exist?*' As if being a beautiful message from the past, it was clearly important that the writer mention the fact to the reader.

Now that we know that Odin *did* exist—*as King Nimrod of Babylon*—it is probably important that we assume the Russell memoir affiliation to be true (a secret kept for obvious reasons)… since it makes them all descendants of King Nimrod of Babylon and Babel.

s.s.O.s.s.

Here is the damning outtake which describes the Russell patriarch, young Viking Rollo who is also strongly believed to be one of the 'finders of the holy grail' in *multiple* other unrelated texts:

> The Bertdrand family were indisputably of the lineage of Rollo. The Count de Toustain—Richebourg, who has investigated the subject with considerable research and industry, represents them as springing from Drogo, or ***Dru, of Normandy**, who appears to have been the same personage as Hrollagur, one of the brothers of the great Rollo, the name being merely softened into Drogo in its passage from Norway into France. When Rollo, in the year 912, proceeded to divide Normandy in fief amongst his followers, he seems to have allotted the northern district of La Manche, in which the bourg of Briquebec is now situated, to his brother Drogo. **This personage took also the name or surname of **Turstain (later evolving into thurstan), in memory of the *supposed* descent of his ancestry from Thor, the son of Odin (remember, *two of the annual S&B members also receive the nicknames* Odin, and Thor).** [Historical Memoirs of the House of Russell: From the Times of the ..., Volume 1, Page 9]

Note*: This * 'Dru of Normandy,' is a phonetic connection to the Ancient Druids, who, like the pagan revelers at Burning Man Festival, left behind little evidence. The Druids were avid wor-

s.s.O.s.s.

shippers of the devil and even sacrificed humans at their creation, *Stonehenge, among many other sites along the same trail of tears.*

Note**: **The very name, *Turstain, means 'Thor.' And since 'Thor' is the 'Son of *Odin* (Nimrod), in essence, the name Turstain literally means, *'Sons of Nimrod.'*

Now that we know that, 'Odin' isn't Greek Mythology, at all, but that, Odin—*Nimrod*—really lived, I would have to assume that King Nimrod's skull too, perhaps, *could* make its home with the creeps at Yale. This would also bring into question the head which the Templar were executed for worshipping—which was said to have had long hair and a long beard....*And,* it too was thought of as unusual for the day, for that reason. (King Nimrod of Babylon, like many of the gruff men that we have identified, had a legendary curly beard, and curly hair.)

One last interesting note about Odin. Here are the two definitions offered for Odin in the Greek Lexicon:

Odin:
1. *the pain of childbirth, travail pain, birth pangs
2. intolerable anguish, in reference to the dire calamities precede the advent of the Messiah

Here is what The Bible has to say about these... *'labor pains.'*

398

s.S.O.S.s.

Matthew 24:5-11 (NIV)
5 For many will come in my name, claiming, 'I am the Messiah,' and will deceive many. **6** You will hear of wars and rumors of wars, but see to it that you are not alarmed. Such things must happen, but the end is still to come. **7** Nation will rise against nation, and kingdom against kingdom. There will be famines and earthquakes in various places. **8 *All these are the beginning of birth pains. 10** At that time many will turn away from the faith and will betray and hate each other, **11 and many false prophets will appear and deceive many people.**

It is said that King Nimrod *(Odin)* became an imposing beast of a man. It was even said that the King was a 'giant,' who somehow activated his pre-deluge *Nephilim* (giants described in The Bible) genes, purposefully, through some lost technology.

In the Bible's defense, from ancient stone depictions of King Nimrod himself, to the Viking Kings, to Bohemond of the Knights Templar, to Native American accounts, there exist countless stories of 'Giant' men, of which The Order's 'schools' have gone through great lengths to hide and discredit. Perhaps, Prescott Bush didn't liken selective breeding of slaves to that of livestock, but instead he was attempting to bring forth these 'Nephilim' traits, which must be hidden among the DNA of all of us. Look:

Genesis 6:4 King James Version

s.s.O.s.s.

4 There were giants in the earth in those days; and also after that, when the sons of God came in unto the daughters of men, and they bare children to them, the same became mighty men which were of old, men of renown.

Athletes such as Shaquille O'neal (among countless others) could substantiate this theory.

To end this section I would like to bring your attention to the meaning and origin of the word 'viking,' itself.

See if you can smell the stink of The Order within the passage below:

> Viking (n.) Look up Viking at dictionary.com Scandinavian pirate, 1801, vikingr, in "The History of the Anglo-Saxons" by English historian Sharon H. Turner (1768-1847); he suggested the second element might be connected to king:
>
>> The name by which the pirates were at first distinguished was Vikingr, which perhaps originally meant kings of the bays. It was in bays that they ambushed, to dart upon the passing voyager.
>
> **But this later was dismissed as incorrect. The form viking is attested in 1820, in Jamieson's notes to "The Bruce."** The word is a historians' revival; it was not used in Middle English, but it

s.s.O.s.s.
was reintroduced from Old Norse vikingr "**freebooter, sea-rover, pirate, viking,**" which usually is explained as meaning properly "one who came from the fjords," from vik "creek, inlet, small bay" (cognate with Old English wic, Middle High German wich "bay," and second element in Reykjavik). But Old English wicing and Old Frisian wizing are almost 300 years older than the earliest attestation of the Old Norse word, and probably derive from wic "village, camp" (large temporary camps were a feature of the Viking raids), related to Latin vicus "village, habitation" (see villa).

The connection between the Norse and Old English words is still much debated. The period of Viking activity was roughly 8c. to 11c. In the Anglo-Saxon Chronicle, the *raiding armies generally were referred to as *þa Deniscan "the Danes," while those who settled in England were identified by their place of settlement.* Old Norse viking (n.) meant "freebooting voyage, piracy;" one would "go on a viking" (fara í viking).

Note*: If it isn't more evidence of the Mark of Dan...It appears as though this is the precise time and place where the vikings molted their old appearance and name. This is the exact moment when the Vikings shape-shifted into the Knights Templar, which, like the name *Russell,* itself, the 'Lost' Tribe

S.S.O.S.s.

of Dan had invented to mask the dirty deeds of their past.

It is now no surprise that the truth had so much trouble gaining traction here.

Fun fact: Several generations prior to the life and times of *King Harald 'Fairhair,'* lived another Russell ancestor named, *King Harald 'Bluetooth,'* after whom the wireless technology, used in all of our devices, is named.

If you turn the '*Bluetooth*' symbol sideways, it doubles as the head of the horned-owl-demon, *'Lilith,'* whose exploits are also supported by air. *The same demon to whom our government officials, and CEO-kings, sacrifice world citizens ('in effigy') to the devil, at Bohemian Grove California.* *King Harald 'Blåtand' Gormsson (mentioned in the second paragraph of this section), who was probably born c. 935, was a King of Denmark and Norway

64. Rollo Russell's Magic Plate

Through the Russell Viking ancestor, *Rollo*, the Russells have also been linked with the *Holy Grail* in *many* independent writings…We will look at the most damnatory of the lot; a telling passage which I discovered to, without question, associate the family who founded Yale (and The Order of Skull and Bones) to have (or at one time) *had* the Holy Grail in their possession.

Below is an outtake from the Russell Memoirs book which further substantiates the *Breastplate of Judgment* to be *the supposedly-fabled Holy Grail:*

> Barneville is stated to have derived its origin and name from Bjorn, the celebrated Norse pirate, son of the younger Regner Lodbrog, and surnamed Côte-de-Fer, **from a magic plate of metal which he was accustomed to wear at his right side, the only part of his body which, according to the popular belief, his mother, a Scandinavian enchantress, had not been able to render invulnerable.** [Historical Memoirs of the House of Russell: From the Times of the ..., Volume 1, Page 9]

We know that Rollo carried around a 'magic plate of metal' which his 'Scandinavian enchantress' mother *(a Viking 'Witch')* had not been able to render invulnerable.' Since the plate was determined to be 'magic' by young Rollo's mother, we can now deduce that, the 'plate' had some sort of divination qualities—*our*

s.s.O.s.s.

Holy Grail fits this description. (Let us also not forget that the period definition for the word grail, is, a *'plate, or platter.'* A grail didn't come to mean, *'chalice,'* or *'cup,'* until the Arthurian Literature told us that that it is what the word meant.)

We can also safely surmise that the object in question *wasn't* impenetrable. And, since we know for certain that the Breastplate of Judgment was made of gold (a soft metal) which was interwoven with other *very old fabric,* it is safe to reason that the object in question wouldn't have been much good in the way of stopping arrows, swords, or spears; rendering the object to be 'not invulnerable' (or deemed vulnerable) as Rollo's *witch* mother had suggested.

It appears that here too Poet Jeremiah Wiffen was begging to tell us the truth about a history which had fascinated him to no end, as much as it has me.

According to another member of the Russell family, *Anna Russell Des Cognets,* in her book, *William Russell and His Descendants,* the surname *Côte-de-Fer* (mentioned above) evolved into De Barneville; to simply Barneville. *Then,* according to *the Author,* the evolution of the Russell name picks up where Wiffen had left off:

"It [surname] derived its distinctive appellation from one of the fiefs which the first chieftain of that name possessed, anterior to the Conquest of England, in lower Normandy, in the ancient Barony of Brique-bec. In 1066 (the year that William **the Conquerer** 'conquered the Normans') they occupied the castle and territory of **Le Rozel**, which was a portion of their appanage, as a younger branch of the Bertrands, Barons of Briquebec; a House the

S.S.O.S.S.

head of which took the title of Sire, being accounted second only in rank to the Barons of St. Sauveur, who were styled Vicomtes of La Manche." [William Russell and His Descendants, By Anna Russell Des Cognets, Page 2]

Below is another outtake from the book above, titled, *William Russell and His Descendants*, which again picks up the Russell lineage where Wiffen had stopped the bloodline (again, for obvious reasons):

"Hugh **Du Rozel**, who appears to have been the first of the name, was born about 1021."

"Soon after the Norman Conquest the **Du Rozel** crossed the channel into England, where they had lands assigned them in **Northumberland, and where the name became Russell**. Robert **de Russell**, in 1141, led his company of Knights, and greatly distinguished himself in the battle of **Lincoln**." [William Russell and His Descendants, By Anna Russell Des Cognets, Page 2]

Let us now make an analysis of the genealogy of this family, as it leads back through the branches, long before the existence of the Raider, *Rollo*:

Note: Each individual is the father of the prior listed—in order from latest to earliest.

s.s.O.s.s.

1—Rollo Ragnvaldsson Duke of Normandy (860 AD—931)

2—Ragnvald Eysteinsson, Earl of Møre (825-894)

3—Eystein the Noisy Glumra (Ivarsson), Jarl av Oppland og Hedmark (810-870)

4—**Ivar Halfdansson**, Opplendingejarl Earl of Norway(780-824)

5—**Halfdan** 'Gamle' Sveidasson, 'the Aged' Jarl av Uppland (estimated before 765-unknown)—Well, well, well, what have we here? This name literally translates to… 'Half Dan!' It seems that we have found the proverbial *missing link! We have successfully tied the bloodline of the Russell Family who founded Yale University, and Skull and Bones, all the way back to the Tribe of Dan from the Children of Israel in The Bible!* By their *own* admission!

Also, look at Viking King #4, after #5 Halfdan, whose name nearly means the exact same thing, *'Half Dan's Son!'* In a previous section we'd discussed the many 'marks' of 'Dan' on the regions of travel in question, and here we have the damning evidence we were looking for

6—Sveidi Heytirsson, Norse King (before 765-unknown)

7—Heytir Heiti Gorrsson King of Kvenland (before 451-unknown)

8—Gorr Thorrasson, King in Kvenland (before 398-unknown)

406

s.s.O.s.s.

9—Thorri Snærsson, King of Kvenland (before 378-unknown)

10—Snær Jokulsson, King of Kvenland (before 299-unknown)

11—Frosti / Jøkull Karasson, King of Kvenland (240-274) (after whom 'Frosty the Snowman' was named)

12—Karl "Wind" Fornjotsson, King of Kvenland (189-240)

13—Fornjot, King of Kvenland aka Fornjot **'The Ancient Giant'** (before 184-unknown)

14—Father to Fornjot of Kvenland (before 184)

We will end this section with the haunting poem which kicks-off The Little Book which helped lead us to this ruthless bloodline of barbarians (*William Russell and His Descendants*):

Like leaves on trees the race of man is *found*,

Now green in youth, now withering on the ground;

Another race the following spring supplies,

They fall successive, and successive rise.

So generations in their course decay,

So flourish these, when those have passed away,

S.S.O.S.s.

—Homer—

Fun fact: This bloodline of Viking Kings can be traced all the way back to Greece and Rome, and even to the Middle East. The first 'race,' who we can trace back to these parts, is that of Antiochus, a Macedonian General for whom the 'Bohemian Trap City,' *Antioch*, was named.

65. Early Viking Presence in America

Academia fervently denies the existence of Vikings *and* Templar in the United States before Columbus (who some argue never even set foot on North America) despite discoveries such as the Tucson Crosses, and the Kensington Rune Stone (http://westfordknight.blogspot.com/2012/02/tucson-lead-artifacts.html). (If you read the article, I would like for you to keep in mind that, the gentleman who is mentioned as an 'expert'—Scott Wolter—is *himself* an admitted Freemason.)

The Tucson Crosses were discovered encapsulated and buried under *six feet* of caliche, which is an amalgam of aggregate stone and earth material—it's as hard as cement. The lead from which they were constructed was also tested for tell-tale pitting which Wolter himself admits, dates the metal items to the Wars of Charlemagne—another fine warrior from the Russell Clan.

One of the most controversial aspects of these finds are the inscriptions which are both in *Hebrew, and Latin.*

I think we all know why these have had such a hard time gaining recognition—remember, Yale's school seal also 'mysteriously' displays Hebrew *and* Latin. The Order *created* Academia, so the institution as a whole has fallen victim to these academic predators' lies.

The inscription on the Kensington Runestone purports to be a record left behind by **Scan-*DIN*-avian explorers** in the 14th century (internally dated to the year 1362).

The text translates to:

S.S.O.S.S.

"Eight Geats and twenty-two Norwegians on an exploration journey from Vinland to the west. We had camp by two skerries one day's journey north from this stone. We were [out] to fish one day. After we came home [we] found ten men red of blood and dead. AVM (Ave Virgen Maria) save [us] from evil. [We] have ten men by the sea to look after our ships, fourteen days' travel from this island. [In the] year 1362."

There has been a drawn-out debate over the stone's authenticity, but the scholarly consensus has classified it as a 19th-century hoax since it was first examined in 1910. Some critics have directly charged the purported discoverer, *Ohman (an old Swedish farmer)*, with fabricating the inscription, although there remains a local community convinced of the stone's authenticity. Once again, the goons' 'scholarly consensus' refutes the stone's authenticity.

Here is a good one….Located in Rhode Island, the Newport Tower, undoubtedly predates the early Anglo-American settlement by 500 years, at least. The structure supposedly 'baffles' historians *and* scientists, alike. I think you can understand why. What no one doubts, however, is that it was built in the style and construction of the Scottish Templar Masons. As you will see, the site has become an important historical site (to the same historians), despite the fact that academia has accepted no truth in the facts which we have discussed.

s.s.O.s.s.

Moreover, what I would like to draw your attention to is, the shape of the sidewalks which have been built with the flag as its centerpiece, to the right of the structure—google image 'aerial view of Newport Tower' to view—*notice the symbology in the design of the sidewalks.* Compare the sidewalks surrounding the American Flag, in this image, to the design in Vatican Square, surrounding the Egyptian stone wiener **(google image 'aerial view Vatican Square').**

Now, look upon the Egyptian Phallic symbol which stands in the center of Vatican Square....Notice the design on the ground surrounding the obelisk....For people who lend no credence to the Templar theory in America, they have certainly taken great care to add an ancient abomination to the property, during our modern times....*Also known as the Wheel of Solomon (or the 'Key' of Solomon),* The addition of this Solomonic Templar symbol, to the modern grounds of the Newport Tower, connects the Ancient American structure to, the *Ancient Templar*, the contemporary *Templar (Skull and Bones), and* it connects these two groups of clowns to the phallic-worshipping Pope. The same symbology makes up the entirety of the 'Union Jack Flag.'

Fun fact: The Minnesota 'Vikings' are the NFL team for the state which produced the Kinsington Rune Stone. Contrary to popular belief, most Vikings did *NOT* wear helmets with horns on their heads; only the Viking *Witches* were known to have partaken in the practice.

s.s.O.s.s.

66. The Greatest Sailor Who Ever Lived

The story of Noah, in The Bible, is a story of the Greatest Sailor who ever lived. After considering that giant stone wieners, continents of people, their belongings, entire Egyptian temples, and endless foreign resources, were transported around the world through manmade seas, it all didn't sound so crazy anymore.

When I realized that these heartless men, who export other peoples' agriculture to the point at which a hundred million people starved to death in India, the story of Noah saving the animals (and our race) doesn't sound nearly as crazy to me. *Does it to you?*

And, to add to that, the supposed extraterrestrial building of the so-called *'great'* pyramids was man's technology a *long time ago too*—there are not aliens, I'm afraid.

The real truth about the 'aliens,' is....We have been made the *aliens* to our own planet.

I'll explain....Over and again we've been eliminated and regenerated from the few of us who'd remained; and our very own ancestors' technology was hoarded and reintroduced to a new batch of *us* as 'marvels.' We have been farmed. An alien, if God chose to make such a thing, would make great ellipses around our airspace whence keen to our foul ways.

The Order enslaved large biomasses of indigenous peoples to dig great canals across our many continents. Great locks now move monstrous cargo ships full of other peoples' livelihoods, uphill, across waterways where land once stood. Many of these mammoth, ancient vessels held as many shackled men, women and children, as the bellies of their holds would fit. These '*modern*

s.s.O.s.s.

marvels' were born, by The Order, out of the necessity for shortcuts across the continents.

Slaves dug manmade seas where land had previously impeded the rate at which, *'progress,'* could be made. But, this was also a progression of atrocious death, torturous labor, famine, slavery, and disease, which carved large swaths across native peoples' lands. All of this destruction was rendered in the name of fulfilling greedy financial interests. This is the work of East India Company.

These horrible people; the inventors of the joint stock venture; the fathers of the modern corporation wagered upon the misery, rape, disease, torture, terrorism, plunder, and murder of others. This is why The Order hides from you *why* the pyramids were *really* made. But, the greedy deeds committed in our own times, in the name of progress, shows us that The Order did *not* need *'alien'* technology for which to move the earth. All which was needed was a throng of greedy, soulless bastards to God, a mass of God's hard-working people, and the ancient technology of God, which was robbed from Noah…by…The Order.

The next time you question whether the animals of our planet may *or may not* have been saved by Noah, aboard His great boat, first consider this—*you,* every Asian, Anglo, African, or East Indian person you see driving down the road, at the grocery store, in the airport, or at that sporting event, were all brought here on a boat, by…The Order!

That flimsy footstool on which your legs currently rest, was brought to you, and one to me, and millions to others, by The Order. One of the tallest phallic symbols in the world, at 1776 feet tall, replacing the towers which were twins, was brought to ground zero, on a boat, by, *The Order.* That giant whore, who guards the

s.s.O.s.s.

giant obelisk, was brought here entirely by boat, by The Order. The London Bridge was moved to Arizona, and was rebuilt stone-by-stone, which were all brought across the world—*you guessed it—on a boat!*

And, every beast in the zoos, around the world, were all delivered, over water, by The Order.

Ham was the son of Noah, and King Nimrod a descendant of Ham. In fact, King Nimrod was Noah's Great-Grandson. King Nimrod was the ruler of Babel, whose highness Manhattan strives for today—remember, *'excelsior,'* on New York's State Flag? When Nimrod's evil deeds scattered God's people, he hoarded the perfect sailing technology of Noah, as it would have been passed down through Ham—Noah's evil seed.

Noah's great, God given sailing technology was used to scatter God's tribes to the ends of the earth. These new settlements could then be independently manipulated for their resources, and again deceived, using the same big lie, over and over again. The result of which were the endless steamers full of God's people, who were all made slaves to The order in one fashion or another, throughout the evolution of our country, America, whose very name means, *'work ruler.'*

These giant floating bowls of misery unsuspectingly floated beneath her cup of fire, which burns in the right hand of the statue of Libertas—The Mother of Prostitutes—and the WHORE OF BABYLON. The Order stole God's Pillar of Fire and Cloud and led our 12 Tribes to the corners of the earth, which is why the Freemason's worship the pillar.

It was by no mistake that the great-grandson of the World's Greatest Sailor governed the city which scattered God's people.

S.S.O.S.S.

Ham's descendants went on to be Templar, Vikings, and Jesuits, who spread their esoteric, cabalist corporate usury to every nation. And after 'scattering' the tribes, they manipulated our markets and wares against each other. These were men appointed by God; those who were expected to witness, teach, and set examples for God's people, by which they could then live themselves.

The Order caused God's people to mistrust and hate one another using the art of propaganda and confusion. The Order taught racial slurs and identified the differences between the traits of man, which fanned the flames of hate, and rendered their corporate logos power—*The Order establishes its structure at very young ages.* The hate generated confusion led God's people to wage war against each other—all so, for profit.

The sick satire in all of this is the following….God's people were scattered by the same means by which God saved our race with Noah's help, after Yeshua destroyed the entire world for the same exact wickedness which the Freemasons now hold dear.

As discussed, the Freemasons virtually worship Noah. Listen to this outtake from the Encyclopedia of Freemasonry 1916 Vol 2 - AG Mackey:

> Noah and the flood play an important part in the "Legend of the Craft." Hence, as the Masonic system became developed, the Patriarch was looked upon as what was called a patron of Masonry, and this connection of Noah with the mythic history of the Order was rendered still closer by the influence of many symbols borrowed from the Arkite worship, one of the most predominant of the ancient

s.S.O.S.s.

faiths. So intimately were incorporated the legends of Noah with the legends of Masonry that **Freemasons began, at length, to be called, and are still called, "Noachidee," or the descendants of Noah, a term first applied by Anderson, and very frequently used at the present day.**

There are those of you who will still say (despite reason) 'oh hogwash….In those old days no one possessed the technology for intercontinental travel.' To that, I would like to introduce you to an American educator from *Minnesota*, named, Robert Asp.

After reading about the discovery of an intact Viking ship in Norway, topping Robert's bucket list was the crazy notion of building his own, to the same specifications as the discovered ancient treasure. The School Counselor then built the ship (which The Order's goons had surmised would have taken 100 skilled laborers a year to build) *by hand in only two years*, nearly *singlehandedly*. But before Robert could shove off for his homeland in Scotland in his homemade vessel, sadly, Mr. Asp succumbed to cancer.

Asp's grieving family agreed to honor their father by living out his dream *for him*. So this adventurous group managed to sail Robert's completed *'dragon ship'* from Duluth to Bergen Norway in only 72 days.

This story too has been buried deep within the digital archives of the World Wide Web, by, The Order….You really should google video search 'Postcards: The Hjemkomst of Robert Asp'…this is amazing!

s.s.O.s.s.

I have chosen a Bible verse to close out this section. The following passage describes the desolation of *New Babylon*, after the 'millstone' destroys her forever:

Revelation 18:23 King James Version
23 And the light of a candle shall shine no more at all in thee; and the voice of the bridegroom and of the bride shall be heard no more at all in thee: **for thy merchants were the great men of the earth;** *for by thy sorceries were all nations deceived.*

24 And in her was found the blood of prophets, and of saints, *and of all that were slain upon the earth.*

Fun fact: The oldest literature ever written dates back to King Nimrod's Babylonian Empire. The story is written on stone, and is titled, 'The Epic of Gilgamesh.'

The story of 'Gilgamesh' describes a single, antediluvian man who had survived the Great Flood. Many credit this evil man with saving and reviving 'the craft' (or Freemasonry), after God had destroyed the world with water for being 'wicked.' ('Gilgamesh' is simply a distorted explanation of Noah's wicked son who had stowed 'the craft' aboard Noah's vessel, causing the widespread havoc we see today).

The hit television program, *Gilligan's Island*, displayed inarguable parallels to this story: Here, you have a man with a similar name, aboard a boat, who had saved himself from a deadly sea of water. There was a 'professor' (which is how the Jesuits re-

S.S.O.S.S.

ferred to their leaders), who was the savior of the crew (through science). We have the dumb captain archetype which is a very good analogy for the politicians who *think* they run our government (when really it was the professor - *the Jesuit*). Thurston Howell III is the British rich guy whose name means, '*Thor*' ; Thurstain being an early version of 'Russell.' Ginger was the 'whore' of Gilligan's Island, and Mary Ann represents the rest of us—*the naive sheep.*

s.S.O.s.s.

67. Kennedy's Fatal Mistake

—Do you now believe that our way of life is under attack?

—Do our politicians and media withhold *facts* which we deserve to know?

—In other words, do you believe that a secret, tightly knit machine which combines, diplomatic, intelligence, economic, scientific, political, and military might, is working toward global organization, in order to manipulate the masses?

If you do your mistaken, because a 'tightly knit machine' already has taken over the world—they did that a long time ago.
What if I told you that John F. Kennedy was killed for trying to warn of this very thing? Would you believe me then? Would you believe Kennedy, if you heard him say these things with your own ears?
In 1963, Kennedy signed the Executive Orders which changed the working dynamics of the privileged families' monopoly of *our* Federal Reserve. The Federal Reserve is *NOT* federally owned as its misleading name implies—it is owned and operated by 12 private banks with our tax dollars. We pay several lucky private families to make our currency, so they can fluff a dollar into 12 lendable dollars, from which interest is then earned on the phony data entry.

s.s.O.s.s.

Believe it or not, John Fitzgerald Kennedy gave his very last speech as a warning against the extreme corruption of the news sources during his times, *and*, secret societies of all sorts, to which here are a couple of outtakes:

Address, "The President and the Press," Before The American Newspaper Publishers Association, 27 April 1961

"The very word "secrecy" is repugnant in a free and open society; and **we are as a people inherently and historically opposed to secret societies, to secret oaths and to secret proceedings. We decided long ago that the dangers of excessive and unwarranted concealment of pertinent facts far outweighed the dangers which are cited to justify it.** Even today, there is little value in opposing the threat of a closed society by imitating its arbitrary restrictions. Even today, there is little value in insuring the survival of our nation if our traditions do not survive with it. And **there is very grave danger that an announced need for increased security will be seized upon by those anxious to expand its meaning to the very limits of official censorship and concealment** (*the Patriot Act comes to mind here*).

That I do not intend to permit to the extent that it is in my control. And **no official of my Adminis-**

s.S.O.S.s.

tration, whether his rank is high or low, civilian or military, should interpret my words here tonight as an excuse to censor the news, to stifle dissent, to cover up our mistakes or to withhold from the press and the public the facts they deserve to know."

[skipped two paragraphs]

"For we are opposed around the world by a monolithic and ruthless conspiracy that relies on covert means for expanding its sphere of influence—on infiltration instead of invasion, on subversion instead of elections, on intimidation instead of free choice, on guerrillas by night instead of armies by day. It is a system which has conscripted vast human and material resources into the building of a tightly knit, highly efficient machine that combines military, diplomatic, intelligence, economic, scientific and political operations."

Soon after signing several pieces of fateful legislation (including the one in which JFK threw a wrench into the cogs of the working dynamics of the Federal Reserve raping which we still enjoy), John F. Kennedy was shot in the head and deemed deceased. Immediately upon Kennedy's demise those pieces of legislation were reversed. Now we know that Kennedy actually *identi-*

s.S.O.S.s.

fied his own killers in his very last speech, and LBJ's actions afterward uncovered their motives for doing so.

In the meantime, there have been countless documentaries, publications, lectures, and pontifications, upon the details of this epic…Who shot from where; the scarfed lady; there was the depository fire from the admitted 'patsy'; let's not forget the grassy knoll and, the many theories, which, as did the cracking of gunfire, still bounce amongst the glass and concrete of Downtown Dallas, today.

But, through all of this smokescreen, no one in The Order's propaganda-blaring news channels reported a letter of the very last speech given by JFK. Which, in its very content, reveals his own killers…Kennedy's final speech *harshly* warned of the times in which we now live (you can hear the nervousness in his voice as his courageous lips purse to blow the whistle). The murder of John F. Kennedy marks the very last gleaming of twilight, which once shone brightly upon the American public's innocence.

Now you too know the truth about 'Camelot,' *and* the so-called 'Kennedy curse.'

s.S.O.s.s.

68. The Nimrod Code

Before The Order killed my Brother, *Joseph*, he would always remark that, 'King Solomon' was his 'favorite Man of The Bible' *('after Jesus,' he would say)*. 'Joey' admired the wisdom of the king. King Solomon is synonymous with wisdom and wealth. Any one of us can learn from this wise man, after all, he wrote several Books of The Bible.

Believe it or not, Solomon even wrote a hit song for *The Byrd's*, which was released in 1965 (right in the heart of the disastrous Vietnam War)…listen carefully to the lyrics of 'Turn, Turn, Turn':

Ecclesiastes 3 King James Version
3 To *every thing* there is a *season*, and a time to every purpose under the heaven:
2 *A time to be born, and a time to die*; **a time to plant**, and **a time to pluck up that which is planted**;
3 *A time to kill*, and **a time to heal**; *a time to break down*, and *a time to build up*;
4 A **time to weep**, and a **time to laugh**; a **time to mourn**, and a **time to dance**;
5 *A time to cast away stones*, and *a time to gather stones together*; a time to embrace, and a time to refrain from embracing;
6 *A time to get*, and *a time to lose*; a **time to keep**, and a *time to cast away*;

S.S.O.S.S.

7 A time to rend, and a time to sew; **a time to keep silence**, and **a time to speak**;
8 **A time to love**, and *a time to hate*; *a time of war*, and *a time of peace.*

'Turn, Turn, Turn'....Is it surprising to you that this song, *about civilizations rising and falling*, was written by The Order's precious King Solomon?

Solomon was the youngest of King David's sons; King David was one of the most respected men in The Bible. From his father, Solomon inherited an empire that extended from the Northeast to the Euphrates, to the southeast of the Gulf of Aqaba, and to the Southwest to the borders of Egypt and Philistia. **A great fleet of ships was amassed and trade was known to have been made as far away as Spain.**

The King also was famous for his copper mines and forgeries. Long before our Civil Wars, 'Revolutions,' and World Wars, which generate money and industry for *our* corrupt metal foundries, Solomon was running the same exact timeworn game— *he invented it.* Solomon was a great king of commerce for an expanding empire, of which Jerusalem was the Capital City. But the cost of maintaining Solomon's court had outpaced his economic engine (exactly like the US has done today). And before long, the financial footings of the great empire began to display fissures in its many foundations. Many of his great buildings were at the cost of striped-backs for his people, who became more and more enslaved as his empire withered (just like us).

Jesus Christ predicted the destruction of King Solomon's Temple when he walked the earth (this is recorded fact), at a time

s.s.O.s.s.

when the men running the place had already turned quite wicked. Remember? One of the charges brought against Christ, by 'The Jews,' was that, Jesus had 'threatened to destroy' their precious 'temple,' which had become a 'synagogue of satan.' *Jesus was only warning the people of the destruction of King Solomon's Temple, which would take place after he descended to Heaven.*

Luke 19:43-44 King James Version
43 "For days will come upon you when your enemies *will build an embankment around you, surround you and close you in on every side,
44 and level you, and your children within you, to the ground; and they will not leave in you one stone upon another, because you did not know the time of your visitation."

Note*: This is what Trump wants to do…look how it worked for these folks…

Christ is estimated to have been sentenced to death by crucifixion between 30-36 AD. If you will recall, Christ taught that, the peoples' evil ways would eventually lead to their own demise (as these practices have crumbled all societies before and since). In 70 AD (not long after Jesus was murdered), Roman legions under **Titus destroyed a great portion of Jerusalem *and* obliterated the Temple of Solomon; just as Jesus had foretold**. And again, a ridiculous amount of praise is sung to Nostradamus for *his* silly writings. And again, a ridiculous amount of praise is sung to Nostradamus for *his* silly writings.

s.S.O.S.s.

Much like the (fitting) chessboard-style floor in Solomon's Temple, Solomon had a checkered past. Solomon kept up to 700 wives (and 300 concubines) in his harem. And though being one of the Great Kings of The Bible, he also fell in-and-out of favor with God. In fact, Solomon built a great temple to Molech to attract young ladies from the corners of his empire, so that they could meet him as they passed their offspring through the glowing arms of the metal statue. The fact that King Solomon even reverted to his old ways of idol worship and human sacrifice, but *still* would have been eligible to return to God's favor, shows that any one of us can be forgiven, no matter what our sins, despite the false teachings of The Order. (Despite writing those Books of the Bible, Solomon *also* wrote a book of magic, in which he describes how to conjure up demons.)

God is extremely loving and graceful.

Here is another small taste of the wisdom of King Solomon; the Wise Man of The Bible, and a worshipped idol of the Freemasons' to this very day (thousands of years after his death). Enjoy…

Ecclesiastes 1:9-11 King James Version

9 The thing that hath been, it is that which shall be; and that which is done is that which shall be done: and **there is no new thing under the sun. 10** Is there any thing whereof it may be said, See, this is new? **It hath been already of old time, which was before us.**

S.S.O.S.s.
11 There is no remembrance of former things; neither shall there be any remembrance of things that are to come with those that shall come after.

Ancient Babylon's *'Former Things'*—
    The Discovery at *'Ur'* is the most amazing archeological site that you have *never* heard of (the hit television show, *Ancient Aliens,* refers to the site as Ancient *'Sumeria')*. There is extensive evidence for technology far-exceeding that which we are taught had existed during Ancient times. At *and around* the site there remains evidence of all of the tyrannical, Templar usury techniques which we *still* enjoy today: checking accounts, real estate listings, lending, taxation, social classing, enslavement, and pretty much everything we have, *save for electricity—and, some report to have found that also (google 'Baghdad Battery')*.
    Baked clay tablets litter the ground of the site. The 'Sumerians' scribed everything from daily events—*newspapers*—to grocery lists. All of this technology was found in a sliver of time in which this technology wasn't supposed to even exist, and we have never heard a whisper about any of it. *Well, except for the Ancient Alien's 'Theorists,' who only show us brief glimpses of the artifacts they want you to examine in order to sell you their load of NWO manure.*
    An original Tower of Babel was discovered in the late 19th Century, and was being excavated more-rigorously by the middle of the 20th Century (after WWII). The Order calls the tower, the *'Ziggurat.'* And, as with the poppy fields of Afghanistan, American Soldiers provide 24-hour security at this precious example of the *Tower of Babel,* which is in…SURPRISE!…*IRAQ!* (Over 90%

s.S.O.S.s.

of the opium 'straw' used for prescription opiates, as well as heroin, comes from the fields in Afghanistan, and are being guarded by *OUR SOLDIERS* (video google search 'U.S. Marines Guard Afghanistan Poppy Fields.') Most *if not all* of the 'wars' fought in the Middle East have taken place in and around this strip of land, which stretches from the spot where Noah beached his boat in modern day Turkey, to the Persian Gulf.

By the way, this is the exact-same route on which every Crusade (including the coalition forces today; the Tenth Crusade) have been carried out.

It is a moment of great satire, when you realize that the destruction of the Ancient Tower of Babel *caused* the scattering of our tribes, *and* the destruction of the 'World **Trade** Center'—*Tower 1 and Tower 2—sparked* the 10th Crusade.

Here is what wikipedia.com *has to say about The Order's precious Tower of Babel:*

> The remains of the ziggurat consist of a **three-layered solid mass of** **mud brick* **faced with** ***burnt* **bricks set in bitumen.** The lowest layer corresponds to the original construction of Ur-Nammu, while the *two upper layers are part of the Neo-Babylonian restorations.* The façade of the lowest level and the monumental staircase were *rebuilt under the orders of Saddam Hussein.*
>
> Note: **The 'Ziggurat' is estimated to have been** *much* **taller, but archaeologists have surmised**

s.s.O.s.s.

that the top portion *'had been destroyed'* (google image 'Ziggurat at UR').

Google Definition for: ***Asphalt**, a mixture of dark *bituminous* pitch with sand or gravel, used for surfacing roads, flooring, roofing, etc.

Look one final time:

Wiki Ziggurat construction explanation:

'...three-layered solid mass of **mud brick** faced with ****burnt bricks** set in ********bitumen*.'

Genesis 11:3 King James Version

"'Come, *let us make bricks and **bake them thoroughly.' *They had **brick for stone**, and they had *****asphalt for mortar**."*

'And the Freemasons were born...'

A tablet depicting Lilith (with owls at her feet) was *also* found at the location known in Bible Times, as, *'Ancient Babylon' (it can be easily viewed using a google image search)*— Babylon also being the Empire which was ruled by the Freemason's *God*, King Nimrod; aka Dagon; aka Odin; aka Ahura Mazda; aka Molech; along with the many other names by which he has been known throughout time.

S.S.O.S.S.

However, once again, putting aside all of The Order's fairy tales, **Lilith too really lived.** I only waited this long in the story, to unmask her, so to minimize the intentional confusion created by The Order. *'Lilith,'* is actually just a resurrection of the legendary **wife of *King Nimrod* of Babylon**, *'Semiramis'* (which is why the two can be seen wearing similar hats in their many ancient depictions).

There is no question as to the existence of this evil Queen, who actually served as 'regent' (temporary ruler) from 811–806 BC, while waiting for she and Nimrod's son (*Thor*) to take the throne. (By the way, after Odin's [or Nimrod's] death, Thor *did* take his seat at the throne of Ancient Babylon.)

This means that, 'Semiramis' (or *'Lilith'*), *actually* **ruled** *the largest Kingdom in the world (at the time)—by far—thousands of years before Hillary Clinton, which is being billed as a great historic evolution. To add to that, there have been several 'black' kings throughout the ages, also, even in Europe!*

In the words of the Great King Solomon, 'nothing is new under the sun,'—'Turn, Turn, Turn.'

Do *NOT* become confused by The Order's shell games.

Getting back to Lilith....As mentioned, **the Statue of Liberty** *is* **simply an evolution of *Lilith*, the** *known* **'Whore of Babylon'** during John of Patmos's times**; our version—*Libertas* is the 'Mystery Whore' of 'New Babylon.'** Having witnessed this old shape-shifting game before, John was sure she would surface with a new face and name in our times; *and she did*!

Keep in mind, when John wrote the Book of Revelation, he would already have wit**nessed many of the forms of this old**

s.s.O.s.s.

'Whore,' *in his times.* The 'Whore of Babylon' predates John's Book of *Revelation* by *eons*.

These two monsters (Nimrod and Semiramis) have taken-on a countless number of new identities (and forms), throughout our civilizations, but in most ancient depictions (at all of these independent locations) *Nimrod even sports the same face and beard.*

And there is one final image to which I wish to charm your attention. It is a map which shows the location where The Bible determines that Noah's Ark had settled, after that fateful deluge and voyage—Mount Ararat.

But first, please read below:

Genesis 11:1-9 New King James Version
The Tower of Babel
11 Now the whole earth had one language and one speech. **2** And it came to pass, as **they journeyed from the East, that they found a *plain in the land of Shinar**, and they dwelt there.

If you look upon a map of Mount Ararat (google image 'Noah's boat landing in relation to shinar'), please look to the southeast of Noah's landing zone (Mount Ararat). If you track your finger down from Mount Ararat, between there and the northernmost-end of the Persian Gulf, it's where ***The Plains in the land of Shinar** and *the 'Ziggurat Tower' were discovered.* Remember that, King Nimrod (who was the great, great, grandson of Noah) was the King of Babylon who *built* The Tower of Babel— Mount Ararat *and* the Tower of Babel *share the same valley.* And now there are countless *towers of Babel* in every inner-city (sky-

S.S.O.S.S.

scrapers). And Nimrod, and his wife, are worshipped (by all of our corporate kings and governors) in *New Babylon's* temple to 'Lilith'—The Queen of Babylon—*in Bohemian Grove.*

Fun fact: America's most extensive collection of Ancient Babylonian artifacts belongs to none other than the sinister *Yale University.*

69. Three Geronimos and a Nimrod

Well, this story began with Prescott Bush 'crooking' a Geronimo's skull and so, it shall end with a Bush reaping yet another Geronimo's head. But...oh how far They have come, from being frat boys with a pick?

We all remember George W. Bush's Nemesis, Osama Bin Laden, whom also got caught up in The Order's magic of war— initially against the Russian's (which we financed), and *he* was later responsible for the unforgettable scene on 9-11, 2001.

Following the killing of Osama Bin Laden, in a mission coined *Operation Neptune Spear* (Neptune being synonymous with King Nimrod who built the tower of Babel), there was a US Navy '*burial at sea.*' We were all led to believe that, for the event, Bin Laden's body was 'encased in concrete' (just as the cadaver of Lincoln had supposedly been) and cast 'into the sea.' Also if you will remember, for the assassination mission, carried out by Seal Team 6, Bin Laden had the distinction of having been assigned the codename, '*Geronimo!*'

Now, Osama Bin Laden's cranium, no doubt, rests in The Tomb on High Street, on the campus of Yale University, right next to the *actual* cranium of '*Geronimo' (the second)* whom shares the very same affectionate handle.

Often I wonder how much this cute frat-boy episode must have cost all of we American people. After all, aircraft carriers have been referred to as 'floating cities,' and carry a crew of around six thousand sailors.

s.S.O.S.s.

In the beginning of this story, *I must admit that*, I think I made a mistake. After Geronimo's family was *'murdered,'* he supposedly made a trip 'deep into Mexico,' from which he returned with a 'new name,' *'Geronimo,' 'one who yawns.'* But, with my research of the Ancient City of Antioch, the City where Bohemond (Russell's) forces boiled and grilled men and children while waiting for his pal on the inside to open the gates, *I discovered a third 'Geronimo.'*

I will begin this explanation with the origin of the name *'Geronimo,'* as per an outtake from etymonline.com:

> Geronimo (interj.) Look up Geronimo at Dictionary.com—cry made in jumping, 1944 among U.S. airborne soldiers, **apparently** from the story of the Apache leader Geronimo making a daring leap to escape U.S. cavalry pursuers at Medicine Bluffs, Oklahoma (and supposedly shouting his name in defiance as he did). Adopted as battle cry by paratroopers in World War II, who perhaps had seen it in the 1939 Paramount Studios movie "Geronimo."
> **The name is the Italian and Spanish form of Jerome, from Greek Hieronomos, literally "sacred name."**

Now that we know that the name 'Geronimo' is actually an 'Italian and Spanish' evolution of the *'Greek'* name 'Jerome,' and really means, *'Sacred Name,'* I sniffed around a little more and discovered that, like *'Bohemond the Giant,'* the earliest use of the

s.s.O.s.s.

name 'Geronimo,' too originates at The Order's Ancient City of Antioch.

The *Italian* Jerome went on quite the pilgrimage before reaching Antioch (where he supposedly found Jesus) in the late fourth century, and he spent a couple of years there. After the brief interloping, Jerome accompanied a gentleman named *Paulinus* (who was now one of the claimants to the Patriarchal right of Antioch) back to Rome, to campaign his position before the Pope, for The Order. (Patriarch means, 'leader'—*The Order also refers to their leaders as 'Patriarch,' i.e. 'Patriarch Bush— to which Prescott Bush was referred, in the bones-man story, in which 'Pat', 'crooked,' Geronimo's head.)*

As the story goes, The Pope took quite a shine to Jerome and appointed him to his Papal council *(secretary to Pope Damasus I)*.

As discussed, *'Jerome,'* is simply the ancient form of the name *'Geronimo'*—look again:

Jerome: "sacred name" (Greek). 'Saint' Jerome was responsible for the creation of the ***Vulgate*, the *Latin* translation of the Bible…**

But, what in the world is a 'vulgate'? The vulgate, as it turns out, is a so-called *'bible,'* which was 'translated to Latin' (by Gerome) and modified for the 'common man.' And, like Yale's *'Wollebius's book,'* the 'vulgate,' was a highly molested form of The Bible. I don't think that you would wanna run out and grab yourself a copy of the… *'Vulgate'*…any time soon.

s.s.O.s.s.

But how did the *'vulgate'* derive *its* name? Here are some outtakes from etymonline.com which shows the evolution of the word *'vulgate,'which began with a form of the word*:

> **vulgar** (adj.)...late 14c., **"common, ordinary,"** from Latin vulgaris, volgaris"of or pertaining to the common people...Welsh gwala **"sufficiency, enough"**...Meaning **"coarse, low, ill-bred"**...

What's more, If you will remember, Jerome became a great pal of the Pope—*Pope Damasus I*—who became *so* impressed with Jerome's *vulgate* that, the Pope adopted Jerome's *'vulgate'as the 'Catholic Bible'* (after several more modifications, of course). Without boring you endlessly with doctrine, *the modifications changed The Bible into a denomination which* **DOES NOT teach salvation by grace through faith in Jesus Christ, but by works alone, which would leave us all in the grave.**

And now you know that the Catholic Bible is a further-molested *version* of Jerome's molested-*translation* of The Bible—*the 'vulgate'*—by *'Geronimo.'*

This is one of the greatest accomplishments of The Order, to date, and explains why the name 'Geronimo' is *so* important to these creeps. It also explains why paratroopers shouted the word 'Geronimo' when jumping out of airplanes, and into the theater of war! It is a great analogy for jumping to your spiritual death.

Geronimo was simply initiated into The Order, and assigned a new demonic name, just like all the rest of these weak and power hungry fellows.

s.S.O.S.s.

In other words, the name 'Geronimo' *is not Mexican or 'Indian' in origin*, it is another regurgitated hero of The Order's.

And....Back to the topic of The Order's never-dying love for King Nimrod and *his* many shape-shifted deities, I would like to make one final point, for this section....It is only fitting that one of our current Presidential Candidates for the United States of America, in such troubling times, also be a famous Nimrod. I'm talking about celebrity skyscraper-builder from New Babylon—aka *New York* City—whose state flag boasts the Latin word excelsior, meaning, *'ever higher!'*

The towhead fellow, who lives at the ***top*** of **Trump *Tower***, is intent on another racial roundup and deportation of at least 2 million people. The same people from whom The Order had originally stolen the entire western portion of this Great Country. Nimrod's presidency, if it indeed comes to pass, would be a fitting ending for the epic drama of the universe, *if the end is indeed as near as it seems.* Can you believe that a modern day tower builder has proposed the building of an 'impenetrable, physical, **tall, powerful, beautiful,** southern border **wall**?'

Revelation 13:5 King James Version
5 And there was given unto him a mouth speaking great things and blasphemies; and power was given unto him to continue **forty and two months.**

This tower-building Nimrod, having spent two years at a Jesuit school in The Bronx (at Fordham University), would make a suitable hand-puppet for The Order.

s.s.O.s.s.

In the unlikely event that Nimrod's 'winning' streak *were* to end, the alternative would make a fantastic *'Whore of Babylon!' She* served as *Senator* of *New* Babylon.

Hillary Clinton's running mate, Tim Kaine, *also* attended a Jesuit school for *four* years. Which makes this election very reminiscent of the Skull and Bones face-off, when Kerry and Bush were assigned to us as our only two flavors, in *that* Pepsi Challenge election. Is it not unnerving to you that one of our choices will ensure a Jesuit President? And our single other option will leave us four pounds of trigger force from having a 'Black (Jesuit) Pope' *and* a 'Black' (Jesuit) President?

One last quote on the topic of the Jesuits:

"The Jesuits are a MILITARY organization, not a religious order. Their chief is a general of an army, not the mere father abbot of a monastery. And the aim of this organization is power—power in its most despotic exercise—absolute power, universal power, power to control the world by the volition of a single man [i.e., the Black Pope, the Superior General of the Jesuits]. Jesuitism is the most absolute of despotisms [sic]—and at the same time the greatest and most enormous of abuses..."
—Napoleon Bonaparte (1769-1821) French Emperor—

The idea of this work was not to analyze every word of the Book of Revelation—my intention wasn't to try and devise an ex-

s.S.O.S.s.

act timeline, as many end-times alarmists will try and impress upon *their* customers.

My motivation was to reveal a demonstrative trail of facts which seem to stream freely, around all areas of history where evil is concerned. Not only to demonstrate to you that the devil has been loose, globally, for around a thousand years, but to give you the exact names (and routes) of the key players who have channelled the evil energy of he and his dark angels, to spread the four horsemens', prophetic 'conquest, war, famine, and death,' to the four ends of earth.

There is now no new ground on this earth for which the four evil ones to gallop upon…again we are all bunched together… and, once more we all speak the same language.

Isn't The Bible amazing? Everyone makes their ideas of the book of Revelation fit forcefully, while a long line of William *the Conquerers* finish the sinister works, right under our noses.

Let us look once again:

> **Revelation 6** King James Version
> **6** And I saw when the Lamb opened one of the seals, and I heard, as it were the noise of thunder, one of the four beasts saying, Come and see.
> **2** And I saw, and behold a white horse: and he that sat on him had a bow; and a ***crown was given unto him**: and **he went forth conquering, and to conquer.**

s.s.O.s.s.

Note*: According to ancient Arabic works, King Nimrod was the first King to ever Don a crown, which explains why the Royal families all took such a shine to the custom.

William *the Conquerer* was the very first William (Russell) ever to be known by the name, *'William.'* William, of course, being the first in what seems like an infinite number of *Evil* Williams, over the years. *Even the surname, 'Williams,' is exactly what it sounds like—a group of Williams.*

Germanic in origin, William is a version of the name Willahelm, which was composed of the elements 'will, desire' and 'helm' 'helmet, protection.' This is ironic, since all of these Williams *will* be in *desperate* need of a *'helmet'* when Yeshua wills the sky to fall upon, and crush, them.

In the wake of 'Brexit,' I have a hunch that, after the Queen dies, another William (Russell) the *Conquerer* (who is now in line for the throne) will initiate some more of The Order's trademarked funny business.

Once again, man finds himself in the same simple predicament. Now that *you* have the *'Knowledge of Good and Evil,'* upon which fruit shall you feast? I hope you will choose to write your name in the Book of Life...

Fun fact: The world's tallest skyscraper, today, is the **Burj Khalifa** in Dubai. The imposing new *Tower* **(of Babel) was built by the Bin Laden Group**, a Saudi Arabian construction company founded by **Muhammed bin Laden—Osama bin Laden's father.** Osama bin Laden's dad's story was another trademarked *'tear-jerker,'*

S.S.O.S.S.
written by The Order; *This Nimrod too* **supposedly** *'began life as a penniless bricklayer.'*

Absurdly, the brain behind '*One World* Trade Center' was, none other than, architect, *David Childs, whose firm Skidmore, Owings & Merrill (SOM) also designed the Burj Khalifa, the tallest building in the world, built by the Bin Laden Group.*

The firm who replaced the old Towers of Babylon was *Tishman Construction.* Tishman famously built and owned the egregious 666 5th Avenue building in Manhattan—on the side of the building was the mark of the beast which was emblazoned in lighted-red numbers, proudly, for all to see. The Tishman's purchased the building *and* Rockefeller Center, right across the street. The company built an atrium connecting the two satanic sites.

Tishman's sold the abomination for a record breaking 1.72 billion dollars—the highest price ever paid for a skyscraper in Manhattan, at the time. (It seems that evil is once again quite fashionable.) After much pomp and pageantry Tishman won the bid to replace the mess that Skull and Bonesmen had made in downtown manhattan. Before the record-breaking sale to Citigroup the building was simply called '*The Tishman Building.*'

s.S.O.S.s.

70. I Will See You Again

The evil ones have discredited a Bible which they themselves *know* to be true. They celebrate, and practice, The Bible's rituals more religiously than we do ours—they are not the rituals of the side of the true God—but those of the dark side of the Holy Chronicles; the History which they themselves so revere. May their ridicule turn to repentance, *or else*, they into God's hated enemy, for the wrath of the Lord and the power of the truth be upon them!

As you can see, the evildoers, who have completely robbed mankind of our identity, real history, and the truth of God's Word, also still honor *their* pagan traditions. These traditions have been guarded, hidden and practiced in secret—in the dark. For deception of the masses and personal gain, they have kept us pure and honest in order to inflict the most damage to the flock.

The Order traded everlasting life for death, and for temporary happiness in this world—knowingly. The Order has indeed stolen our inheritance, many of our lives, our efforts, and a *great many* of our souls, through trickery. The Great Pyramids themselves, which these creeps worship, are a great symbol of exercise in futility for generations of Men, who surrendered their entire lives to toil, for basic human needs—*food and shelter.*

We must forget the slurs of our past and honor our unique histories, and 'genetic traits' with which God has colored his beautiful, multi-hued tribe. Beware of The Order of the Tribe of Dan, because he is hidden in the blood of all of our *old* scattered tribes. But, now he will be easily recognized, so fear not. They have

s.s.O.s.s.

caused us to hate one another—my brothers and sisters from the same tribe—*Judah*. *Rejoice, for we are one tribe.* **We....Are... all...*Judah! (if we only choose to be).***

Let the good done to others warm your own heart with the amount of God in which the muscle can withstand, *as I have mine.*

May the Lord be with thee, for once again, we find ourselves in times of challenge as Christian Believers. I will see you soon, here....*or thereafter—*

"Yes, I am coming soon." Come, Lord Jesus. The grace of the Lord Jesus be with God's people.
Amen.

Lest you ever forget, that *we are all of the immortal tribe of Judah*—children of Jesus Christ and *The Almighty,* our Creator!

For those of us who *believe* in Christ, there is....

....No End...

Thanks for listening,

Judah!

s.S.O.S.s.

The Way

—The Way—

For gold, glory, or liquid worth;
They by twilight stormed the ends of earth;

For truth, for faith, for peace of mind,
Crusaders right the wrongs of thine;

From Molly Pitcher's bitter brew;
To Adolf's plans and though he knew

That judgement passed by Franklin's crew,
To his delight, killed millions too;

To those who happened upon Dahmer's day,
Whom stoned with horror, lost their ways;

All their years and all their feats,
They laughed, they cried, they're zesty treats;

Some charter scouts, or look to Frost,
Sent trailblazing…
Now safe, but lost.

s.S.O.S.s.

Judah—**written around the age of 17**

John 14:6 King James Version
6 Jesus saith unto him, I am the way, the truth, and the life: no man cometh unto the Father, but by me.

The Real 'Rules'

The 'Knowledge of Good and Evil' truly isn't rocket science. The secret to the ancient magic of 'The Order' is this: If you possess the age-old ability of creating an infinite number of fraternities, who all take open-ended oaths and do whatever one is told lest the consequence of death, you have the ability to control the world. When you combine with that the possession of endless false religions which all contradict one another, you have robbed a spiritual and innate part of man's mind, which has been reprogrammed for radical ideas and potential actions. These 'potential actions' and 'ideas' allow a central dark force to control the world, in every way and from every angle. And, whether you believe it to be spiritual or subconscious, evil is evil, and evil *is* controlling *this* world; that cannot be denied.

The following are a list of rules which, if obeyed, prevent the dreaded 'desolation' described in the bible from one end to the other; whether you believe it…or not:

The Ten Commandments

I—**You shall have no other gods before me.**

II—**You shall not make idols.**

III—**You shall not take the name of the LORD your God in vain. (Which means, declaring *yourself* to be Jesus, like the Jesuits and the Pope do.)**

s.S.O.S.s.

IV—Remember the Sabbath day, to keep it holy.

V—Honor your father and your mother.

VI—You shall not murder.

VII—You shall not commit adultery.

VIII—You shall not steal.

IX—You shall not bear false witness against your neighbor. (This means, taking scripture out of context for personal gain, or creating new 'false' religions; the Jesuits and the Pope bear 'false witness.')

X—You shall not covet. (Which means, don't yearn for your neighbors' property, which *leads* to 'stealing' it.)

Now doesn't that sound easy?

Can we not agree that the notion of a band of clandestine Knights who traveled to the other side of their world, just for an alabaster cup, is absolutely absurd? Even for a silver chalice this sounds silly—did Christ's personal drinking-cup say, *'Jesus'?*

Think of this....How would The Order even positively identify the cup's providence, *if* found? I admit that copies have also been made of the Breastplate of Judgment—the story of Micah (*The Idol and the Ephod*) is proof of that.

s.s.O.s.s.

But, at least, if you *did* find Aaron's original Ephod gear, you would certainly have the ability to identify it as such.

Despite the beast's ancient superstitions, if you haven't already arrived at the conclusion on your own, Aaron's Breastplate is *not* the *'Holy'* Grail, either. The Holy Grail, and everlasting life, are both very real things which The Order has *'crooked'* from you, since the dawn of man. Jesus Christ is the Holy Grail, and, only through His Name, *Jesus Christ,* can one can take of the fruit of the tree of life, and truly live forever…for the wages of sin is death, and, it is indeed payday for the wicked.

Below you will read the true source of The Order's Holy Grail fable:

John 4:14 King James Version
14 But whosoever drinketh of the water that I shall give him shall never thirst; but the water that I shall give him shall be in him a well of water springing up into everlasting life.

s.S.O.S.s.

Suggested Reading List—

Before you move on...If you liked this work, will you please rate it on Amazon, and share it on social media? The reading list:

The Holy Bible—Read The King James 1611 version of The Bible, with a heavy emphasis on the books of Mathew, Mark, Luke, John—read *John first!* Then start from Genesis. The book of Revelation will also be a fantastic read. The prophetic book describing the end, to this modern day Bible Story, will probably be pretty hard to keep you away from, now that you are with eyes open.
By: God, Christ,
And our Brothers in Christ

The Windows of Reality
By: Timothy Allen Zigler
This book chronicles Tim's insanely desperate journey out of the darkness of opiate addiction. ('I got clean in a basement in Tijuana Mexico, with people I had never met in my life.')

—And the essay which started it all: located on the homepage on TheWindows*Of*Reality.com **website...**
  This essay began the unfurling of the golden thread of culpability for the House of Russell. After becoming clean from prescription opiates, myself, using an African root bark which is illegal in the US, my eyes were peeled wide open. As you can imag-

S.S.O.S.s.

ine, I was dumfounded that there was a cure out there, *which is an illegal Schedule I narcotic!* My feculence meter began to vibrate spastically.

As I peeled back the layers, over time, I realized that each cure for the prior opiate epidemic became the next demonized Opiate Dynasty. In every case, the deceived addict was forced to take on a dark persona who was no-longer them. When The Order ushered in a subsequent Opiate Dynasty, another wave of 'criminals' were created for their beloved court systems, after their victims were left cut off from their supply. The prisons became full and so did their wallets, using *legal* slave labor. Prisoners have no rights, and, therefore, no minimum wage. Our brothers who didn't survive were sacrificed to Skull and Bones members' god, Baal.

With my awareness of the Warren Delano (Grandfather of FDR) involvement in dope-dealing for The Order, the stink meter began to rise rapidly; when I got to Samuel Russell of Russell & Company and then to Skull & Bones at Yale, the entire Bible Code began to unfurl like grandma's favorite sweater.

The discovery of the Book, *The Memoirs of the House of Russell*, caused me to begin writing like a madman. A few months later the manuscript which you are currently reading was ready for delivery.

Join me at the beginning of this epic, at a time when I didn't even know what freemasonry, Secret Societies, Skull & Bones, or The Order, even were.

Secrets of the Tomb
By: Alexandra Robbins

s.s.O.s.s.

Great Read~and much thanks to Alexandra for all of her brave work, much of which was quoted, or paraphrased, in section 10, *'Fifteen Known Men'*

The Synagogue of Satan
By: Andrew Carrington Hitchcock

Fleshing Out Skull & Bones
By Four Separate Authors: One of my favorite Authors, Antony C. Sutton, Daniel Hopsicker, Kris Millegan, and Webster Tarpley

America's Secret Establishment (can be downloaded as a free PDF online, I believe all of Sutton's books can be, and, though I have not read them all, I am looking forward to doing so)
By: Antony C Sutton

Jeb! and the Bush Crime Family
By: Roger Stone

The Deliberate Dumbing Down of America
By, "Whistleblower," and former Senior Policy Advisor in the US Department of Education: Charlotte Thomson Iserbyt

Adventures you can take on your own...

Visit the murals at the Denver Airport, and see how many of the clues (which we have learned about today) are in the images...

s.S.O.S.s.

And finally, if you can take a couple of hours out of your day, the following gentleman seems to have had a similar awakening as I. And he seems to have researched the things which I didn't. This adventure will not only confirm and add to my findings, but will reveal to you the mechanics of The Order, around the world. It will show you how they all work together as a giant machine.

'Leonard Ulrich' also debunked the 9/11 job, better than anyone possibly could. You really should google video search for Leonard's self-funded documentary of the truth!

s.S.O.s.s.

—Dedication—

Last in this book, but first in my life, I humbly commit my work, my life, and my soul, to my one and only personal savior, *Jesus Christ.*

Printed in Great Britain
by Amazon